The War on Music

The War on Music

RECLAIMING THE TWENTIETH CENTURY

John Mauceri

Yale UNIVERSITY PRESS

New Haven & London

Published with assistance from the foundation established in memory of
Amasa Stone Mather of the Class of 1907, Yale College.

Yale University Press books may be purchased in quantity for educational,
business, or promotional use. For information, please e-mail sales.press@yale.edu
(U.S. office) or sales@yaleup.co.uk (U.K. office).

Set in Adobe Garamond type by Integrated Publishing Solutions.
Printed in the United States of America.

Library of Congress Control Number: 2021944874
ISBN 978-0-300-23370-4 (hardcover : alk. paper)

A catalogue record for this book is available from the British Library.

This paper meets the requirements of ANSI/NISO Z39.48-1992
(Permanence of Paper).

10 9 8 7 6 5 4 3 2 1

For Michael Haas,

who (in 1990) asked,

"Why, John, after a half-century, do we not play the music Hitler banned?"

Here, I hope, is the answer.

Though I cannot tell why it was exactly that those stage managers, the Fates, put me down for this shabby part of a whaling voyage, when others were set down for magnificent parts in high tragedies, and short and easy parts in genteel comedies, and jolly parts in farces—though I cannot tell why this was exactly; yet, now that I recall all the circumstances, I think I can see a little into the springs and motives which being cunningly presented to me under various disguises, induce me to set about performing the part I did, besides cajoling me into the delusion that it was a choice resulting from my own unbiased freewill and discriminating judgment.

—*Moby-Dick,* HERMAN MELVILLE

Fifty years is ample time in which to change a world and its people almost beyond recognition. All that is required for the task are a sound knowledge of social engineering, a clear sight of the intended goal—and power.

—*Childhood's End,* ARTHUR C. CLARKE

Contents

The War on Music

Introduction

In the first months of the third decade of the twenty-first century, an executive order emerged from Washington, D.C., that was called "Making Federal Buildings Beautiful Again." It mandated that new federal buildings in the United States must be designed according to the classical architectural style of Roman temples as the "default style." Predictably, this caused outrage among many and set up fake battle lines between America's conservatives (the Republicans and President Donald Trump) and liberals (the Democrats and so-called progressives). Predictably, on February 24, 2021—a mere five weeks after his inauguration—Democratic President Joe Biden revoked the order. Beauty was the justification for the Trump administration's order. Consistency and reference were the means to that end.

All this brought back one of the most contentious, ironic, and little-understood periods of art and music: the de-Nazification of Europe after World War II, the Cold War, and the then Republican administration's official support of a very different artistic style—the avant-garde—portraying it as a fundamental example of freedom of expression in art and music, thus countering the Soviets' official stance against it. The Soviets supported visual art that was representational—a painting of an apple looked like an apple—and music that continued a long tradition of tonal music: music that could be full of edginess, conflict, and challenge, but that would inevitably end in victory and uplift. Most importantly, Soviet music had to be comprehensible to the public. And just as the regimes of Mussolini and Hitler supported very similar anti-experimental concepts of art and beauty, the U.S. military believed that any composer who had written nontonal music during the war was neither a Nazi nor a Fascist and a get-out-of-jail-free card was handed to the composer. The unintended consequence of that policy was that any composer who wrote non-avant-garde (if such a phrase can be accepted) classical music—symphonies, operas, chamber music—was required to prove his innocence of having been a Nazi or a Fascist.

The Cold War became a battleground between the Soviets' view of an ever-evolving traditionalism and the West's embrace of the radically new, the challenging, and the iconoclastic—one that viewed beauty in music as being both inappropriate and banal. The concept of "new," however, was based on theories that derived from 1909 and its *Futurist Manifesto*. Never mind that the public did not embrace the new music—either in the 1910s, the 1960s, or, it should be noted, in the 2020s. This was and continues to be a battle of philosophies—and politics.

Perhaps music and art have always been, to some extent, pawns of politics: the plaything of kings and popes. The archbishop of Salzburg liked Mozart's music, until he didn't. The public has always had its songs and dances, and the rulers had theirs—though they sometimes intersected, as when King George II commissioned London's popular composer George Frideric Handel to compose the *Royal Fireworks Music* in 1749.

Architecture shares some of the aspects of music, but just some. Both are experienced through time. Both are inherently structural, though music's structures are temporal and not visible. Buildings change over time since they are open to the elements and subject to erosion, and sometimes, explosion. Music disappears by silencing it—which, as we will see, can be the result of an overt action or simply of general lack of interest. Even the greatest architectural achievements can be radically changed, like the great Catholic cathedral built in the sixth century that was transformed a century later into a mosque in which the bells and altar were destroyed, the Christian mosaics plastered over, and minarets constructed on its exterior. Istanbul's Hagia Sophia was then reconstituted as a secular museum in 1935 and in 2020 reclassified as a mosque, with the potential of further architectural changes. Music is always in a state of transformation since it depends on repetition to exist, and even if that repetition is exact because of recordings, the perception of the exact repetition will not be the same since it must be interpreted by an ever-evolving listener.

We expect a bank, a church, or a school to indicate by its external appearance what goes on inside. This does not require a provocative executive order. Rather, it seems like common sense. Buildings that are modern references to ancient Rome "say" something about our collective expectations. As we shall see, European culture, out of which comes much American and international culture, is full of "fake Roman temples," to use a phrase in a *New York Times* editorial's headline.[1]

Many government buildings in Washington, D.C., are good examples of those Roman monuments, but so are Berlin's Brandenburg Gate and Paris's Arc de Triomphe. They are all fake, insofar as they were not built during the reign of Julius Caesar, but they do say something about what people expected architecture to do at the time of their construction, and they are beloved symbols—just as the radical architecture of the Eiffel Tower, Antoni Gaudí's Sagrada Família in Barcelona, and Frank Gehry's Guggenheim Museum in Bilbao are. It is not necessarily about conservative versus modern.

It might also be pointed out that much imperial Roman architecture is itself fake, since the columns were generally not needed for structure once the Romans perfected the use of concrete around 200 B.C.E., but still clung to the "look" of Greek architecture. Those impressive Roman columns were merely ornaments. All these so-called fake architectural expressions gave the population a real sense of foundational power, victory, and stability.

In 1984, the AT&T Building of Philip Johnson—a thirty-seven-story skyscraper on Manhattan's Madison Avenue—was capped with a non-functional pediment that echoed the top of the Parthenon, thus joining a modern architectural achievement with the classical principles of ancient Greece and Rome. Shocking to many at the time, it came to represent a rejection of the strict doctrines of modern architecture, which itself had rejected ornament and, one could say, history. Johnson's skyscraper was neither a fake Roman temple nor a "less is more" international-style building. Genius will always transcend doctrines and executive orders.

When, however, a former church is turned into a brewery and pizza parlor, as was Pittsburgh's Church Brew Works, the mind and spirit are confronted with something "wrong," which adds to a feeling of participating in a communal heretical act—naughty enough to be hip without feeling the need to enter one of the former church's confessionals carrying a pint and a slice. And a symphony that begins with a thunderous E-flat-major chord sets up very different expectations from another that starts with a Big Bang—the familiar *fortissimo* cluster of dissonances that starts so many avant-garde orchestral works of the Cold War period.

Whatever the result of any national architectural guidelines as to what is appropriate for new federal buildings, architects and citizens will converse, as they always have, meetings will be held, compromises will be achieved, and decisions will be made. The delicate balance between reference and xerographic copies has always been at play in art and music. Was the simple tune that Brahms composed for the last movement of his First Symphony an homage to Beethoven's famous "Ode to Joy," the choral finale of his Ninth Symphony, or was it an accident? (Brahms acknowledged the resemblance with a terse "Any ass can see that.") Brahms's genius is that the theme did two things at once: his finale not only recognized the monumental edifice created by his esteemed predecessor, it also reclaimed the symphony from requiring a chorus and four vocal soloists to express its musical narrative.

Making anything official in art and music will inevitably work both ways, as we shall see. "Don't think of an elephant" will result in only one thing—a pachyderm with real staying power. In the case of classical music from the last century, we are still living in the residue of its dictates and the battles for cultural supremacy that were part of the arsenals of its global wars.

It would undoubtedly come as a surprise to many people in the twenty-first century that classical music—or any music, for that matter—was used as a strategic element in the great wars of the last century. The ultimate collapse of the political value of music in international politics is partially due to the global reach of music to easily transcend borders in our technologically connected world, even though that process has been going on for as long as mankind has moved from one place to another.

That said, we live in a time in which there are no living symphonists that Austria and Germany can claim to represent their superiority over the rest of Europe. There are no living ballet composers that Russia can point to as representing its inherent superiority over the United States. And if Italy has a group of living opera composers to carry on its legacy as the inventor of the art form, those composers are unknown—if they exist at all. Classical music, like the deutsche mark, the franc, and the lira, is a currency with no currency.

That is because something profoundly significant happened to music in the twentieth century. It was not merely a matter of aesthetics or changing tastes, and it played on the unique aspects of music that separate it from all other art forms.

Music has power to control behavior, and those who wished to conquer the world sought to harness its power. Music is dangerous because it possesses an invisible force that can represent emotions and create tribal affinities. Hitler, Stalin, and Mussolini were in the business of controlling behavior and therefore felt the imperative to control music. Additionally, the style of music became an essential symbol of nations, political philosophies, and a potent metaphor of cultural and racial unity—and power. Though late in the game, the United States learned to use certain kinds of music to win over nations as part of its weaponry during the last of the great twentieth-century wars, the Cold War.

When the Greeks first described music, some 2,500 years ago, they noted the power of music using a certain scale (or "mode") to encourage violence, whereas music in a different mode could bring calm. In the eighteenth century, Benjamin Franklin's invention, the glass armonica—a series of glasses that rotated in a pool of water operated by a foot treadle and were made to vibrate by putting one's hands on their rims—was outlawed in certain regions of Europe for *causing* mental illness. It is therefore not surprising that this was the instrument Gaetano Donizetti originally used in the famous mad scene from his 1835 opera *Lucia di Lammermoor*. In the twenty-first century, music has proven to be an effective therapeutic tool in combatting post-traumatic stress syndrome. Like radiation, which both causes and cures cancer, music is not something to be taken lightly.

Aristotle (384–322 B.C.E.) believed that "music ought to be used for many benefits (including) serving to relax our tension and give rest from it." Indeed, it is said that in Confucius's time (551–479 B.C.E.) music was not considered to be an art. Rather, it was part of public administration. People have written about music for centuries—discussing what it is, what it has been, what it should be, how it works, how to compose it properly, how it relates to our physical universe, what it does or does not represent, and why it exerts its extraordinary power.

There remains a fundamental question (the ultimate subject of this book) as to what constitutes "good" music. Unique among the arts, music is invisible. It is mysterious and has a way of overtly or covertly affecting us in profound ways, as the missionary Jesuits, Napoleon Bonaparte, and Pete Seeger knew, and every politician knows today. It can warn us, make us proud, incite riots, lead us into war, make us joyful, encourage lust, bring us closer to God, and, as many believe, make us better human beings.

That said, who, after all, should decide what is *good* music? Everyone would like to think that good art is good because it *is*. However, we all know that fashions change and what was once deemed great may be long forgotten. Composer Johann Adolf Hasse (1699–1783), for instance, was judged by music historian Charles Burney "without injury to his brethren . . . to be superior to all other lyric composers."

On the other hand, a negative assessment can be also be refuted over time. Consider the American artist Jean-Michel Basquiat (1960–1988). "He had everything but talent," said art critic Hilton Kramer in a 1997 article for the *Guardian.* Tell that to the man who spent $110,500,000 for Basquiat's *Untitled* in 2017. A contemporary exhibition of an artist's work can and will change the evaluation of his or her importance because it is being seen in a new context and judged again. Expert opinion can indeed be outvoted by time—and, inevitably, by the public.

Which brings us back to music—and its Achilles heel: it cannot be known unless it is heard.

You can go to a museum and peek into a gallery and decide immediately not to go in by a quick perusal of its contents. You can spend hours—indeed, a lifetime—staring at and communing with a painting you love. You may visit it at a museum, look at a reproduction of it in a book, or even own it. You cannot do that with music. Music is delivered to us through time, and it requires its own time and ours to experience and judge it. There is no fast-forwarding through the societal experience of attending a live performance of Richard Wagner's *Parsifal* or Olivier Messiaen's *Turangalîla.* But like a reproduction in a book, music can only be partially experienced in a recording, which is merely an aural replica that removes the unpredictability and power of a live performance. Anyone who has stood before a painting by Picasso or Van Gogh, rather than a picture in a book, knows this difference.

If aesthetic evaluations fluctuate as wildly as they do, it is worth observing how music of the last century fared, given the impact of global warfare and the use of music in those wars. When Arnold Schoenberg joined the Austrian army in World War I, he saw it as his mission to stamp out French *music* and its famous Parisian resident, Igor Stravinsky, whom he derided as "the little Modernsky." Four thousand miles west of Schoenberg's Vienna, as America prepared to enter the Great War in 1917, New York's Metropolitan Opera stopped performing Wagner because his music was understood to express the very spirit of the Austro-German Hun—even though the composer had died in 1883. It would not be the last time Wagner's music would be used for political purposes.

After World War II, America sent a group of jazz artists, most of whom were African-Americans, along with the Boston Symphony Orchestra to Europe as representatives of the United States and its broad cultural life, countering the impression held by many European intellectuals and Soviets that America had no real culture. America, supported by private-citizen groups and the CIA, was determined to demonstrate that freedom of expression and a profound immigrant heritage had created a vast and vibrant artistic community that could interpret Europe's eternal masterpieces at the highest level and also create new and vital art.

The twentieth century was a century of war: World War I, World War II, and, equally important, the Cold War. What had developed within Europe over centuries—the perception of musical styles and genres as the unique cultural legacy and pride of nations—became part of the weaponry of identity and superiority in the twentieth century. By the time the world entered the twenty-first century, much twentieth-century classical music had become collateral damage of those wars. Frequently described as "the international language," music was in fact judged by military victories, defeats, political philosophy, public policy, unpredictable alliances, and the understandable emotional responses to the music itself.

We can only imagine how painful it must have been for exhausted and defeated Germans and Austrians in 1945, living in the unimaginable squalor they had brought upon themselves, to accept a single note of the music composed by four of their most famous—and one could say greatest—living composers, Arnold Schoenberg, Erich Wolfgang Korngold, Paul Hindemith, and Kurt Weill, all of whom had survived the war in an enemy country. Heralded in their homelands in the 1920s, they had subsequently been outlawed and might have been killed had they remained in Germany, Austria, or any of the other countries that constituted the Third Reich. Hearing their new "American" music, most of which was complex and also uniquely beautiful, was simply unbearable. The newly minted intellectual and passion-free music emanating from the young Europeans was far easier to tolerate and discuss, even as the core repertory returned to Beethoven, Brahms, and Mozart.

And then there was Hollywood. From 1933 onward, and almost without exception, its major film scores were composed by refugees who had fled racism in Europe and Russia. These men were defined as Jews by the Third Reich, though most were non-religious. They were, however, brilliant musicians who had been trained in Europe's greatest conservatories. What then did the vanquished make of Hollywood and its epic symphonic music composed by their former wunderkinds, who now were Americans, living in paradise under palm trees—and rich?

In 1991, the Decca Recording Company proposed a series of records of music banned by the Nazis (who labeled it *entartete Musik,* or degenerate music) and subsequently forgotten, in which I was to be one of two principal conductors. Simultaneously, the Los Angeles Philharmonic Association and Philips Records created a new orchestra at the Hollywood Bowl, which I led, and we committed it to play music composed in Los Angeles. The steep learning curve for the composers and their music was daunting and exposed a double legacy of forgotten music along with the extraordinary discovery that the names of the founding composers of Hollywood could also be found on Hitler's list.

For someone like me, who graduated from Yale College in 1967 as a music major (theory and composition) and served on the faculty from 1968 until 1984, this discovery was a profound shock. I was trained in musicology, the art of composing and analyzing contemporary music, making use of the electronic music studio, the computer lab, and the procedures of twelve-tone composition first articulated by Schoenberg in the 1920s and subsequently embraced and expanded with ever more complex procedures in the post–World War II era. The relationship between the European composers who emerged in the 1920s and the Hollywood music of the 1930s, however, was totally unknown to me in the 1990s. So was the impact of refugee composers who taught in American music schools and universities well into the 1950s, along with that of their students and colleagues. Few people were aware that Schoenberg had been George Gershwin's last mentor or that Hindemith had taught a young man named Mitch Lee, who would go on to write the Broadway musical *The Man of La Mancha*—giving credit to Hindemith for his success.

Odder still was the discovery of music composed in the United States by refugee classical composers whose names were generally known, but whose music was never the focus of attention—like the late tonal ("American") music of Schoenberg and the "American" symphonies that Hindemith composed when he taught in the same rooms at Yale in which I was studying and teaching. It was a personal struggle to understand why this enormous repertory was missing from the experience of someone who had been attending concerts and operas and buying records since my childhood in the 1950s.

This book is about classical music and what we have come to define as such. It is not about the many other kinds of music that have developed and triumphed during the last century, though it can be argued that because of the narrow definition of what constitutes contemporary classical music, other genres of music have flourished while orchestras and opera companies have been in what many call a "crisis."

Music is ultimately uncontrollable, but because of technology, some music that was removed from consideration as not being "classical" has partially survived in the echoes of brilliance occasionally submerged below the dialogue of early sound films. All the while, another kind of new music filled our concert halls and opera houses. This is the music of the "institutional avant-garde"— an oxymoron if ever there was one. The music excluded from serious consideration that was *not* composed for films is simply missing altogether, awaiting someone to bring it back. That said, it surely is time to ask why so much contemporary music played by our greatest musical institutions—and supported overwhelmingly by music critics—is music that the vast majority of people do not want to hear—and have never wanted to hear.

This, then, is a story of continuity in spite of political power and historical

pressure to control what the public should accept as appropriate art music—
one that transcends the fake categories of pitting classical against popular. The
moral center of this book is about fairness and about loss. It is something
we can and must address. What follows is the product of more than a half-
century of curiosity and experience, stretching from the middle of the twentieth century, when I grew up in New York during the aftermath of World
War II, through the Cold War to my present vantage point in the third decade of the twenty-first century. It is naturally a personal story, one, however,
that derives its narrative from global experiences.

In 1990 I began to put those experiences into words, with a speech delivered in Glasgow to the International Society of Arts Administrators called
"Failed Futures." That speech, which challenged the idea of futurism as a model
for evaluating music of the twentieth century, was subsequently published as
the cover story in *Musical America* in what would be its last print edition.
Speeches and articles in London, Berlin, Vienna, New York, Los Angeles, and
Washington, D.C., followed over the years—speeches about the mysterious
disappearance of recent classical music repertory ("Where Has All the Music
Gone?"), the music and composers of film music ("No Sin in Cinema"), the
total lack of any discussion of its merits in journals ("The Music That Has No
Name"), and the music banned by Hitler and why it was never successfully
returned to concert halls and opera houses after the war, even as the paintings
stolen by the Nazis continue to be returned to the families who originally
owned them, and many of which are now hanging in museums.

My recordings and concerts—including hundreds of modern premieres
of abandoned music—along with articles, speeches, and media appearances,
have been heard, published, and read by millions of people for three decades.
For sixteen seasons, from 1991 to 2006—and before a combined audience of
four million people—the restoration of Hollywood refugee composers was the
core of our concerts with the Hollywood Bowl Orchestra. And while World
War II was the center of discovery—with World War I seen as something of
a preview—it took a long time for me to understand how important the last
of these twentieth-century wars, the Cold War, was in creating the bonding
of the avant-garde with the very institutions it was created to annihilate.

In addition, this book has emerged from a journey that did not start out
to prove some point. The point only became a thesis after many years of liv-

ing, hearing, thinking, and doing. We always try to make sense of things. Call it an endearing human folly. Yes, some things have changed since I began trying to understand my century in 1990. Telling this story from the vantage point of both an observer and a participant might prove valuable as that century fades further into the past.

The points of departure are love and loss. The loss, it must be said, feels incalculable. When a new production of Korngold's 1927 opera *Das Wunder der Heliane* (The Miracle of Heliane) was declared a masterpiece in Berlin in 2017—countering decades of dismissal and derision—the composer's daughter-in-law wept and said, "It is so sad because it comes so late." Then ninety-three years old, Helen Korngold well remembered the brutal treatment meted out to "Papa," who had died in 1957, a bitter and broken man.

At the same time, perhaps this book will make the reader curious to hear music that remains unknown. It may also encourage a lively debate—one that is sorely missing in our journals and intellectual discussions. It is all well and good for some current music writers to say that all those silly discussions about style from the last century are over or exaggerated, while some have the temerity to pretend that they always valued the music that has been neglected and derided, as if the generally held assessment of the last century was based on *our* ignorance, and they are here to point us in the right direction—in spite of their previous writings and aesthetic positions. In fact, those same aesthetic theories are alive and well and still inform the discourse on what constitutes "good" music. In 2019, the *New York Times* dedicated a number of articles to the avant-garde German composer Karlheinz Stockhausen's *Helicopter String Quartet*. First heard in 1995, adored by some and ridiculed by others, the work was still deemed worthy of column inches and serious discussion. (Yes, each instrumentalist is required to be in a separate helicopter.)

Rewriting history is different from reclaiming it. When the then chief operating officer of the Los Angeles Philharmonic, Chad Smith, stated that his orchestra had always been playing the music of the refugee film composers, it was totally untrue, as their archives can demonstrate. Indeed, the Philharmonic had a similar attitude toward two other important local residents, both refugees, who did not write for Hollywood—Schoenberg and Stravinsky. The Los Angeles Philharmonic could take a lesson from two other great orchestras, the Berlin and Vienna Philharmonics, that have revealed their mid-century histories. We today cannot take responsibility for the actions of the last century, but if we do not confront what our institutions actually did, then we become complicit. Music critic Alex Ross wrote in the *New York Times* in 1995, "A love for Korngold will always be a guilty pleasure." Telling the truth might remove any sense of guilt.[2]

And the unquestioned acceptance of a never-ending avant-garde is not just about music. As recently as August 2017, the *New York Times* travel editors recommended a visit to Brussels *because* of its "graffiti, avant-garde installations [and] conceptual creations." The concept of an eternal avant-garde is taken for granted—a *reason* to visit a city—whereas it might be important to question whether this philosophy, formulated in the years before World War I, is still a viable way to justify any art 100 years later. After all, Alexander Scriabin imagined that his unfinished tone poem *Prefatory Action,* begun in 1903, would begin with "trumpeters on Mars" and "bells hanging from clouds over the Himalayas." Helicopters would come later.

QUESTIONS AND NO ANSWERS

Conductors spend their lives in search of music and repertory. New works are always being written and the repertorial pool gets deeper and wider every day. Some conductors become specialists and others are generalists. Specialists explore what makes various works within their field different from one another. Generalists look for common denominators in the large field they explore. Since music expresses continuity, I chose to be a generalist. The center of the wheel—the great classical canonic works—remains constant even for generalists: the vast majority are Austro-German, Italian, French, and Russian. This is known as the standard repertory, which begins around 1710 and comes to an end around 1930, with a few works that transcend those outer boundaries. Having explored what remained within this phenomenon in my book *For the Love of Music: A Conductor's Guide to the Art of Listening,* it seems only logical to explore the mystery of what disappeared. As writer Rich Cohen put it in the *Wall Street Journal,* "As a rule, a museum tells more by what it leaves out than by what it includes."[3] Why, therefore, did the classical music canon end when it did—unlike every other art form that has continued to grow with new and seemingly timeless works throughout the twentieth century and into the twenty-first?

While much of my time as a young conductor had been spent performing the music of living composers as well as the works of the core repertory, something began to emerge in those early years that was hard to explain: great Austro-German composers, previously lauded in Europe, who had survived the Holocaust as refugees in America, where they lived and composed, had left a large and varied legacy, worthy of anything they had composed in Europe. That they each died as American citizens should be a source of pride to Americans and possibly a source of curiosity, if not of "difficult conversations," for Germans and Austrians.

It struck me as suspicious that World War II's refugee composers seemingly had written music in the United States that should be avoided because of different, and in some cases opposite, aesthetic justifications. The conclusion, however, was exactly the same: Do not play this music. It is as if something had happened to them when they left Europe that made their music's intrinsic artistic value disappear. Something certainly did happen, and the clues were bringing me to some truly uncomfortable conclusions.

CHAPTER I

A View from 30,000 Feet

On a recent flight to Europe, I brought along Norman Lebrecht's 1997 exposé *Who Killed Classical Music?*—a controversial book that attempts to explain, as the jacket copy states, "the poignant fate of classical music, an art that has sold its soul and lost control of its future." The flight attendant noticed the book sitting on my tray table. She smiled and asked, "Are they still writing that anymore?"

It took me a moment to understand what she was asking. Are people still writing *classical* music? "Uh, yes," I answered, but that "uh" had exposed a very large issue. Mercifully, she did not follow up with "And who is writing it?" or "How come I have never heard any of it?"

The gist of Lebrecht's book is that classical music is in crisis because of corporate, money-grabbing, art-stifling, and ignorant policies. Without discussing his thesis, we might ask a larger question: Is new classical music really dead?

It is true that even before the coronavirus pandemic of 2020–21, in city after city and country after country, symphony orchestras were struggling to survive because of shrinking audiences, dwindling private and public support, and unsustainable ticket revenue. On November 15, 2016, the *New York Times* reported statistics from the League of American Orchestras that indicated, as the headline put it, "It's Official. Many Orchestras Are Now Charities," since American orchestras depended more on philanthropy than ticket sales "to buttress them." But the very same "crisis" had been one of the central concerns of as diverse a group as Handel, when Londoners in the 1730s stopped being interested in his Italian operas; Mozart, when the symphony was going out of fashion in 1785 Vienna; and, as noted by Alex Ross in his *The Rest Is Noise,* in the 1930s, when "classical music could be sold to the masses [in Germany] only with pressure from above. German listeners had felt the pull of Americanized popular music in the Weimar era, and they kept demanding it under Nazism."

The situation in which classical music currently finds itself might not be a unique function of an aging cohort of arts patrons in the first quarter of the twenty-first century. One could optimistically point to the fact that there are more orchestras worldwide today than in the nineteenth century, and that new symphony orchestras are being created in a number of countries, including many in China. We could simply be going through a readjustment phase, one that has merely been accelerated by a global health crisis. As music critic Anne Midgette wisely put it in the *Washington Post:*

> When an orchestra closes, it's seen as an assault on Beethoven and Brahms. By contrast, when a restaurant closes or a car company goes bankrupt, people may bitterly bemoan it, but they don't see it as a threat to food, nor do they think that cars are endangered. . . . Change isn't always good, by any means, but it happens. Yet in classical music, there seems to be a belief that every single institution is worthy of preservation, even though the logical extension of this would be a landscape so littered with old institutions, shored up beyond their actual useful life, that there would be no room for anything new.[1]

In the early 2000s, the Los Angeles Philharmonic built a new framework for its legacy by creating a business model based on the opening of Walt Disney Concert Hall in 2003 and the artistic/business partnership of its chief executive, Deborah Borda, its music director, Esa-Pekka Salonen, and the hall's architect, Frank Gehry. Meeting together every week for two years, they created a new vision for the orchestra, one that started with Gehry's idea of making the new hall something like "a living room" for its audience, and the expansion of the orchestra's repertory to include world music, jazz, film music built around the participation of John Williams, and new music, as well as the standard repertory.

Nevertheless, it is difficult to be sanguine over the general state of our musical institutions and blithely put them into a context of "classical music has been losing money for people for 500 years"—a memorable line from the Amazon cable television series *Mozart in the Jungle*. Opera companies in major American urban centers have disappeared. Historic musical institutions in the United States have declared bankruptcy or resorted to lockouts. And in Europe, drastic cuts in governmental support for classical performing arts institutions have shaken the very foundations of what constitutes the responsibility of governments to define the value of their artistic legacy, a situation exacerbated and clarified by the global impact of a microscopic virus. Classical music, as it is currently defined, does seem to be fading further into the past, even though its core repertory seems impervious to assault.

There are a number of theories that attempt to explain this—while others deny it. In 2014, the *New York Times* ran a large story reporting not only that orchestra subscriptions were significantly down, but that they would most likely continue to decline for decades. The causation offered was the change of habits in modern society, and what were suggested as solutions by the artistic leaders of the New York and Los Angeles Philharmonics, and by the newspaper's chief classical music critic, were, first, shorter concerts; second, events at non-theatrical venues, such as bars; third, informal clothes for the orchestra; and fourth, single-event concert programs (that is, fewer repeated concerts, as if this model could in any way be viable, considering that the costs of rehearsing would remain the same while the income from the concerts would be significantly cut). In other words, there was no discussion about changing *what* was being played, just how the institutions might package it.

Meanwhile, other branches of the arts and entertainment appeared to be flourishing. Attendance at museums, jazz and rock concerts, live theater, movie theaters, and, above all, sporting events, as well as television viewing (on its various platforms), was bringing in more people (and money) than ever in the new century. The 2018 Broadway season, for example, brought in 1.8 billion dollars with its best-attended and highest-grossing year in history. And lest this be chalked up to crass commercialism, it was a season of dramas, comedies, and musicals—both old and new, simple and complex, some with large casts and some with a cast of one. Entire towns in the United States vie for season tickets to both amateur and professional football and basketball games—analogous to what the classical-music world calls subscriptions. International football and soccer leagues, with their multi-billion-dollar entertainment industry and media dominance, are perhaps the greatest example of the continued viability of subscriptions and time commitment throughout the world.

In the last years of the twentieth century, one major excuse offered for dwindling attendance in classical performing arts—besides a personal favorite: "difficulty parking"—was the attention span of young adults who grew up watching *Sesame Street,* with its short segments for preschoolers. This theory is contradicted by the fact that young adults (now grown adults) were staying up all night to read enormous books, such as the *Harry Potter* series, *The Lord of the Rings,* and *A Song of Ice and Fire* (also known as *Game of Thrones*) epics. It has become quite normal for people to spend over three hours watching movies of a length formerly reserved for special films of the past such as *Gone with the Wind, Ben-Hur,* and *Cleopatra*—and then viewing "extended" versions of those films plus "extra features." This does not even address the hours people spend playing video games or "binge watching" entire seasons of television series. Attention-span deficit does not appear to be the problem.

There is, perhaps, another reason. Rather than explore the beautiful and comprehensible music composed during and after World War II, orchestras have remained wedded to performing the same "classic" repertoire our parents and grandparents enjoyed, much of which without question represents the masterpieces of civilization's musical arts. Then, sandwiched rather uncomfortably between these ever-aging eternal masterpieces, are the works commissioned from living composers. And who would not want to encourage new music?[2]

The new music that has been presented as new is, almost without exception, non-tonal (sometimes incorrectly called "avant-garde"), enormously complex, and incomprehensible to most people. It appeals to very few music lovers—and, it should be added, was frequently intended as such.

How many times have people come up to me to express their dislike for "modern" music and ask me to explain it? Frequently they blame *themselves* for not having the capacity to understand it. Sometimes they express a sense of panic at being trapped in a middle seat at the philharmonic as the incomprehensible and frequently offensive music is being performed. This phenomenon has repeated itself for more than a century. A review in Philadelphia during Leopold Stokowski's years as music director (1912–41) started with, "There was a stampede at the Academy of Music last night, when late comers to Maestro Stokowski's program of modern music encountered those walking out early."

Meanwhile, on those rare occasions when orchestras perform contemporary music that the public *does* want to hear (for example, new music from film scores or video games), the music itself attracts passionate, sell-out audiences who are seen as separate from the classical music public. The music is viewed as of transient interest, denigrated and, more often, ignored by the press, and thus eliminated from any serious discussion. Performed on an absolute minimum of rehearsals (frequently only one), it is orchestral music that is treated as commerce, not art. In 2000, two Russian-American fellows—visual artists—at Berlin's American Academy became exasperated with me on the subject of contemporary music and said, "Why do you support music that needs no support?"

Commercial music can be defined as music that makes money for itself and its composer. All the operas of Verdi and Richard Strauss, the concertos of Beethoven and Mozart—indeed, let's face it, *all music* is commercial in one way or another, whether it is a Gregorian chant composed by a monk who got room and board for his services or a contemporary composition that is commissioned by a symphony orchestra. In a 1781 letter to his father, Mozart wrote, "Believe me, *my sole purpose is to make as much money as possible;* for after good health it is the best thing to have" (emphasis added). Joseph Haydn lived at the Hungarian palace of Prince Nicolas Esterházy, where he composed music for the family and the court. Richard Wagner captured the heart and mind of King Ludwig II of Bavaria, who bankrolled him with a brand-new theater, a stipend for living expenses, and a house. In the twentieth century, composer, music theorist, and professor Milton Babbitt was employed by various American universities, allowing him to write electronic music, publish articles, and live in a totally secure environment, free from freelancing. In other words, Wagner and Haydn moved in with princes, while Babbitt moved into Princeton.

Should contemporary instrumental music that is beloved by a large public be as valid an expression as the rarified art of Pierre Boulez (1925–2016), certainly the most influential figure in classical music in the second half of the twentieth century? Can we admit into the circle of approbation the popular symphonic music of John Williams, Hans Zimmer, Alexandre Desplat, Ramin Djawadi, and Hildur Guðnadóttir, the first woman to win the Academy Award for Best Score (*Joker,* 2019)—a circle that currently includes the music of George Benjamin, Thomas Adès, Kaija Saariaho, Nico Muhly, and other living classical composers whose voices are supported with commissions, awards, grants, and artistic residencies?

If there are two "kinds" of music in your universe, popular and serious, and those two categories are seen as opposites and determinants of *quality,* then it might be worth considering that those two adjectives are not in fact opposites in any language or philosophy. You might wonder how and when that came to be. We shall solve that particular mystery later on.

Clearly, serious music can be popular. Puccini's *La Bohème* is a good example. Beethoven's Fifth Symphony is another. Simple music, like Ravel's *Boléro,* can elicit a profound response, and complex music, such as Messiaen's *Chronochromie,* can leave some people cold. Classical music can be funny and light (Prokofiev's "Classical" Symphony), while popular works can be serious, like Rodgers and Hammerstein's *Carousel,* Kander and Ebb's *Cabaret,* Leonard Bernstein's *West Side Story,* and Anaïs Mitchell's *Hadestown*—while some might find these works trivial and superficial.

In politics, we frequently see the binary appellation of liberal versus conservative, whereas these are not opposites either. Everyone is both. The issue is what you wish to conserve and how you wish to support it liberally. In describing music of the last century, "conservative" is still viewed as retrogressive, while the word "modern" and its various appendages—post-modern, modernist, modernistic, along with "experimental"—are deemed good and appropriate.

However, if you were asked if it is day or night, you might want to choose another way of seeing the world, something we might call the kinetic/spectrum view. In that model, the day is always becoming something that is the opposite of what it is. It is becoming night (during the day) and becoming day (during the night). In the northern hemisphere, the days are getting longer in winter, even though the temperatures are dropping.

The difficulty with the yes/no, on/off world of categories was best expressed by New York University's Jonathan Haidt at the Manhattan Institute regarding universities and identity politics—but it is also true of music. "A funny thing happens when you take young human beings, whose minds evolved for tribal warfare and us/them thinking, and you fill those minds full of binary dimensions. You tell them that one side in each binary is good and the other is bad. You turn on tribal circuits, preparing for battle. Many students find it thrilling; it floods them with a sense of meaning and purpose."[3] In March 2015, the Finnish-born composer/conductor Esa-Pekka Salonen spoke of his mentor Pierre Boulez: "Young people are attracted to black-and-white statements. At least I was. And Boulez was like a black-and-white statement machine. He said, 'This is wrong, and this is right.'"[4]

All borders are porous. Wagner, who will become a major character in the drama that follows, once described composition as "the art of transition." We could expand that statement to "the art of *living* is the art of transition." Music and the responses to it are closer to a Wagnerian paradigm—a series of transitions—and cannot be wrestled to the ground on the basis of one thing or the other, except on a singular and ever-evolving personal level, about which we shall also speak.

When George Gershwin died suddenly on June 11, 1937, at the age of thirty-eight, it was Arnold Schoenberg who delivered the eulogy on American radio. Schoenberg's emotional speech included the following: "There is no doubt that he was a great composer." In a binary world of popular versus serious music, you would have to choose between Gershwin and Schoenberg. However, if they didn't, why should we? And it might be of tremendous interest to program late Schoenberg with late Gershwin in a concert. This might help an audience hear how they influenced each other, which they certainly did.

Are there perhaps universal principles in which music celebrates our common humanity, while simultaneously recognizing that we are all different? Political commentator David Brooks rightly pointed out that in defining the world in binary terms "will tear a diverse nation apart."[5]

What is true of a nation is true of music.

THE LONG TRADITION

Classical music passed through the twentieth century and into the twenty-first, surviving wars and upheavals. However, the natural continuance of a long and ever-developing tradition of art music composed to express a dramatic process that dates back to before Bach, Handel, Haydn, Mozart, and Beethoven was annulled in the middle of the twentieth century, within the democratic West, when contemporary music that did not rise to its newly defined functionality was removed from concert halls and opera houses. We shall investigate the possible reasons for this, which are complex and centrally related to various official dictates from the Nazi and Italian Fascist regimes and the responses to them after World War II.

During that post–World War II period, the well-meaning patriots and patrons, conservatory and university instructors, conductors and composers, music critics, government functionaries, and private foundations that were funneling governmental monies accepted an exclusionary and confrontational definition of what constituted the appropriate and valued art of our time. Their aesthetic judgments were not a natural progression of art but a form of political action and personal survival.

A number of young, creative people growing up in a devastated Europe embraced a new, unemotional, and intellectually challenging music, and, it should be said, many profited mightily from it. Their young lives emanated from a cold, dark place that demanded rules (*new* rules) to make sense of life and culture after a war they barely understood but the effects of which were everywhere to be found. When I first visited Europe in 1966, it was shocking to see the number of men in wheelchairs and on crutches as I made my way through the streets of Munich, where much of the city was still mountains of destruction, and the pounding noise of jackhammers was the "music" heard at every street corner—and that was more than two decades after the bombings had ceased.

The one thing that was inadmissible to many young Europeans was sentiment. The horrors of war made beauty inappropriate. For them, beautiful was synonymous with vulnerability and was rejected as kitsch. Beauty could only be experienced as a guilty pleasure. As the enormously influential German philosopher Theodor Adorno (1903–1969), who helped shape the intellectual underpinnings of West Germany, wrote provocatively in his *Aesthetic Theory,* "There is more joy in dissonance than in consonance." After two world wars, there was a sense of numbness in that post-traumatic world. A new musical universe, justified by complex intellectual structures rather than emotionality, offered a certain artistic protection within the chaos. In retrospect, we can offer another conclusion: that this dissonant music is redolent of loss—of family, home, and community—forcibly removing a population from its recent past transgressions. It was music as medicine—it tastes terrible, but deep down it will do you good—not unlike like the self-punitive architecture that was being constructed in bombed-out Cologne.

The composers who came of age during the war, as well as their students and protégés, took ownership of this position and did not let go of it. Speaking as someone who was taught and encouraged to compose during the 1960s, this music was admittedly fun to write and create. There was a sense of freedom and futurism in those years that titillated those of us caught up in it. We were the best and the brightest, and composing music that made use of mathematical manipulation, electronic sound oscillators, and a brand-new machine called a "computer" was like learning to play a very advanced three-dimensional board game. And, as we were very smart and very creative, we could dazzle, amuse, and confound you all at once. We won awards, earned post-graduate degrees, and got exceptionally high grades for it.

At the same time that the young intellectual (and frequently angry) voices of Europe were being supported, classical music ensembles began to turn away from the former crowned giants of "serious" twentieth-century music—Heitor Villa-Lobos, Howard Hanson, Samuel Barber, Gian Carlo Menotti, Aaron Copland, Paul Hindemith, Ralph Vaughan Williams, and countless others. Those who had achieved universally accepted greatness up to about 1930 (the music we still call "classical") remained, after which a narrow line of composers who wrote in a complex and non-narrative style (no more stories or descriptions of nature) rose to the top and maintained their position well into the twenty-first century. The amount of twentieth-century music and the number of composers who were discredited remains one of the great mysteries—and tragedies—of that century. Was this merely the zeitgeist, or was it something else?

But that is only part of the conundrum for those looking for compositions to fill out the great—and missing—repertory of Western art music. The new works that won the prizes and major commissions received their world premieres and, like the giants listed above, also disappeared. It would be difficult to create a list of unquestioned symphonic and operatic masterpieces written between 1960 and 2000. That alone should be a cause for inquiry. As a potent example, consider the repertory currently played on classical music radio stations and streaming systems throughout the world. There you will rarely find the new music that won the awards and received the grants.

Has not the gigantic hole in the classical canon, now stretching past seventy-five years, created the disconnect with contemporary audiences? When I was born, Strauss, Rachmaninoff, Stravinsky, Weill, Sibelius, Shostakovich, Prokofiev, Hindemith, Korngold, Bartók, Schoenberg, and Britten were alive. Whose names will be on the list of living composers for those born today?

It is also important to recognize that during the second half of the twentieth century, when non-tonal modernism came to dominate the new music played in our concert halls, a vast amount of symphonic music continued to be composed by musicians who generally did not participate in the modernist classical music discourse at all. They just wrote music, sometimes defensively, creating the unique phenomenon of our current era: the two parallel universes of contemporary instrumental music, one that is written about but few people want to hear, and one that is almost never written about and people want to hear, but is not considered "classical."

This latter music, listened to in concert by millions of people (who might be called "the audience" but who are usually dismissed as "fans"), demonstrates the indestructible continuity of dramatic music from the late nineteenth century into the twenty-first, written by immensely successful composers who have a thorough knowledge of the experiments and achievements of the twentieth century—but who are rarely concerned with winning approbation from those who rejected the very music that carried forth these traditions. This music is sometimes described as sounding like or being "movie music." It is not, as we shall see.

Although these two worlds exist simultaneously, there has been a general lack of discussion and debate on this phenomenon. Perhaps it is time to shift the narrative and understand that a tradition of classical music was disrupted, but not broken, in the mid-twentieth century.

As already noted, art and politics have always intersected. In the mid-twentieth century a worldwide power was asserted over aesthetic judgments regarding style and function. These judgments came to dramatically influence what music we hear and what music is granted official status by our national and international institutions. At the start of the century, the avant-garde was formed to confront and overthrow our institutions. But by the late twentieth century, our institutions provided the support *for* the avant-garde with festivals and major commissions in Europe and the United States.

And, in the middle of this story, music emerged as both a political weapon and a target. Both unwanted and, to quote the former director of Vienna's Konzerthaus, "inconvenient," a huge cache of great and varied music simply disappeared for more than half a century. How does one eliminate music once it is composed? What happened to all those symphonic composers whose music is no longer played? Why do we struggle to name our greatest living composers when, if that question had been asked a century ago, the names would have rolled easily off the tongue? Puccini, Ravel, Saint-Saens, Elgar, Villa-Lobos . . . Why was the last Italian opera to enter the standard repertory—Puccini's *Turandot*—composed in 1924, even though the art form continued with enormous success well into the 1940s and beyond? And why, if the Nazis lost the war, do we still not play the music Hitler banned?

CHAPTER 2

Brahms and Wagner

THE TWILIGHT OF TWO GODS

The tumultuous twentieth century emerged out of the forces at play during the close of the nineteenth, when two German composers, Johannes Brahms (1833–1897) and Richard Wagner (1813–1883), dominated the intellectual conversation within the world of classical music. The aesthetic arguments that emanated from their purported rivalry became a recurrent theme throughout the new century, with its debates about the value of old (Brahms) and new (Wagner), pictorial music (Wagner) and non-descriptive or "absolute" music (Brahms), and Wagner's concept of the "music of the future."[1]

The genius of Wagner lay in his vision of creating a "total artwork," one in which every aspect of the musical and dramatic experience was controlled by a single person—himself. And in 1876, against all odds, he succeeded. He first conceived an enormous four-part epic poem that hearkened back to the earliest German and Scandinavian myths, which he wrote in an invented pseudo-archaic German, and then composed the music to it. He supervised the design for the most modern theater in the world—one in which the orchestra was hidden from sight and where a total blackout was possible, allowing unprecedented control of the lighting within the confines of the auditorium.

In the Bayreuth Festspielhaus, as the theater was called, Wagner directed all the visual elements, making use of both the latest and traditional stage technologies, including gas lights, gauze, smoke, steam curtains, and "magic lantern" effects, as well as three-dimensional and two-dimensional scenery. He perfected the use of what is known as the leitmotif—a term that Wagner did not use but that refers to short and memorable melodic, rhythmic, or harmonic fragments that represent characters, objects, and situations in the music drama, and which are subsequently repeated throughout the work as "memory themes." And he composed it all with the staging in his mind, demanding the total synchronization of gesture with music from his singers.

The great German helden-baritone Hans Hotter was taught the words, the music, *and the gestures* when he learned the roles of a Wagner opera, so that all of it was one organic muscle memory. "The hardest thing about singing Wotan for Wieland [Wagner] when Bayreuth reopened after the war," Hotter told me in 1989, "was to unlearn how I used the spear when I sang." Wieland, the composer's grandson, created new productions of the Wagnerian canon from 1951 until his death in 1966, eliminating Wagner's required and expected synchronized gestures from his staging.

After twenty-eight years of gestation and composition—and after taking a respite to compose *Tristan und Isolde* and *Die Meistersinger von Nürnberg* (The Master Singers of Nuremberg)—Wagner's fifteen-hour opera cycle *Der Ring des Nibelungen* (The Ring of the Nibelung) premiered at the newly constructed Festspielhaus (Festival Hall) in August 1876. Over four nights the audience experienced a Romantic retelling of the ancient myth of a magical ring forged from the gold of the Rhine. First, the gold is stolen by cursing love and forged into an all-powerful ring. Then the ring itself is cursed when it is stolen from the dwarf who made it. Generations of loves and lies, compromises, broken oaths, and the machinations of gods, demi-gods, dwarves, two giants, two dragons and, above all, humans—both evil and heroic—bring the world to the destruction of the old gods with the death of humanity's greatest hero, Siegfried, and the self-immolation of his human wife, a former Valkyrie named Brünnhilde, who realizes that human love is the greatest power in the universe. In the end, nature, which had been lovingly described throughout the storytelling, is returned to its primordial balance when the twice-cursed ring is returned to the bottom of the Rhine and the earth is cleansed of its evil.

Wagner's achievement was on an unprecedented scale in music theater—

and his influence remains incalculable even in the twenty-first century. At the same time Wagner was translating on a monumental scale the coalescence of all Western art as embodied in the foundational philosophy of Greek drama, which included sung poetry, visual design, costumes, movement, and important historical and social issues, he was also composing music that was "futuristic" in that it broke with many of the conventions of opera and also expanded harmonic function and melodic phrase lengths so as to achieve "endless melody."

His supposed antagonist—binary historical models, such as Newton's Third Law of Motion, seem to demand that everything in the universe have an equal opposite—was Johannes Brahms. Brahms's overt musical inspiration was the actual past—the lineage and legacy of classical music, rather than Wagner's imagined past of retelling ancient stories with his simultaneous commitment to composing music of the future. While Wagner was interpreting the philosophy of the ancient Greeks, Brahms was busy collecting the handwritten manuscripts of the composers of previous eras and using generally abandoned musical forms like the fugue, brought to perfection in the 1700s by Johann Sebastian Bach, and the early seventeenth-century variation form called the passacaglia as a way of linking his music to a living, contemporary, and ever-evolving German tradition.

Brahms's interest in older musical forms and his search for continuity became part of a new academic study: musicology—a field that has fed music departments in almost every university in the world and for which a person can achieve the highest academic degree, a doctorate in philosophy.

For centuries, composers studied with their teachers and only heard other *living* composers' music. Equally important, they did not expect their music to last past whatever performances they could arrange before moving on to their next piece. They received no royalties, and if they sold their music, it was to a publisher who earned money for his company. Although this situation began to change in the nineteenth century, music was seen as a disposable art form and audiences were used to hearing only new music. By the end of the nineteenth century, however, composers were beginning to understand how to earn money from their works even when they were not present to perform them. That, too, is part of the rise of musicology and the sense that old music composed for the stage and concert hall had a value, not only as something to be studied but also as something to be performed for profit even after the composer's death.

In the simplest of terms, one can say that Wagner and Brahms were seen to be representing the future and the past of music—a false dichotomy and one that was fueled by Vienna's most powerful critic of the time, Eduard Hanslick (1825–1904). That Wagner wrote operas almost exclusively, while Brahms wrote everything but operas, made this exaggerated difference easy for many to accept. Wagner, after all, told stories. All his works had titles and scenery. Brahms published his works by generic categories (symphony, quartet, etc.) and opus numbers, rarely using a descriptive title, as he did with his "Tragic Overture," Opus 81. This has helped set up an exaggerated battle between the future and the past.

It might be hard to understand Hanslick's influence today. Even if a few contemporary critics are thought to influence the public, theirs is nothing like the influence that Hanslick exerted during a time of great and varied musical output in Vienna, "the City of Music." Born in Prague, and having studied law and music, Hanslick was a towering figure in the music world, looming over it and judging it for fifty years from 1854, with the publication of his book *Vom Musikalisch-Schönen* (The Beautiful in Music), to his death in 1904. His anti-Wagnerian aesthetics, seen as conservative by Wagnerites, held that music could be beautiful whether or not you liked it; that emotion is not present in music and music does not even *represent* emotion, even though it may awaken feelings; that music is sound and motion, and its beauty is based on its form and form alone. Music does not describe anything at all.

Hanslick was an ardent supporter (and friend) of Brahms, and he came to hate the musical theatrics of Wagner and Wagner's self-proclaimed "music of the future." Hanslick's is an aesthetic philosophy that ran counter to the way the Greeks defined and described music, and echoes of Hanslick's voice can be heard well into the twenty-first century. Those who hold to his position believe that good music is "absolute," regarding it as pure, whereas music that somehow tells a story ("program" music) is of significantly lesser value. It is ironic that Hanslick's anti-futurist conservative philosophy was subsequently taken up by the modernists of the twentieth century who also railed against program music, epitomized in music for the cinema but also prevalent in many works composed for the concert hall. At the same time, these modernists were embracing the symphonies of Gustav Mahler, who wrote to the German writer and music critic Max Kalbeck, "From Beethoven onwards, there is no modern music that has not an inner program." Ironies abound when it comes to the twentieth century, as we shall see.

Thus, Wagner, whose music was able to describe water, a rainbow, tumultuous storms, heroic deeds, curses, dragons, spiritual and carnal love, and one hopping frog, was the very opposite of a composer of absolute music. Brahms, who wrote music for instrumental ensembles and called his symphonies by numbers and without descriptive names, was the great living representation of Music itself.

In reality, Brahms profoundly admired Wagner. We have four letters between the two geniuses regarding Brahms's owning part of the manuscript of the 1861 Paris Opéra version of Wagner's opera *Tannhäuser*. Wagner wanted it back (ostensibly for his son Siegfried to have) and suggested that it could not mean much ("a curiosity") to Brahms. Brahms replied that he did not collect curiosities, and that young Siegfried had plenty of musical manuscripts by his father, but as a fellow composer he could not refuse the request. Here's where the correspondence gets interesting: Brahms asked for something in return, "perhaps the *Meistersinger*," and signed his letter "With the greatest respect and esteem."

Wagner, after receiving the manuscript that had been used (and abused) by the French copyists to create parts for the orchestra, thanked Brahms and then noted that all copies of *Die Meistersinger* had sold out. Wagner hoped Brahms would accept instead a leather-bound display copy of *Das Rheingold*, stamped in gold, that had been exhibited at the Vienna World's Fair of 1873. Wagner pointed out that his music had been accused of being mere "stage scenery" (Hanslick!), and that *Das Rheingold* had exposed him to this reproach, since there was much descriptive music in that opera, from its first five minutes of water music to the rainbow bridge at its end. Wagner jokingly inscribed the much-handled *Rheingold* score to Brahms with the following: "To Herr Johannes Brahms as a well-conditioned substitute for an ugly manuscript. Bayreuth 27 June 1875. Richard Wagner." He ended his letter: "Greetings with highest esteem from your very devoted and indebted Richard Wagner."

The final letter of the four is the moment when the two greatest German composers of their time—and supposed enemies—meet in a sacred place of reconciliation. A war that would rage for a century to follow has ceased as two magisterial kings stand on the field of battle and demonstrate respect for the other—but without giving an inch.

That letter, written by Brahms in June 1875, refers to Wagner's gift as a "splendid present." Brahms notes that he prefers *Die Walküre* to *Das Rheingold* and hopes Wagner does not take that comment amiss. It is important to remember that by 1875, Wagner had yet to premiere the final two operas from his *Ring* cycle but had also completed both *Tristan und Isolde* and *Die Meistersinger.* Thus, Brahms, like many others, was impatiently awaiting the completion of Wagner's mammoth undertaking and the opening of his new theater in Bayreuth. Brahms writes,

> We have, after all, a strange, if stirring, enjoyment of watching this unique work of yours raise itself gradually and come to life—much as the Romans have, when a colossal statue is being dug up. In your less pleasant occupation of witnessing our astonishment and disagreement, the only things that help, of course, are a deep feeling of conviction, and the ever-spreading, ever-growing esteem your imposing creativity calls forth.
>
> I thank you very much again and am, with the
> > greatest respect
> > Yours very truly
> > Johs. Brahms[2]

In this moment the received wisdom of the ages is confronted by surprising facts. The duality of the world becomes clouded by complexity, and we are grateful not to perceive the world in terms of black and white. We are permitted to love both Wagner and Brahms and not take sides in an old and questionable aesthetic battle. That Brahms admitted to knowing Wagner's operas and actually owned (therefore purchased) Wagner's handwritten manuscript, sitting in his collection alongside autographs of Mozart, Haydn, Gabrieli, and Bach—among the greatest composers of the past—says all one needs to know. While Wagner seemingly did not know Brahms's music at the time of their correspondence, we know he subsequently asked to see one of his symphonies—

in both full score and piano reduction—and clearly he saved Brahms's letters, just as Brahms saved the letters from Wagner. It may reasonably be assumed Wagner studied Brahms's First Symphony, but that is only a guess.

When Wagner died in February 1883, Brahms was in the middle of composing his Symphony No. 3, and anyone with ears to hear will find multiple quotations from Wagner's greatest works half buried in the score—a broken memory from *Tristan* just before the end of the first movement, surrounded on either side by silence; the love motif from the *Ring* as an unexpected song that rises to an unprecedented level of emotion during the recapitulation section in the second movement—like those Roman statues Brahms alluded to in his letter to the master, and safely hidden from Hanslick's "pure" vision of music by the man he saw as epitomizing it.

In 1933 Schoenberg published an article entitled "Brahms the Progressive" in which he set out "to prove that Brahms, the classicist, the academician, was a great innovator in the realm of musical language, and that, in fact, he was a great progressive." Clearly the lines were already blurring between the two so-called antagonists, and Schoenberg was leading the charge. Wagner might have been composing music of the future, but Brahms was composing "progressive" music. It was this new way of hearing Brahms that was avant-garde code for justifying its value—as if anyone who loved Brahms needed a reason. Ironically, Schoenberg himself remains a victim of black-and-white portraiture. He was far more interesting—and important—than that, as we have already noted.

Today, more than a century after the Wagner/Brahms battles in the press, we can see how similar these two men were. Both searched the past to justify and inspire their new music. Wagner looked to ancient myths—not only their subject matter, but also poetic structures that frequently depended on questions and answers to move the story forward, as well as the dramatic procedures of Greek drama. Wagner's opera *Siegfried,* which takes over four hours to perform, never has more than two people on stage at one time, a requirement attributed to Aeschylus. Brahms looked to musical forms from the German past. Both composers understood that nothing is really new and nothing can ever be repeated. New and old are a part of the same entity—merely convenient (and frequently misleading) points of view.

1900: THE FUTURE ARRIVES

Fourteen years after Wagner's death in Venice, Brahms died in Vienna on April 3, 1897. Soon afterward, the world entered a new century that carried with it the complex technologies of not just a "modern" world, but a world of "futurism." Futurism was an ambiguous concept that nonetheless pitted experimentation against tradition and saw new as better, even if "new" was a concept that was difficult to define.

The preoccupation with The New became more and more important as a method of valuing any work of art in those years—as it frequently is today in reviewing contemporary classical music—partially because of a misunderstanding of Wagner's theories of the future of German music. This criterion would have been irrelevant to Bach or Mozart, whose preoccupation was with what they would compose next, not what was new. The next composition *was* new.

Europe has always been a self-referential culture. Painters and artists made copies of famous works so that the rich could have them in their palaces and grand estates. Are these works real art or new fakes? The terms "copies" and "forgeries" have to do with commerce, but what of intrinsic artistic value? The Brandenburg Gate is the architectural symbol of Berlin. It consists of twelve Doric columns and is based on the gateway to the Acropolis in Athens, which was completed in 432 B.C.E. The Brandenburg Gate was completed in 1791. Is it art or a fake—or both? In German, the word for art—*Kunst*—and the word for artificial—*Künstlich*—are derivatives, as is true in English. The issue of authentic art versus ersatz and imitative art would, after all, become a fundamental and poisonous issue for eliminating "Jewish" German music during the Nazi regime.

Travelers to Cologne inevitably visit its gigantic cathedral. Workers began building it in 1248 but stopped in 1473, leaving it incomplete for almost 400 years. Recommencing in 1842, work on the cathedral was finally completed in 1880. Although it looks like the Cathedral of Notre-Dame in Paris (1163–1345), the Cologne Cathedral is actually a relatively modern completion that was spurred by a Romantic *idea* of the Middle Ages—the same spirit of the age that inspired Wagner to compose his *Ring* cycle, his *Tristan,* his *Meistersinger,* and his *Parsifal.* Indeed, after the devastating fire that practically destroyed Notre-Dame on April 15, 2019, the world learned that it, too, was a result of years of architectural intervention and modification, including its iconic spire, which was designed by Eugène Viollet-le-Duc in the mid-nineteenth century.

In other words, when you visit the Cologne Cathedral today, think of the Mass composed in the 1360s by Guillaume de Machaut, as well as the Seventh Symphony (1881–83) by Anton Bruckner, because both the music of the Middle Ages and the music of the late Romantic era are present in the completed building's architecture—what Goethe called its "frozen music." Again, is it old or new? Is it authentic or a cheap replica?

Within a generation after the completion of the Cologne Cathedral, Europe was consumed with early twentieth-century "isms"—futurism, cubism, expressionism, vorticism, constructivism, and surrealism. Other *isms* from the previous century—Marxism, socialism, communism, and, perhaps most important of all, anarchism—persisted as the new century marched inexorably into the Great War that engulfed much of the world. Marking the centenary of that war in 2014, many new books added to the plethora of information that can be summed up with one sentence. The most powerful countries in the world and their empires were entangled in so many treaties and ancient feuds that one incident—the assassination of Archduke Franz Ferdinand in Sarajevo on Sunday, June 28, 1914, at the hands of a nineteen-year-old named Gavrilo Princip—brought the world into conflict on a scale never before seen.

The Great European Civil War, as many have called World War I, ended empires and monarchies, redrew the boundaries of countries, and sliced up new pieces of the pie for the powerful, including the creation of countries such as Iraq, with little or no regard for the populations that became citizens of those countries. Music was a part of the international reorganization, before, during, and after.

The run-up to the Great War was a time of frenetic artistic vitality and variety. A multitude of thoughts fueled the passionate debates about art and music in those years and the era's overriding spirit, which was to find something new by breaking and/or rejecting something old.

What that new thing was in music involved rejecting certain aspects of music through a series of experiments, while preserving others. Thus, Schoenberg began composing music that unmoored music from its tonal system, but still kept the same number of notes within the octave. Stravinsky began creating music that was in more than one key at the same time, and with disjointed and unpredictable rhythms that disoriented the listener. But, like Schoenberg, Stravinsky was still writing narrative works—works that told a linear story on a stage. Schoenberg made use of expressive vocalizing—rhythmic speech, singing, and occasional shouting—and Stravinsky did it in terms of dance and mime.

With thousands of newspapers being published every day and new monthly music journals in Europe, the press could fuel the debates. At the same time, we must also understand what was actually being programmed and supported by the public in those years. Audience response is often cited in reviews, such as ovations, the demand for encores, and so on. In the case of operas, the number of repeat performances and productions in other opera houses were a reflection of audience response, not of a good or bad review. Therefore, we can actually understand more clearly what was successful during those years— and it was not the experiments, though they got a lot of attention in the press, and still do today.

In the years before World War I, existential questions were asked that most certainly had not been at the forefront of composers' minds in preceding centuries. Does music have a purpose? If it does, what might that be? Aristotle believed that music was meant to soothe us, but maybe it should teach us or shake us out of complacency. Maybe it should open our ears to the sounds of the modern world that surrounds us, rather than to the closed environment of a concert hall. And, after all, why should a composer write what people want to hear?

There was a collective sense that *something* was looming. Reading diaries and articles from the time as quoted in the many histories of that era, it is clear that an excitement/dread was building with each news story of another strike, another incursion, another war in the Balkans, another beheading of Christians in the waning years of the Muslim Ottoman Empire. Some saw an inevitable war that would finally cleanse society, much as wars were justified in ancient myth and old histories, while others found the crescendo of violence abhorrent. Still others thought it was all a bluff and there could not possibly be a war within Europe. They were wrong.

Music responded to and collaborated in the run-up to the Great War, a war that would ultimately expose its avant-garde to accusations of complicity in the madness that killed so many millions of people and marked the precipitous fall from grace of Europe and its self-regard as being the great civilizing force in the world, epitomized by its culture and, above all, its music. "Western music" is called by this name because it was the music first described in the *writings* of the foundational fathers of what is still called Western civilization, the Greeks. "West of what?" is the logical question. Although this appellation ignores the fact that music—all music—is the result of our very human desire to mimic what we hear, it is used in this text as a shorthand for music that developed in Europe and then, because of its enormous popularity, spread back into the world from which it came.

The classical music that developed in Europe is a glorious compendium of the world's cultures collected over many thousands of years, beginning with the indigenous music of the first humans, and carried on trade routes by commerce, religion, war, and our human curiosity—and a desire to find pleasure.

The 4,000-mile Silk Road had existed for 2,000 years when ancient Romans first purchased the magical fabric made from the larvae of silkworms. Those who sold it also brought music with them—the music of China, Persia, India, and nomadic tribes—and the Romans paid for it with physical currency, as well as an intangible gift: the music of Rome, itself a compendium of music from the Greeks and global Roman conquests in northern Africa and the Middle East, which then traveled back across deserts and mountains—a journey said to take four years—toward the white mulberry trees of China, where the silkworms lived.

Music of those ancient times continued to collect, imitate, and adapt, setting the stage not only for the notes composed more than 1,000 years later by Bach and Wagner, but also for the instruments they wrote for. It took 35,000 years, from the Stone Age to the mid-nineteenth century, to achieve the modern flute. Gold and bronze trumpets have been found in the tombs of the pharaohs. As in European music, there are twelve pitches within the octave in traditional Chinese music, which, as the *Encyclopaedia Britannica* states, are "acoustically and proportionally in the same relation as is found in the Greek Pythagorean system, one of the classic tuning systems that was used extensively in the West." Ancient systems based on groups of twelve (as opposed to ten) are historically linked to units of time, like the signs of the zodiac and the hours of the day that the Babylonians used. What we call classical music, then, is a product of alternating cultural currents of adaptation, assimilation, inexact mimicry, and the desire to create and hear music and make it one's own. Embedded in this music are our collective memories, our humanity, and our instinct to share them.

Music, from the Greeks onward, was understood to be an expression of civilization—and also to be *civilizing*. After the disastrous Great War, music was the subject of even more passionate debates than those that had been waged before its outbreak in 1914. But before we skip ahead of ourselves, we will examine two historic musical events on the eve of World War I.

Vaslav Nijinsky replicating a final gesture from his 1910 *Prelude to the Afternoon of a Faun* for the Ballets Russes. Photo by Baron Adolph de Meyer (1912). (Public domain)

The climactic pose from Nijinsky's 1913 ballet *Jeux* (Games) as rendered in pastel by Valentine Gross, first published in the magazine *Comoedia illustré* in 1913 and subsequently used as a souvenir program. (Public domain)

The original set design for *Jeux* by Léon Bakst, realized here as a composite image by James Edward Burns in 2013, reconstructed and supervised by Kenneth Archer for the University of North Carolina School of the Arts. Note the exaggerated, jungle-like foliage of London's Bedford Square observed from an architecturally neutered version of 18–19 Bedford Square. One window symbolizes the voyeuristic nature of the ballet and three electric lights create an unnatural ambiance for nocturnal activities.

Vaslav Nijinsky as the Rose in Léon Bakst's costume, first seen in 1911 and repeated on the Ballets Russes' program following the world premiere of Stravinsky's *Le Sacre du printemps* (The Rite of Spring) in 1913. The original monochrome photo by Charles Gerschel was colorized to match the costume's overall dusty-rose appearance. (Public domain)

Poster designed by Ludwig Tersch for the Nazis' *Entartete Musik* (Degenerate Music) exhibition in 1938. Private collection. (Album/Alamy Stock Photo)

Raphael's *Queen of Sheba Paying Homage to Solomon*. The fresco was recreated in *tableau vivant* for the 1812 Vienna premiere of Beethoven's Fifth Piano Concerto (the "Emperor"). (Public domain)

Nicolas Poussin's *Swooning of Esther* (sometimes called *Esther before Ahasuerus*) was the second biblical scene re-created in *tableau vivant* for the Vienna premiere of Beethoven's Fifth Piano Concerto. We do not know if the tableaux were presented before or during the musical performance, which, in any case, Beethoven attended. (Public domain)

Cologne, Germany, in 1945. The bombing by Britain's RAF began in 1940, and after 262 air raids in which some 13,000 civilian homes were destroyed, only the spires of the Cologne Cathedral stood watch over the destroyed city. Photo by Margaret Bourke-White for *Life* magazine. (Getty Images)

CHAPTER 3

Stravinsky and Schoenberg

OVERTURES TO THE GREAT WAR

Music history of the second decade of the twentieth century tends to focus on two composers and two cities: Igor Stravinsky (1882–1971) in Paris and Arnold Schoenberg (1874–1951) in Vienna. Ever since the mid-nineteenth century, when classical music had these two capitals, the world paid attention to what was going on there, especially to what was new and provocative. Perhaps it is no accident that Stravinsky and Schoenberg would emerge as the two most interesting composers of the avant-garde with works that premiered within months of each other (October 16, 1912, and May 29, 1913) and soon split the forward-thinking musical world into two opposing camps.

Although France and Austria would be enemies in the war that broke out in 1914, both countries had enormously cosmopolitan capitals that were international magnets for artists, writers, and money. What happened in those two cities was important and was covered in national and international newspapers. Quite simply, column inches needed to be filled, and there was always something worth reporting and commenting on for readers who were interested in the latest developments in music and the performing arts.

A DANCE TO END ALL DANCES

In 1907, a Russian showman, impresario, and self-described charlatan named Serge Diaghilev presented five concerts in Paris of Russian music that had never before been heard in the French capital. The next year, he went further by bringing a troupe of Russian singers and dancers, plus scenery, costumes, and a symphony orchestra, to give the first performances outside Russia of Modest Mussorgsky's opera *Boris Godunov,* electrifyingly performed by Feodor Chaliapin in the title role. And then, in 1909, he focused on ballet and changed the world of classical music and theater design forevermore. For Parisians, Russia was a far-off place, an anachronism, a semi-medieval state in the modern world. The passion, the brilliant colors with the super-realism of the graphic art and design, plus a kind of visceral dancing that was unknown to French ballet fans, made the season of the Ballets Russes an essential annual event.

For all the exoticism Russia brought to Paris, France was politically bound to it by secret treaties. The Franco-Russian Alliance of 1894 protected the two countries from Germany, which was itself bound to Austria-Hungary. In addition, the 1907 Triple Entente joined the French Republic with the Russian Empire and the Kingdom of Great Britain and Ireland as a counterweight to the Triple Alliance of Germany, Austria-Hungary, and the Kingdom of Italy.

Perhaps we shall never know precisely how these political alliances greased the wheels that brought Diaghilev to Paris, but there is no question that a passionate affair between the two countries was cemented in the French capital during that period. The moment when Diaghilev knew he was onto something that touched the very nerves of the Parisians occurred during the 1909 season. The one-act ballet *Cléopâtre,* an epic tale of a deadly one-night stand with the queen of Egypt, was performed within the fantastically sensuous and opulent designs of Léon Bakst and with the full-body expressivity of semi-nude dancers that thrilled the public. Equally important was the French premiere of Act II of Alexander Borodin's opera *Prince Igor.* The "Polovtsian Dances" is the centerpiece of this act, and the athleticism of the half-naked men and women, evoking primitive Russia, and its set designed by Nicolas Roerich, caused a sensation, with men from the audience excitedly storming the stage door when it was over.

The commercial value of sex and violence at the ballet was obvious to Diaghilev, and he knew what he had to do to fill his theaters. In the nineteenth century, ballet had been a woman's world, albeit from the vantage point of men. The magical and precious prima ballerina, who appeared to be lighter than air by having a male partner behind her, controlling her gravity-defying descent from a leap, or managing the appearance of balancing her entire body on one toe, was the graceful fantasy world of classical French-Russian ballet. Now, with the Ballets Russes, women were the sexual predators, with men as their sex slaves.

In 1910, it became a man's game, both athletic and openly sexual, when Diaghilev let his young superstar lover, Vaslav Nijinsky, choreograph Claude Debussy's ten-minute symphonic poem *Prelude to the Afternoon of a Faun.* Nijinsky created a two-dimensional ballet centered around himself as a sexually aroused faun—half man and half animal—with disjointed and ungraceful balletic movements presented in profile, seemingly lifted directly from Greek vases and Egyptian paintings. The extraordinary music from 1894 of the young Debussy—hazy and sensual—and Bakst's untamed forest setting created multiple scandals. The first concerned the choreography itself, which in no way seemed to represent or respond to the music: it confronted it. And then there were the costumes.

The nymphs appeared in loose-fitting Greek chemises that allowed light to pass through them, giving the audience the impression of seeing naked bodies. Nijinsky wore a specially designed leotard that exposed parts of his torso, a little erect tail at the tip of his spine, horns in his wig, and purple grapes intended to lead one's eye to his pubic area, where, it is said, he wore no supporting undergarment, exposing what one writer called his "*rotundités complètement impudiques*"—the shocking outline of his male genitalia just below his tights. Removing the little skirt male dancers traditionally wore had gotten Nijinsky fired the year before by Russia's dowager empress when he did this very thing while dancing in *Giselle* in St. Petersburg.

Enshrouded in misty lighting, Nijinsky's faun was an aroused, naked, alien creature encountering semi-nude nymphs in a glade at sunset. The final moment in his choreography, seen in profile, had the faun lowering his body onto a veil that had been left behind by one of the women, and slowly pressing his groin into it, as the delicate music finished—a tuned finger cymbal and harp harmonics tinkle. The faun arched his back, his mouth open. Curtain.

Riot! Press! Ticket sales! More, please! And not to mention: Sensation. Scandal. Notoriety. What followed was a tour to London and Germany. If the police were called into the hall, Nijinsky made the ending look more like "The Nap of a Faun."

What was missing from the equation, however, was new music to accompany something really violent and/or really sexual. For sex, Diaghilev had gone to Rimsky-Korsakov's 1888 score to *Scheherazade* and produced, in 1910, the most successful ballet in the history of the Ballets Russes. The sensation of this erotically charged version of *Scheherazade* would endure for decades, even to the point of being parodied in 1936, when George Balanchine created "The Princess Zenobia" ballet for the Broadway musical *On Your Toes.* For sensuality, Diaghilev turned to Ravel and the Greek myth of Daphnis and Chloe, but the 1912 audience did not care for its middle-of-the-road depiction of love in ancient Greece. If only that final, propulsive music had been choreographed as an orgiastic bacchanal, instead of a merry *danse générale.*

Waiting in the wings, however, was the young, smart, and aggressive Stravinsky, who had created two exotic but sexless story ballets for Diaghilev: *The Firebird* (1910) and *Petrushka* (1911). "He is the kind of young man who steps on your foot as he kisses your hand," Debussy said of him. Diaghilev had an instinct about where to go for what would become the apocalyptic work of its time.

Nijinsky would create the perfect response for the Parisian public's desire for more sex and violence at the ballet, and Stravinsky, who claimed that the initiating situation came from a dream ("I had dreamed a scene of pagan ritual in which a chosen sacrificial virgin dances herself to death"), would compose its score. Together with the painter and archeologist Nicolas Roerich, they would create what came to represent a time and a place: not ancient Russia, but the subconsciously untamed and voyeuristic Paris of 1913—*disguised* as ancient Russia—during the frenzied months preceding the outbreak of World War I. That work is *Le Sacre du printemps* (The Rite of Spring). "The Ritual of Spring" would be a more accurate translation of the French, but "The Coronation of Spring" was the original intent of its title in Russian.

The story of *Sacre* is actually a series of pictures set to dance and mime, and the work's subtitle is in fact *Scenes from Pagan Russia*. It takes us to primitive Russia just as spring is first sensed, arousing feelings of lust and violence among the various tribes. After a twisted and winding introduction for woodwinds and brass, the curtain parts to depict tribal behavior during daylight: an ancient soothsayer, virgins dancing, and a ritual of abduction in which groups of men seize the virgin girls. There is a springtime "round dance," a competition of rival tribes (an early inspiration for the "Dance at the Gym" in *West Side Story*), and a dance of the earth. The curtain falls, and when it rises again, it is night—the night of the Great Sacrifice. We see the mystic circles of adolescent girls, an evocation of the ancestors, and finally, the old men choose a teenage virgin who is glorified and, shaking with terror, required to dance herself to death as an offering to spring.

Setting a story in ancient times and in a very foreign land was an effective device in getting past censors in Europe. An opera that took place in Spain, for example, let the composer off the hook since Spain was seen as a lawless outpost of European civilization, one that conveniently had no notable operatic tradition of its own. Thus, Mozart's *Don Giovanni,* Beethoven's *Fidelio,* Verdi's *La Forza del destino,* and Bizet's *Carmen* could be seen without too much official objection. Verdi had to go even farther afield in one opera (*Un Ballo in maschera*), moving it from Europe (Sweden) to America (Boston) to keep the audience (and the censors) in check from responding to the assassination that takes place in the last act.

Audiences, however, are not stupid, even if censors behave as if they are. The new Diaghilev ballet may have been set in ancient Russia, but it gave a bloodthirsty Europe the excitement and provocation it profoundly wanted. Its so-called scandal was its glorious success.

Describing violence had been rare in Western music, though not in drama. The most violent acts in classical drama, however, took place offstage so that the audience did not witness them. Opera plots included murder and tragedy, but the music itself did not describe them—they happened during a recitative (Handel's *Giulio Cesare*) or with a single chord (Mozart's *Don Giovanni*). One would not know in Verdi's *Un Ballo in maschera* that the king had been stabbed from merely hearing the music—only from the text and the stage action.

All that began to change with Wagner, who was a master in terms of musical metaphor. In *Tannhäuser* (1845), he composed music to describe spiritual love (using a hymn tune) and invented music to describe sexual love (never before done, until his pulsing, chromatically rising music reaches a climax in the overture, before the curtain rises). Significantly enough, he added an onstage orgy for the Paris premiere on March 13, 1861, which, predictably, caused an uproar and was pulled from the stage after three performances. Historians claim the uproar had to do with Wagner putting his ballet in Act I rather than Act II, as demanded by tradition. While that may be partially true, the descriptive nature of the music, and its visual acting out, was a choice that must also be reckoned with. After all, Wagner could have written a lovely ballet in Act II as a prelude to the song contest. He did not.

Seven years earlier, Wagner had been required by his own libretto to describe an onstage murder when the giant Fafner bludgeons his brother Fasolt to death in the last scene of *Das Rheingold*. In three measures of unprecedented brutality played by the timpani, with support from the lower strings, Wagner once again made history. (And he never did it again, even though other characters in his *Ring*—Siegmund, Mime, and Siegfried—would die in full view of the audience. In Wagner's dramaturgy, those murders are swift and done with a single stroke, and therefore are barely articulated in the orchestra.)

However, in the first decade of the twentieth century, violent actions—and their description in orchestral accompaniment—became more prominent in classical music, especially opera.

The first twentieth-century opera that joined the standard repertory was Puccini's *Tosca,* which premiered in Rome on January 14, 1900. Notoriously derided by some critics, it is a masterpiece and, if one had to choose, Puccini's greatest opera. There are many reasons for saying that, including its perfect balance between action and poetry, the brilliance of its orchestration, its tapping into a primal story of a woman who attempts to seek mercy for her brother/husband/lover from a corrupt public official/person of a higher estate, who demands sexual favors in return (see Shakespeare's *Measure for Measure* and the screenplay to Ernst Lubitsch's *To Be or Not to Be*), and its basis in historical incident. For our purposes, however, it is the musical depiction of violence that marks *Tosca* as a prescient and particularly twentieth-century view of the folk tale.

Violence is never far from the environment of *Tosca,* and, unlike Beethoven's *Fidelio*—which also takes place during Napoleon's corrupt empire building—when *Tosca* is over, it is most definitely over. The three main characters are dead. One is stabbed and dies in paroxysms as he suffocates on his own blood, another is shot by a firing squad, and a third commits suicide by jumping off a parapet—and all of it before our eyes. In Beethoven's hands, the corrupt official is arrested at the last minute and the husband and wife are saved, as the chorus joins in a final hymn to freedom and God's mercy. The American musicologist Joseph Kerman famously called *Tosca* a "shabby little shocker," but it is neither shabby nor little. *Tosca* was the first big musical shock to hit the twentieth-century stage, but it would hardly be the last.

Richard Strauss also felt the tug to compose two operas in which violence is a main component: *Salome* (1905) and *Elektra* (1909). Strauss had honed his abilities to describe objects, characters, and natural occurrences in his tone poems (composed in the previous century) and was universally viewed as Wagner's heir even before he began to compose operas. *Salome* reaches its grisly climax with an offstage beheading of John the Baptist in which the orchestra describes the sound of his head falling to the ground, followed by a sex scene with his dismembered head and the crushing to death of the teenage girl under the weight of Roman shields—with clarinets squealing like a slaughtered pig, brass fanfares, and the percussion section taking its cue from the bludgeoning of Fasolt in Wagner's *Das Rheingold.* And, as in *Tosca,* the curtain falls immediately upon her death. There is no epilogue, just a shocking execution performed in full view of the audience.

Elektra is different since it is based on Sophocles' play in which murder is a purifying act that cleanses the House of Atreus. As in all Greek drama, the murders take place offstage, but the brutality of the twentieth-century orchestral description—and the screams of the victims—were without precedent on the musical stage. And when Elektra dances herself to death before our eyes, her sister Chrysothemis calls out to their brother Orestes while battering the doors of the palace. There is no answer—only a violently triumphant C major, punctuated by a repeated three-note rhythmic figure played with maximum strength by the percussion section. Again, as with *Tosca* and *Salome,* there is no comment at the end, only a shocking death.

EDGING CLOSER TO WAR

All of this brings us to Paris in 1913 and the eagerly anticipated return of Diaghilev's Ballets Russes. For the new season, the company took up residence in a brand-new theater, the Théâtre des Champs-Élysées. Modern and considered profoundly "un-French" (read "German"), this theater was at the cutting edge of contemporary design. The two world premieres of that season are emblematic of the aesthetic split in Europe of that time. On opening night of the new season, May 15, 1913, Debussy's *Jeux* (Games) received its world premiere. Exactly two weeks later, the very same company presented the world premiere of Stravinsky's *Le Sacre du printemps.* Each of these premieres was nestled (perhaps "hidden" is a better word) between other works on the program that were already known to Parisian audiences.

Stravinsky admired Debussy and had sought his approval. Debussy was never sure of this young man from Russia. After the premiere of Stravinsky's *Firebird* in 1910, Debussy, when asked what he thought, said, "One has to start somewhere." Stravinsky had practically quoted the French master's description of clouds (*Nuages*) in the opening bars of his opera *The Nightingale* (begun in 1908). And when Stravinsky had completed a four-hand piano version of *Sacre,* he brought it to Debussy and the two sat at the piano and played it, with Debussy sight-reading the lower part.

Jeux and *Sacre* would be presented by the same company, on the same stage, with the same conductor (Pierre Monteux), and choreographed by the same man—Vaslav Nijinsky. But that is where the similarity ends.

Unlike *Sacre,* which the program stated takes place in "ancient Russia," *Jeux* is set in the future. The diaphanous and mysterious opening chords alternate with a foreign-sounding rhythmic figure that predicts an unusual series of games—"foreign-sounding" because the rhythm is colored by non-Western percussion sounds—xylophone, suspended cymbal, and tambourine—which playfully answer the "normal" and ethereal sounds of Debussy's trademark orchestral palette. All settles back down again as the curtain rises on a park at sunset—modeled on London's Bedford Square—and the last "natural" light that we shall see. A startling visual image playfully intrudes on Debussy's and designer Léon Bakst's aural and visual environment: a tennis ball arcs through the sky from the right, bounces on the stage, and then disappears to the left.

A team of elephants could not be more shocking, and because of the surprise, the audience laughs. The games have begun.

The original scenario for *Jeux* was a playful erotic encounter of three people (two women and a man) dressed in tennis attire under the unnatural electric lights that had only recently been installed in London's public parks. If one reads the printed text in the published piano score, the climax of the work was to be a triple kiss, interrupted by a second tennis ball that bounced onstage, causing the three to run away into the night. Debussy composed a score that is atmospheric and sensual, with a quotation of the fundamental love motif used in Wagner's *Ring* cycle that is harmonized and distended into something far more sexual and predatory than any version of it in Wagner's original setting. Debussy hated violence and was horrified that Stravinsky and others of his generation saw the possibility of an impending war as something that might cleanse European civilization. Stravinsky was quoted in a French magazine at the time saying that war would be a good thing since it would purge society of its weaker elements, leaving the world a stronger place. He was not alone in this sentiment. It was, after all, a fundamental part of the Italian poet Filippo Tommaso Marinetti's *Manifesto del futurismo* (Futurist Manifesto) of 1909.

In point of fact, Nijinsky, who was simultaneously choreographing both *Jeux* and *Sacre,* was equally uncomfortable with violence, and, as he set Debussy's music with his developing choreography, something in his plan changed dramatically. The climax would no longer be a sexual one. That climactic moment, preserved in the drawings, paintings, photographs, and reviews of the time, is a pristine and symmetrical joining of the man (Nijinsky) with the two women standing on either side of him, their arms entwined like a Greek statue.

What precedes this moment is a series of panic gestures of the two women and the man, who at one point falls to the ground as the three try to dance a waltz together.

The music may have originally been meant to describe the sexual arousal of the three, but in fact the rising emotions in the completed ballet are of foreboding and protection.

The second tennis ball is not the discovery of the three *in flagrante delicto,* but something more like a shocking attack from above. Originally, Nijinsky had spoken of an airplane crashing upstage, and Diaghilev and others thought it was just some incipient madness on the dancer's part.

Nijinsky, perhaps because he was also working on *Sacre* and was a profoundly sensitive man, seemed to have foreseen a war that would leave one man alive for every two women in the belligerent countries when it finally ended in 1918. During the period in which he was creating *Jeux*, he spent a significant amount of time at the London home of Lady Ottoline Morrell. She, her husband—a distinguished member of Parliament—and her lover, Bertrand Russell, were all pacifists during the run-up to World War I. It is certainly possible that the ballet's scenario and its visual environment were inspired by Nijinsky's meeting the painter Vanessa Bell and her sister Virginia Woolf, and intently watching the ambisexual artist Duncan Grant play tennis in Bedford Square during the Ballets Russes' 1912 tour to London.

At the end of the ballet, the second tennis ball interrupts the three young people who are lying on the grass. The scenario indicates that they are surprised and frightened, and leap "into the depths of the nocturnal park" (*"dans les profondeurs du parc nocturne"*). Debussy repeats the mysterious opening harmonies and adds a murmuring figure within its orchestration. For thirty seconds—a very long time in music!—the audience watches an empty park at night, wondering perhaps at the source of this second tennis ball (Another "game"? Another voyeur [besides us]?), and also perhaps imagining what might be going on somewhere in the dark among the two women and the youth, who have discovered something about each other.

Jeux did not cause a scandal, though it surely would have had the gestures of the women (who, as the libretto states, are meeting in the park "to share confidences") represented a consensual sexual union with the man. Anything like the final masturbatory gesture from Nijinsky's *Faun* would have fulfilled and topped that particular expectation. Instead, Nijinsky created movements that were refracted gestures from playing tennis presented in symmetrical patterns. The various pairings were based on popular dance forms—the tango, the waltz, and the two-step—with influences from Cambodian ritual formations and references to classical ballets such as *The Sleeping Beauty*. The influences from ancient Greek and Egyptian art were intermixed with the procedures of cubism.

The set by Bakst was jungle-like, with the roots of trees exaggerated and twisted upward. In the background, a white residential building, indicating that this jungle was in the middle of a city, looked down at the park, with one open window for the unseen voyeurs—us! The three dancers were dressed in white, and Nijinsky, whose shirt was left open at the neck with sleeves rolled up, sported a bright red tie and a belt on his tennis trousers. Clearly the designs were created for a ballet about gender blending and the open relationships embraced by the Bloomsbury Group.[1]

The point here is that *Jeux* was a work that started out as a potential scandal-project enlisting the most sensual designs and music, and instead became a warning against violence. The opening night of the Ballets Russes' 1913 season had begun with a reprise of the 1910 hit *The Firebird. Jeux* followed after the first interval, and the evening ended with *Scheherazade,* Diaghilev's biggest hit. Surrounded by such overwhelming color and panache, *Jeux* was dwarfed and its importance all but lost on its glittering audience. As such, it remains relatively unknown, though its score (Debussy's last completed orchestral score) is a masterpiece.

Two weeks later, a well-documented scandal would come to the Ballets Russes with the premiere of *Le Sacre du printemps.* Like *Jeux, Sacre* was presented between other Ballets Russes successes. The historic evening began with *Les Sylphides* (music by Chopin orchestrated by various composers, including Alexander Glazunov and Stravinsky). An intermission followed and a ninety-nine-piece orchestra crammed into the pit for the tumultuous world premiere of the new ballet. After *Sacre,* Nijinsky, who had been in the wings for his premiere, went to his dressing room, where he put on his pink leotard, pinned on the roses, and applied makeup and lipstick to appear as the erotic memory of a rose given to a young girl at her first dance.

Le Spectre de la rose (performed to *Invitation to the Dance,* Carl Maria von Weber's 1819 piano piece in the 1841 orchestration by Hector Berlioz) was immediately followed by another safe and successful hit, the *Polovtsian Dances,* the violence of which was somewhat mitigated by its melodious nineteenth-century score by Borodin. Little attention has been given to what was danced that night after the premiere of *Sacre,* though it must be said that subsequent performances of the program (there were five more in Paris, before going on to London) were not greeted with whistles and the throwing of programs or the occasional fistfight of the opening-night audience. Gertrude Stein, who attended the second performance, reported a bit of noise but nothing like a "riot." All subsequent performances, judging from the extant reportage of the time, were quiet, and in London Nijinsky thanked the public for *not* rioting.

A great deal has been written about *Sacre,* and there is no need to repeat the many stories here. While *Jeux* took place in the future and *Sacre* took place in the ancient past, both can be seen as complementary images representing Europe in 1913. Perhaps two other points should be made.

First of all, *Sacre's* scandal feels more like the product of a successful public relations campaign than a reflection of its shocking artistic influence. Scandal at a world premiere was not all that unusual. The world premieres of *Tosca* in Rome (1900) and *Madama Butterfly* in Milan (1904) were greeted with demonstrations and controversy, as was that of *Salome* in Dresden (1905). Equally infamous were the world premieres of *La Traviata* in Venice (1853) and *Carmen* in Paris (1874). When Victor Hugo's play *Hernani* was first produced at the Comédie-Française in 1830, a battle between the conservative classicists and the new iconoclastic Romanticists broke out each night in fistfights and other violent acts.

America, which usually brought the latest important works to its shores from Europe within a year—and sometimes months—took seven years to perform *Sacre* in concert and another five as a ballet. The so-called opening-night riot in Paris (no one was shot and no one died, but people booed and whistled) seems to have had far more to do with the ballet itself and the ballet audience's expectations than with its music. The next year, Paris heard *Sacre* in concert at the Casino de Paris, again conducted by Monteux, and Stravinsky was hailed by the audience and carried through the streets of Paris (much to the annoyance of Diaghilev, who, upon learning about the police presence, said, "Our little Igor now needs a bodyguard, like a boxer"). What makes that story particularly poignant is that many of the young men who carried Stravinsky through the streets would be dead within a year, once the violence espoused by its score became a reality.

Second, and separate from the "riot," *Sacre* remains a singular masterpiece. Like *Tosca, Salome,* and *Elektra, Sacre* presents violence unapologetically. At the conclusion of the ballet, the teenage girl, encircled by the old men who have chosen her, dances until her heart stops beating and drops dead. They then lift her body to the sky and there is a blackout. Under any other circumstance in Western ballet, there would have been an epilogue to justify the action. A final tableau—something like the ending of *Swan Lake* or the more recent *Firebird*—would have shown us the blessings of the sacrifice: the earth would come to life, flowers would bloom, and there would be another fruitful year, justifying this annual ritual. Mother Earth would show her pleasure and there would be a general dance. Curtain. Applause.

Nothing of the kind! The violence of *Sacre* is simply what it is, no further comment provided. It is an artifact of a time when many thought violence was "in the air," and not only does it express Stravinsky's naïve philosophy—supporting a cleansing war—it can also be seen as both accepting and encouraging what many consider the very worst in human tribal and sexist behavior.

More than 100 years after its premiere, *Sacre* remains the work on which Stravinsky's fame rests (even though his sensuous and colorful *Firebird* is his most popular and performed work). From a personal point of view, if I may, I clearly remember how I felt *while* conducting it and *after* having conducted it. What a conductor must become in order to perform *Sacre* makes us find that thing in our nature we work so hard to reject as civilized human beings. After a performance in London, I decided that the work was just too terrible and that I never wished to go there or be that person again—and, it should be said, neither did the composer.

It would be hard to find an example of any other composer who, having found his or her "voice" and concomitant worldwide fame, stepped away from that voice while attempting to maintain that fame. And, in spite of all that has been written about *Sacre*'s influence, there are only a few works that sound anything like it—until much later, as we shall see.

Any conductor, however, who completes a performance of *Sacre* and smiles has no idea what this work is about. We would never accept a singer's smile after completing Schubert's tragic song cycle *Winterreise* (A Winter's Journey), and yet *Sacre* has become more of a technical proving ground—the faster the better—rather than what it actually is: a terrible journey into the depths of primitive behavior.

It is true that, with *Sacre*, Stravinsky invented a unique and fascinating *way* of composing that indeed influenced other classical composers. It would be hard for a non-musician to actually hear that method without carefully being tutored in listening for it. For one thing, *Sacre* belies its composition at the piano. Composers who write at the piano make use of how their fingers and hands fall on the keys, which allows them to hear the music in the air rather than in their heads.

The history of how a composer gets his/her ideas and then develops them is varied and fascinating. Prokofiev, for example, was proud of the fact that his "Classical" Symphony was composed away from the keyboard. Puccini, Debussy, and Handel composed at the keyboard. Berlioz allegedly composed on the guitar.

What is clear from *Sacre* is that Stravinsky experimented on the piano, simultaneously playing "normal" chords with each hand but with the chords belonging to different keys. This was something like a chemistry experiment. Magnesium powder is very stable, and so is water. Put them together and you get an explosion. That's what happens in much of *Sacre,* and the technical word for this kind of harmony is polytonality. In general, however, polytonal works after *Sacre* were comic, since the melody and the accompaniment were playing in different keys. This "wrong-note" setting is funny because it sounds like a series of mistakes made by beginning students who don't read the key signatures or the clef in the musical notation.

Equally interesting, Stravinsky created long sections of music in the new ballet by compiling various extremely short musical motifs, or "cells," in unpredictable, repeated patterns. This, I believe, was his way of imagining ancient music and perhaps even the way birds create patterns in their calls to each other. The music of the Czech composer Leoš Janáček is constructed this way, as is the motoric music of Bernard Herrmann's score to the movie *Psycho*.

In general, however, the public awareness of *Sacre* had to wait until Walt Disney's artists stripped away its original story and replaced it with nothing short of the creation of the universe and the violence of the earth's first 300 million years (and all in less than a half-hour). After the music's appearance in the 1940 animated feature film *Fantasia,* all kinds of *Sacre*-sounding works emerged, not necessarily in concert halls but rather in movie theaters in scores by Franz Waxman, Bernard Herrmann, Jerry Goldsmith, and John Williams, and on Broadway, with Leonard Bernstein's score to *West Side Story*—whose harmonies and orchestration on the word "somewhere" in the Act II nightmare ballet are another clear reference to Stravinsky's tale of macho violence.

But for Stravinsky, *Sacre* was a self-created dead end. The reason for this,

I believe, was an awareness of how utterly wrong he was about the war and, in some deep sense, an understanding of his culpability in supporting and encouraging it. As we shall see later in this book, Stravinsky, like many of his contemporaries, ultimately found his own voice—one that was uniquely his, but far less dense (read "noisy" and "brutal") and more transparent (his chords became simpler, built with larger spaces between the notes).

After *Sacre,* he settled into various stylistic "periods" that included modern reinterpretations of other people's music, his "discovery of the past"— *Pulcinella* (1920), *Le Baiser de la fée* (The Fairy's Kiss; 1928), Symphony in C (1940), *Monumentum pro Gesualdo* (1960)—drawing inspiration from and featuring references to Baroque, pre-Baroque, Classical, and even Romantic composers, including lesser-known music by Tchaikovsky in which he altered "normal" chords—as if passing them before a fun-house mirror—by adding intrusive notes here and there and distorting traditional Classical rhythms. After 1918, Stravinsky's music generally became devoid of the excessive passions depicted in his *Sacre.* This musical language, often referred to as neoclassicism, showed a wry sense of humor, an emotional detachment, and an occasional spirituality. Above all, it was free of overt violence, while nonetheless maintaining a complexity of rhythmic notation that is the true echo of his *Sacre*—one, it should be said, that is hardly noticeable to the listener but is a well-known gauntlet run by those of us who perform his music.

Stravinsky lived a very long and public life. Early on, he tried his hand at conducting, and his recorded legacy is seen by many as being the definitive interpretation of his music. While this makes a certain logical sense—the composer as interpreter of his creation—many composers are not competent conductors and their views of their own music inevitably plead a case for their works and their relevance.

Stravinsky made a good living as a conductor of his music. His various recordings of *Sacre* (1928, 1940, 1960) are always worth examining. Stravinsky the conductor became more secure as the years went by and orchestras became more able to play the complicated music. However, with each new recording, Stravinsky also seemed to be reinventing *Sacre* to fit into a changing world of aesthetics. Each subsequent recording is more and more detached due to his inflexible and unbending tempos, making it less emotionally evocative— less "Romantic," if you will—and emphasizing its impersonal brutality.

As he stepped away from its obvious storytelling (it is, after all, based on a dreamt *scene*—Stravinsky's word—and its story was developed with a *visual* artist, with each section having a title), he finally announced, a half-century after its premiere, that *Sacre* "is not a picture postcard of ancient Russia." All of this feels like an attempt to keep the work new and in line with the intellectual assessment that "pure" music is better than programmatic music (Hanslick again, and kept current by the equally influential German, Theodor Adorno), the overwhelmingly accepted dictum during the 1960s. As described in the 2017 online *Encyclopaedia Britannica,* "The movement of the twentieth century was generally away from the descriptive [in classical music]." We can call it whatever we like and perform it however we want, but *Sacre* is a great story ballet, and its music is a titanic description of violent human behavior. Period.

Aside from the brutal power of its harmonies and massive orchestration, it is *Sacre*'s unpredictable rhythms that are unprecedented. When Wagner called Beethoven's Symphony No. 7 "the apotheosis of dance" in his book *The Artwork of the Future* (1849), he could not have known that a ballet would emerge in the future that was, in fact, the antithesis of dance music. If we describe all music as being fundamentally a song or a dance, then *Sacre* is the work that ends the development of dance music, because the very essence of dance—its unchanging and dependable tempo and meter—is constantly upset, fooling and challenging us, and making it impossible to predict the next strong beat.

1–2–3, 1–2–3, 1–2–3 is a waltz. It never changes. 1–2, 1–2, 1–2 is a polka or a samba. A tango stays a tango. Dance bands do not need a conductor because the leader of the band can give a short countdown ("uh–1–2–3–4") to get it started and that's that. However, in *Sacre* the pulses are so irregular that Stravinsky could play them on the piano but was unsure how to write them down. In fact, he kept rewriting the music (not how it should *sound*, but how to indicate that sound on paper) for decades after its 1913 premiere. Many conductors, even today, rewrite its beating patterns to make it easier for all to perform.

Here is an example of beats in the final section of the score: 1& / 1&& / 1&&/ 1&& / 1&& / 1& / 1&—2&& / 1&—2&—3& / 1&—2&—3& / 1.

Earlier in the score, just before the section called "The Glorification of the Chosen One," four timpani, a bass drum, and the entire string section playing with slashing down-bows strike eleven equal hits at maximum loudness. Why eleven, you may ask? Eleven is a prime number that cannot be grouped by the brain into repeated groups of twos, threes, or fours. Stravinsky makes his use of eleven into an ear-splitting repetitive noise that seemingly has no end—and is unprecedented as something one might call "music." It is followed by a dance pattern (if you can call it that) that goes like this: 1&—2&& / 1&—2&& / 1&&—2&&—3&& / 1&—2&& / 1&—2&—3&&—and so forth. No listener can predict this wild and mad explosion of tribal ecstasy at having found the girl who will die. For me, those eleven hits shake my very soul, because part of me is committing a violent murderous act, while another part of me feels as if *I* am literally being hit eleven times. A conductor is exactly that: the one who conducts the energy of the score, leading it and being the immediate recipient of it. There is no more terrible moment for a conductor than this bar of music, because you are simultaneously the perpetrator and the victim.

Even if the world did not get a series of *Sacres* after 1913—the way Beethoven's Ninth inspired so many dramatic symphonies, or *Tristan*'s ghost haunted so may operas and symphonic works in the decades after the opera's premiere in 1865—*Sacre* can be seen as the apex of complexity in Western dance music. Many great works of dance were composed after it, but one would be hard pressed to find another masterpiece that gets anywhere near its anarchic rhythmic structures.

If *Sacre* brought Europe to an end point with its violent orchestration and complex dance rhythms, what about Europe's great song tradition in the pre–World War I experimental musical world? *Sacre*'s place in avant-garde history has little to do with its melodies, which are made up from snippets of Russian folk tunes and a few new ones by Stravinsky. When it comes to vocal music and melody, one would have to go somewhere other than Paris for the latest experiments in music that confronted the status quo. Something equally apocalyptic was emanating from Vienna and, as one has come to expect, it created the other camp in modern music, one that dismissed Stravinsky as a creator of kitsch.

A SONG NO ONE CAN SING

It is important to remember that Vienna is at the eastern end of western Europe, and in the early twentieth century its population was a heady mix of ethnicities and influences, far more varied and "non-European" than Paris. People spoke French in Paris, which was also the official language of diplomacy. Vienna, which was the primary capital of the Austro-Hungarian Dual Monarchy, had, by contrast, eleven official languages. The empire's population included Germans, Czechs, Montenegrins, Poles, Romanians, Hungarians, Italians, Ukrainians, Croats, Slovaks, Serbs, Slovenes, Bosnians, Ruthenians, and Herzegovinians. Music, art, philosophies, myths, and traditions all mixed together in its capital city, which, like Paris, was a magnet for artists and intellectuals.

Following the 1867 constitution and the formation of the Austro-Hungarian Dual Monarchy—and the completion of Jewish emancipation—Jews from across the empire flooded into Vienna to take advantage of their new freedoms. As their numbers expanded (to 10 percent of the population by 1880), their success in business and the professions resulted in ever-increasing anti-Semitism, which was finally allowed official expression on March 12, 1938 with the *Anschluss* to Nazi Germany.

Vienna was also the city of Sigmund Freud and his discoveries of the deep and violent subconscious, the city of the distorted poetic and visual arts movement known as expressionism, and the birth city of composer Arnold Schoenberg.

Schoenberg's early music, which was highly admired by both Gustav Mahler and Richard Strauss, carried on the epic sweep of late nineteenth-century Austro-German Romanticism. However, he claimed that "an inner compulsion" drove him to move further away from evolutionary developments in his music and, during 1908–09, he began writing songs that had no reference to a key whatsoever.

Just about every classical work up to that point could be said to be in a "key." Beethoven's Fifth Symphony is published as being "in C minor." Bach's great Mass is called "the B-Minor Mass." Schoenberg took a step into the unknown with the setting of mystical poems by Stefan George that had no home key and could wander in a rootless metaphoric world devoid of one of the fundamental forces of nature—gravity. Soon he began writing large-scale works that continued the implications of those first steps, and ultimately became known as the leader of what is known as "The Second Viennese School"—the first being that of Mozart, Haydn, and Beethoven from a century before.

Tonal music, which is the music we hear every day and which developed over centuries, is quite simply "normal" music—whether it is the language of a simple nursery rhyme tune, your national anthem, a song by the Beatles, a gigantic symphony by Mahler, or the score to a new video game. Throughout the centuries, classical music had stretched the tonal language of Western music to take journeys that wandered farther and farther afield, only (inevitably) to come home at the end. In the first decade of the twentieth century, Schoenberg cut the umbilicus and began writing music in which there was no "home key" to return to. And there were no rules by which to navigate a world of total harmonic freedom—which could also be perceived as harmonic chaos.

There can be no sense of home without memory, and without memory, as we well know from those suffering from dementia, there is no home. The new music was free of all rules, except it could/should NOT sound like tonal music. It was, to most people, also free of audibly perceivable structure. Without structural memory, the listener feels lost, since music is experienced through time and can only be understood if that listener can perceive and remember.

"The intentional fallacy" is a phrase that challenges the idea that an artist's intent can be understood from a work of art, or, in the case of "the biographical fallacy," that art is an expression of that artist's life situation. A musician can be unhappy and yet compose "happy" music. However, Schoenberg's life story at the time of his brave walk into weightlessness surely influenced his musical output. While it is true that his earlier, highly Romantic music was occasionally injected with surprising dissonances, a crisis in his life seems to have pushed him into a complete psychological unmooring that made his non-tonal music inevitable.

Schoenberg's wife, Mathilde, whom he had married in 1901 and who was the mother of their two children, abandoned him in 1908 to continue an affair with a young painter named Richard Gerstl. Seen by many as the father of expressionism, Gerstl lived in the same building as the Schoenbergs, painted portraits of the family, showed a deep interest in Schoenberg's music, and even taught the composer how to paint. Mathilde ultimately returned to her husband, presumably for the sake of their children.

On the night of November 4, 1908, during a concert of music by Schoenberg's students to which Gerstl was not invited, the rejected twenty-five-year-old painter burned whatever he could find in his studio, stripped himself naked, and hanged and stabbed himself while watching his image reflected in a full-length mirror he had set up to view his final self-portrait.

During this period, Schoenberg, like a man possessed, wrote music. In 1909, he composed an astounding amount of it—a fifteen-part song cycle called *Das Buch der hängende Gärten* (The Book of the Hanging Gardens), which tells the tale of adolescent love that ends with the departure of the young woman and the destruction of the garden; *Orchesterstücke* (Five Pieces for Orchestra); a one-act monodrama called *Erwartung* (Expectation); and a series of piano pieces, Op. 19. When there were texts to his music, the words expressed the devastation that a human being can withstand—and still live— as in his own text to *Erwartung*:

> On the entire long road nothing lives. . . . There is no sound. . . . The wide, pale fields are without breath, as if dead. . . . No straw moves. . . . And yet, always in the city . . . no clouds, not the shadow of a night bird's wing in the sky . . . this borderless death pallor . . . I can hardly go further.

Publicly, Schoenberg frequently spoke of this new music as "the emancipation of dissonance," as if it were a technical achievement and not an expression of his emotional state and the total humiliation he felt. There is, to be fair, a certain disagreement about when the composer knew of the affair and kept it a painful secret. From his professorial point of view, the new music created a world in which there was no such thing as dissonance. It would have formerly been *called* dissonance when placed in the context of consonance or harmonious music. However, just as there is no night without day, no quiet without loud, Schoenberg believed that non-tonal music was its own complete universe of sounds in which the very concept of dissonance was inoperative—except for the fact that complex waveforms stimulate the ear, send information to our brains, and have real consequences as to whether we like them or not.

Schoenberg was already famous for his unique music when he reached a milestone with his 1912 melodrama *Pierrot lunaire* (Moon-struck Pierrot)—a setting of poems recited and acted out by a woman dressed as Harlequin, accompanied by a chamber orchestra hidden from the audience's view. The sad, white-faced clown that was a common figure in pantomime and *commedia dell'arte* appeared in full costume speaking, singing—and sometimes shrieking—a series of poems that expressed the longing of the clown who is both moon-drunk and homesick. He has visions of being a grave robber, a blasphemer, a condemned man about to be decapitated, and a poet, crucified on his words by the public.

The work was not premiered in Vienna, but in the city that would replace Vienna in the post–World War I years as a music center—Berlin. Wherever Schoenberg's new music was played, there were demonstrations. Six months before the famous "riot" at the 1913 world premiere of *Le Sacre du printemps* in Paris, Vienna had its own *Skandalkonzert,* also known as the *Watschen-Konzert* (slap concert), at the Great Hall of the Musikverein on March 31, 1913. The violent response to hearing new music by Schoenberg (his Chamber Symphony No. 1) and his students, Anton Webern and Alban Berg, led to the concert's being terminated before its scheduled final work by Mahler, as objects were being hurled and furniture destroyed.

There were also those who passionately supported the new music. What is clear is that, no matter what side of the argument you took, everyone of importance went to experience *Pierrot lunaire:* Stravinsky traveled to Berlin to hear it while he was composing *Sacre.*

And if you did not go to Berlin, *Pierrot* came to you. Immediately after its premiere, the composer, his cabaret-star performer, and the little chamber orchestra traveled to no fewer than eighteen cities, including Vienna, Leipzig, Dresden, Prague, Hamburg, and Düsseldorf. The work received over 100 reviews, now all dutifully archived at Vienna's Arnold Schönberg Center. Within a decade, it traveled throughout Europe to London, Paris, Amsterdam, Brussels, Rome, Venice, Milan, and Barcelona, and across the Atlantic to New York City. In addition to those by Schoenberg, performances were conducted by

Hermann Scherchen, Darius Milhaud, Leopold Stokowski, Otto Klemperer, Fritz Stiedry, and Fritz Reiner. Even Mahler's widow, Alma, hosted a performance in Vienna in 1923 in her home, conducted by Schoenberg, whom Mahler had seen as his musical son.

From the beginning, the new music of Schoenberg was associated with Vienna's avant-garde, expressionism, and the theories of another Viennese Jew, Sigmund Freud, as can be gleaned from the early reviews of *Pierrot*. This one of the premiere, from the *Berliner kleine Börsenzeitung*, is succinct in its assessment. Dated October 12, 1912 and uncredited, it reads:

> Songs of Pierrot lunaire. Futurism in music. An equivalent to a Kandinsky exhibition. A sad document of our times, a wish from the newly valued art and a helpless Not-to-be. The music: a chaos of dissonance; the recitation—painterly—an hysterical scream or whisper—an enraged public applauded—A sanatorium for all the futurists and their hangers-on, that's the only way for this new art.

For all its expressivity, Schoenberg knew this new non-tonal music (and his subsequent twelve-tone music) was severely limited in *what* it expressed. There are no successful non-tonal comedies. There are no uplifting twelve-tone finales. His student Berg's two operas, *Wozzeck* and *Lulu,* are about torture, murder, mental derangement, sexual obsession, and degradation.

WESTERN MUSIC'S BIG BANG

In the months just prior to the outbreak of World War I, Western classical music reached a crucial juncture: the moment when classical dance became undanceable, classical song was unsingable, and all the rules of harmony developed over 1,000 years of European culture were abandoned in two cutting-edge works that made other composers take note. Puccini, Milhaud, Gershwin, and countless others journeyed to hear Schoenberg's daring leap into a totally new world of music. Stravinsky rejected Schoenberg and then Schoenberg rejected Stravinsky. For Stravinsky, once Schoenberg had espoused his twelve-tone procedures a decade later, his Austrian rival was more of a chemist than a composer. Schoenberg viewed Stravinsky as being superficially modern and not truly revolutionary.

Both *Sacre* and *Pierrot lunaire,* significantly, were in the service of images (visual and verbal) that attempted to recreate the mindless primitive—either through violent stage action or as a poetic journey into the darkest visions embedded in the human psyche. The overt tribal behavior of *Sacre* was curiously similar to the collective nightmares embedded in our subconscious as expressed in *Pierrot.* The civilized world was on the brink of finding out just how civilized it was, and for many writers what was new in art and music was profoundly important to our understanding of who we were and where we were going.

Pierrot and *Sacre* together constituted what was for many the artistic equivalent of the Big Bang, because music history is generally described as a journey toward ever greater density and complexity. Ironically, it was in 1912 that the American astronomer Vesto Slipher first observed the "redshifts" in galaxies that led to what physicists call the Big Bang. Once the musical experiments of 1912–13 reached total density of harmony and complexity of rhythm—or, at least, reached the point at which most music lovers could no longer recognize form or find beauty—classical music had coalesced into a molten pre-echo of an imminent global war that would destroy many of Europe's long-standing structures. Music would emerge from this more-or-less simultaneous event and expand away from it in new directions throughout the century.

How are we to understand Western music after this point is reached—after two modernist composers achieved total saturation and unpredictability? Do we still adhere to the theory of ever-greater complexity, once the mind and the ear already had experienced an incomprehensible complexity in which all twelve tones of the chromatic scale could be played either simultaneously or sequentially, and dance music was possible without predictability of tempo or beat?

The concatenation that occurred just prior to World War I can still be felt more than a century later and is at the heart of what musical arbiters of taste—the academy, critics, and major institutions—consider worthy music, not only of the last century, but of this newer one. A century after *Pierrot lunaire* shocked the world in 1912 with its newness, British composer George Benjamin's *Written on Skin* premiered, telling an adaptation of the *Tristan* legend of a cuckolded husband who murders his wife's young lover and then serves her the young man's heart for dinner. The opera was hailed as a master-piece by the international press. Anne Midgette of the *Washington Post* describing its music as "mercifully free of attempts to seduce listeners with sugary melody but often fall[ing] agreeably on the ear, pulling apart textures to reveal moments of soft gentleness before piling up layers of instrumental sound, as the screws of the plot tighten, until the brassy orchestra screams aloud."[2]

In 2016, Thomas Adès's non-tonal opera *The Exterminating Angel* adapted the story from Luis Buñuel's film about a dinner party in which the guests are trapped, incapable of leaving a locked room, by expressing it with ear-splitting dissonances, pounding rhythms, and extended vocal ranges that turn every vowel into "ah" and therefore render the text incomprehensible without reading it. The *Los Angeles Times* review by its music critic, Mark Swed, reporting from the Salzburg Festival, bore the headline "'Exterminating Angel' the Most Important Opera of the Year, Proves It's Here to Stay."

If we put aside the unquestioned priority given to the avant-garde, the next wave, and the constant re-experimentation that gets so much intellectual attention, what does the remainder look like? What would it tell us of the century that called itself modern, but may in fact have been the flowering of Romanticism in a new technological age? An equally provocative argument could be made that the great composers who entered the world's stage as composers of enormously dense music—such as Hindemith, Weill, Prokofiev, Stravinsky, Copland, and Shostakovich—moved away from their Big Bang moments to create their own twentieth-century voices that were unique, versatile, effective, successful—and superficially simpler. While it might be easy to confuse early atonal Weill with early atonal Schoenberg, and 1918 Bartók with 1916 Prokofiev—when they were experimenting and flexing their young musical muscles—there would be no confusion once they found their own voices, moving away from "having it all" and discovering that "all" was rather useless for an artist. The avant-garde, however, went on without them.

After the Great War ended in 1918, who could have imagined, among other things, that both Stravinsky and Schoenberg would live much of the rest of their lives in Los Angeles, California, writing music (and not speaking to one another!) and dying as American citizens?

And lest we forget the larger picture, Puccini, Sibelius, Strauss, Ravel, Rachmaninoff, Vaughan Williams, Poulenc, Prokofiev, and countless others from that time, while curious about what was getting some people so excited, just continued to write their music—the music we continue to play in our concerts, perform in our opera houses, and broadcast on our classical music radio and streaming services. It is the music we all refer to simply as classical.

CHAPTER 4

The Lure of Chaos

The attraction of throwing out 1,000 years of tradition—the rules of counterpoint, the voice leading of tonal harmony, the conservatory exams in writing fugues, the consistency of rhythmic downbeats and upbeats, everything except the notes on the page (there were still twelve of them)—was a profoundly revolutionary idea, eliciting a kind of ecstasy akin to being let out of school. It was, for some, impossible to resist.

In the summer of 1914, Germany, which was allied to Austria, invaded France. Paris had been given an artistic jolt provided by wild and creative Russian designers, dancers, and composers, whereas Austro-Germany, the towering center of classical music, was home to the most *avant* of the avant-garde composers, Arnold Schoenberg. What had been unlikely to some soon became a reality—the Great War that took most of the world into a war "to end all wars." Part of the warriors' response was to ban the *music* of their enemies. The significance of this gesture should not be underestimated.

The forty-one-year-old Schoenberg joined the Austrian army and imagined that an Austro-German victory would somehow "teach the kitschmongers to venerate the German spirit and to worship the German God." The kitschmongers included Maurice Ravel and, as already mentioned, Schoenberg's rival in modernity, Igor Stravinsky.

The thirty-nine-year-old Ravel was too tiny in stature and weight to join the army and be outfitted in a military uniform. Instead, he tended the wounded and learned to drive, spending much of the war with his truck, which he named Adélaïde, delivering supplies under incredibly dangerous conditions for the French. He developed a heart condition, contracted dysentery, had to be operated on for a hernia, and developed insomnia, a condition from which he suffered until his death in 1937.

The fifty-two-year-old Claude Debussy, who was dying of cancer, was frustrated at not being able to join the fight: "My age and fitness allow me at most to guard a fence. . . . But, if, to assure victory, they are absolutely in need of another face to be bashed in, I'll offer mine without question." The Germans had developed an enormous siege cannon that could hurl gigantic shells from seventy-five miles outside of Paris for their spring offensive of March 1918. Debussy, too weak to be carried down to the basement, died hearing the explosions and the violence he so dreaded in life and art.

Ralph Vaughan Williams was forty-one when the war broke out, and he enlisted in the British army, serving as a stretcher bearer in France and Salonika. His exposure to gunfire caused permanent hearing damage and ultimately total deafness.

The thirty-two-year-old Stravinsky, who so favored the possibility of war, did not volunteer to fight for either Russia or France, and made a hasty retreat to wait out the war in Switzerland with his children and wife—who bore another two—on the shores of Lake Geneva.

When the fighting was over near the end of 1918, four years after it started, some 20 million people had been killed, and another 21 million wounded according to the Centre Européen Robert Schuman.

Consider what you just read, even as you proceed to the next sentence. The once supremely confident Europe that had created and developed a profound musical legacy would never be the same. One of the results of the war was that each surviving country reaffirmed its various cultural institutions and used them to bolster a sense of worth and identity—somehow trying to make sense of something as senseless as the Great War. The ubiquitous post-war watchword, "self-determination," was applied to art and music as a representation of the national self. In earlier centuries, musical style could represent a country and a people—but now, perhaps for the first time, it could also represent a political philosophy.

The empires of Russia, Germany, Austria-Hungary, and the Ottomans were gone, and Russia, the site of what became known as "the Great Revolution," was bent on a worldwide revolution of workers demanding equal rights to access the fruits of their labor—an idea that would attract millions throughout the world. Equally important to our understanding of this period is that when the war was over, it was hardly over. As Margaret MacMillan noted in *The War That Ended Peace:*

> Europe paid a terrible price in many ways for its Great War: in the veterans who never recovered psychologically or physically, the widows and orphans, the young women who would never find a husband because so many men had died. In the first years of peace, fresh afflictions fell on European society: the influenza epidemic . . . which carried off twenty million people around the world; starvation because there were no longer the men to farm or the transportation networks to get food to the markets; or the political turmoil as extremists on the right and the left used force to gain their ends. In Vienna, once one of the richest cities in Europe, Red Cross workers saw typhoid, cholera, rickets and scurvy, all scourges they thought had disappeared from Europe.[1]

To some extent, classical music and its avant-garde component confronted its relationship with the war, while the public sought to embrace the new world created by various treaties, the most famous being the Treaty of Versailles. Among many other results, American power and American art were injected into European culture. Where there had been a glittering multicultural Austro-Hungarian Empire with its waltzes, polkas, and csárdáses, there was now a group of separate nations, each with its own cultural past, but little political power. Germany, blamed for the war, was crippled with reparations that were immense, made all the more impractical because of tariffs placed on German goods.

American musical culture was, however, omnipresent with its ragtime and jazz. Not unlike Bryan Magee's explanation of the vast cultural impact resulting from the opening of Europe's Jewish ghettos, the emancipation of African-American slaves in the nineteenth century brought with it an equal explosion of musical creativity—beginning with the ragtime of Scott Joplin and others in the 1890s. One could argue that owning slaves and necessarily controlling their living quarters, whether Egyptian slaves, Hebrew slaves, or Roman slaves, meant that the concentration of their culture would inevitably seep into the culture of the enslaving regimes. By 1918, the music of Black America had entered popular (white) culture and soon conquered the world.

Classical composers at first played with this new popular music with ragtime-inspired works by Debussy, Ravel, Stravinsky, Hindemith, and, later, Shostakovich. From 1927 on, Germany was opening one "jazz opera" after another, beginning with *Jonny spielt auf* (Jonny Strikes Up), Max Brand's *Maschinist Hopkins* (Hopkins the Engineer; 1929), Ernst Toch's *Der Fächer* (The Fan; 1930), and jazz bands appeared in Erwin Schulhoff's *Flammen* (Flames; 1932) and Alban Berg's *Lulu* (left incomplete in 1935). After this brief flirtation, however—and under pressure from Hitler's arts policies—most classical music composers turned away, leaving only George Gershwin to remind us of a time when ragtime and jazz's long-form potential could fuel piano concertos (*Rhapsody in Blue,* his *Second Rhapsody—Rhapsody in Rivets,* the Concerto in F), a tone poem (*An American in Paris*), and the opera *Porgy and Bess.*[2]

Although music was a plaything of politics in World War I, the only practical way to control it was not to play it—as New York's Metropolitan Opera did with German music in 1917. If New Yorkers did not hear Wagner and Beethoven, perhaps they would not be seduced by it. The invisible art form can easily sneak past borders without a passport. The proof of that is obvious enough with the triumph of the music invented by former African slaves in the United States, Cuba and South America. The non-Black public overwhelmingly found this infectious, visceral, and free music both intoxicating and liberating—and still does.

Black American music developed out of its "negro spiritual" period, which both Antonín Dvořák and Frederick Delius found deeply moving, into ragtime, gospel, jazz, rock and roll, and, in the last quarter of the twentieth century, hip-hop—in spite of being ignored or shunned by classical snobberies. In the first decades of the twenty-first century, hip-hop culture and rap music—created out of Black and Latino urban rage—found its way into music created under the most repressive regimes in the world. There is Syrian rap and Arabic rap, and recently, with the support of the U.S. State Department, hip hop has emerged in Uzbekistan.[3]

It is therefore not surprising that with the arrival of the Americans to end the Great War, a weary and despondent public entered a wild period in which the new in popular music was American music—it was escapist, and it was naughty fun. As Philipp Blom says in his book *Fracture,*

> After the Great War, the once vigorous cubist movement had abruptly faltered, as if the artists had lost both nerve and appetite for presenting splintered bodies and disintegrated selves. Picasso, both reflector and initiator of artistic currents, had begun to paint in a neoclassical manner as early as 1918, and others were soon to follow. In Russia, the young Sergey Prokofiev premiered his Classical Symphony in the same year; in Paris, Jean Cocteau was using a similarly simplified neoclassical idiom for his drawings and stage designs; and Igor Stravinsky turned from the extravagant modernity of his *Sacre du Printemps* to tame variations on eighteenth-century Italian musical forms. A pall had fallen over the seemingly boundless experiments of the art world, and many artists joined the great Western project of making humans whole again, rescuing the New Man from the shell-shocked ruins of the old.[4]

Ravel composed works that continued to echo his wartime experiences for the twenty years that remained in his life, including his *Le Tombeau de Couperin* (The Tomb of Couperin), a series of short pieces dedicated to his colleagues who had been killed; a piano concerto for a wealthy pianist who had lost his right arm during the war (Concerto for the Left Hand) that is a devastating portrait of the war; a tone poem originally called *Vienna* but renamed *La Valse,* which ends with the Viennese waltz turned into a nightmare of cacophony; and the endlessly repetitive sound of a factory—*Boléro.*

Giacomo Puccini, who was in his mid-fifties when war broke out, could not escape the politics of the war, even as he attempted to compose operas to follow the enormous successes of *La Bohème, Tosca,* and *Madama Butterfly.* This was not to be. The Metropolitan Opera commissioned his next work, *La Fanciulla del West* (The Girl of the Golden West), which premiered in New York in 1910 and was considered to be his masterpiece at that time, showing that the composer was well aware of the latest developments in French and Russian music.

However, a commission from Vienna to compose an operetta (*La Rondine* [The Swallow]) caught Puccini in the middle of the acrimony of the war, with accusations that he was supporting German-Austrian aggression. The work had to be refashioned for a premiere in Monte Carlo and is the least successful of the composer's later works. One month after the armistice, Puccini unveiled a triptych of one-act operas at the Metropolitan Opera. *Il Trittico* contains a highly emotional drama of murder and adultery, a religious melodrama of revenge, suicide, and redemption, and a comedy about greed. There is one common denominator in the three stories: death.

Stravinsky composed a number of small works, some of which made use of Russian themes, and one particularly war-themed piece called *L'Histoire du soldat* (The Soldier's Tale). Composed for narrator, three actors, a dancer, and a small instrumental ensemble, it is perhaps a response to his *Sacre* as well as the vest-pocket portability of Schoenberg's *Pierrot lunaire.* The world premiere of *Histoire* in Switzerland took place six weeks before the end of the war, on September 28, 1918.

It was on this date, according to various sources, that a British soldier, Private Henry Tandey, encountered a wounded German soldier in France who was in retreat during the Fourth Battle of Ypres. Tandey felt he could not kill a wounded soldier and decided to let him go. The German soldier was Lance Corporal Adolf Hitler.

L'Histoire du soldat tells a story of an exhausted soldier marching home from the war. He is seduced by the Devil with promises of wealth in return for giving up his most precious possession: his violin. Obviously, the work is a response to the war, but it can also be seen as expressing Stravinsky's conflicted emotions regarding his pre-war beliefs and his own non-participation in it. Composed for only seven instrumentalists (rather than the nearly 100 required by his *Sacre*), it nonetheless keeps rhythmic complexity at the forefront of the piece, and, as with *Sacre,* there is no comment or uplift at the end. The Devil wins.

Schoenberg, having served in the army that lost the war, returned to a Vienna that was no longer the capital of an empire. He founded a private society to present complex and challenging contemporary music under ideal rehearsal and performance conditions—free of any dependence on popular appeal—and then went on to create a compositional technique known as the twelve-tone method (also called a "system"), thereby ensuring his fame and his infamy forevermore.

Pulitzer Prize–winning composer Mel Powell (1923–1998) suggested that the twelve-tone system was Schoenberg's attempt to control the wild beast he had unleashed before the war, when non-tonal music was "freely" atonal, that is, it was composed without rules or systems. Without going into too much detail about tonal music, there are really two important focal points in any key. The first is the home note (by which we name the key, like C—and the chord based on it—and which is the lowest note on the scale built from that note). The second most powerful note and the chord built on it is a fifth above it in the scale (G in the key of C). You can simply count up, if C=1, D=2, E=3, F=4 and G=5. All the other notes in the key have subsidiary functions and power. If the home key is G, then the second most important note is the fifth note in the scale built on G, which is in this case D.[5]

Throughout the centuries of Western music, returning to the home key remained a fundamental part of music and its comprehensibility. Schoenberg, having traveled into a musical world where there was no home, decided to go even further. He created a way in which all twelve notes within an octave would be absolutely equal, with no one note having more "pull" than any other. And here is what he proposed:

1.   Take all twelve notes inside the octave and give them a unique order. C could be 1, F could be 2, A-flat could be 3, and so on, until all twelve are in a unique sequence. This is the *tone row* for your new piece, and from it all the notes in your composition are selected, *but only in the row's order or series.*

2.   The complete row can be sounded in four basic ways: the row (1 through 12), the reverse (12 through 1), upside down (so that one plays it in a mirror image of the row) and upside down *and* backwards. ("Upside down" means you are basing the third and fourth version of the row in terms of their intervals—the distances between the notes rather their names. If two pitches in the original row go upward a half-step, then the mirror image version goes down a half-step.)

3.   The notes can be played at the same time, like a chord, or can be heard as the melody, or a mixture of both.

4.   Notes can be played in any octave, but they must adhere to the order determined at the beginning.

Because a composition is making use of a specific series of notes, this technique is often called serial music.

Even if you haven't quite understood these rules, you probably can imagine the response from those who had been dubious about freely atonal music in the first place. It was a mixture of total horror, amusement, dismissal, in contrast to the passionate support the twelve-tone system elicited from those who saw a Promised Land for music, especially German music. It was pure. It was strictly controlled. It did not sound like all that Romantic music of the past, and for Schoenberg and his students, principally Berg and Webern, it was still deeply expressive. In its own way, it was as Romantic as Wagner and Mahler, only it did not sound like them at all. And in this sense, it was new.

Astonishingly, it is unlikely that a listener can actually perceive the difference between music composed using the twelve-tone system and freely nontonal music. Using this system, however, ensures harmonic consistency. It also inherently creates compositional structures from which to build a piece of music. Because it is a method, it does not and should not determine if a work that uses it is good or bad. We might be interested in how Beethoven composed each day and how long it took him to compose the first movement of his Fifth Symphony (a long time!), and how he threw out various versions of it and tinkered over it until it felt organic, memorable, and inevitable, but it is the work itself that either speaks to you or not. If you find the music attractive, you may want to know more about the composer and how it was composed, but only if you are attracted to the piece in the first place. It usually does not work the other way around.

Another equally brilliant Viennese composer, however, was blithely continuing the language of German classical music of Wagner, Mahler, and his mentor, Richard Strauss. He offered an alternative to the new dissonant music being played to Schoenberg's private society. His name was Erich Wolfgang Korngold. His music was enormously complex but, unlike the compositions of Schoenberg and Berg, mysteriously uplifting. Unafraid of soaring melodies, this young man wrote in a language that emerged out of *Tristan* and *Parsifal,* as well as the unabashed sentiment of Viennese operetta, much as Strauss did in his 1910 opera *Der Rosenkavalier.* Korngold's chromatic wanderings always led to enormously satisfying harmonic consonances.

A rare meeting of the two antithetical Viennese composers—Schoenberg and Korngold—included a lesson by Schoenberg on how his twelve-tone system worked, in an oft-told story still repeated by the Korngold family today. Holding a pencil pointing downward, Schoenberg said to Korngold, "If this is the row," and then pointed the pencil upward, toward the ceiling, "this is its inversion." Korngold did not wait for the rest of the lesson before interjecting, "*Ja*, but Schoenberg, you can't write with it!" And then, without saying another word, Korngold went to the piano and played Schoenberg's Op. 19, his Six Little Piano Pieces from 1913, from memory. "You could never overestimate Papa's memory," his ninety-five-year-old daughter-in-law said in 2019. "It was an almost supernatural gift."

Ultimately, the public, and not the critics or the experts, judged the twelve-tone music of Schoenberg. They also judged Stravinsky's post-*Sacre* music. They judged it on how it sounded and not on how it was written—and, it should be said, whether they wanted to hear it again.

As it turns out, the greatest beneficiaries of Stravinsky's music and Schoenberg's most famous students were not French, Russian, or Viennese, and were mere children at the time of the twelve-tone system's creation (1921–23). They had no idea how they would ultimately meet, study, and be inspired by the "Father of Modernism," Stravinsky, and the "Father of Atonality," Schoenberg, thousands of miles west of Paris, Berlin, and Vienna in as unlikely a place as anyone could have imagined.

THE NECESSITY FOR CONTROL

In 1922, other developments would lead to that irony, and lead to a monumental tragedy for humanity and European culture. In that year, the thirty-nine-year-old Benito Mussolini—appointed by Italy's King Victor Emmanuel III—became the youngest prime minister in Italian history, and within three years turned Italy into a totalitarian state. Fascist Italy would be the first Western country to officially recognize the Bolshevik leadership in Russia. Seeking a common denominator of Italian culture, Mussolini imposed the Roman salute—the outstretched arm—in Italy's schools. America at first welcomed Mussolini as someone who would bring order and stability to his country. Hitler saw Mussolini as a role model—thus, the Nazi appropriation of Mussolini's appropriation of the Roman salute, which is now known as the "Nazi salute."

The German mark had dropped to one-trillionth of its pre-war value by 1923, and Hitler added "National Socialist" to the name of his political party. He would at first fail in his attempt to take control of Germany, be jailed for it, and not become its chancellor until 1933—eleven years after Mussolini's regime began in Italy.

Also in 1922, Lenin made Iosif Vissarionovich Dzhugashvili the general secretary of the Soviet Communist party. The personality of this tough enforcer led to a simpler name: "Man of Steel"—Joseph Stalin. Lenin soon grew to distrust Stalin and wished, upon his death, for the Communists to be ruled by a collective leadership. He died in 1924 and within three years Stalin had taken control of the government, which he ruled until his death in 1953.[6]

All three of these dictators came to control music. Two of them, Hitler and Mussolini, admired many aspects of America, and all three loved Hollywood movies—which they would show in their residences. Imagining Stalin watching Tarzan films after state dinners, or Hitler viewing *Snow White and the Seven Dwarfs,* makes one ponder their need for fantasy and their admiration for America's often derided entertainment industry. Mussolini built a cinema city in Rome, Cinecittà, so Italy could join other countries in making movies. Mussolini's 1937 motto was "Movies are the greatest weapon." Cinecittà would become a detention camp in 1945. Then, in peacetime, it was where Federico Fellini filmed *La Dolce vita* and Hollywood made *Ben-Hur* and *Cleopatra.*

The myth of control, however, in which the three dictators so firmly believed, is constantly exposed by the reality of what was achieved—and irretrievably destroyed—in the decades after their regimes fell. Tragedy and loss of incalculable proportions are commingled with persistence and triumph. None, however, is more ironic than Hitler's attempt at murdering the Jews and their music, which inadvertently contributed to the worldwide proliferation of music composed by Jews, and through the medium he so enjoyed after dinner—the movies.

At the center of this part of musical history is the man who seems to be omnipresent—Richard Wagner. That his reprehensible anti-Semitic articles inspired Hitler is well known. That Wagner's family curried favor with the Führer to keep their Bayreuth Festival alive before and during World War II is also known to opera lovers. What is less known is how Wagner's *music* and his immense achievements in creating a method by which one could compose endless melodies in an ever-developing orchestral framework became the lingua franca of Western music—delivered to the world during the war and into the next century by Jewish composers who openly carried on those musical traditions, never commenting on the master's hateful personal thoughts on race and religion. For those composers and their families, there was enough anti-Semitism in Los Angeles to cope with without delving into several articles written by one of the greatest geniuses in German music—and who had died years before they were born.

But before we get ahead of ourselves, we need to understand what Hitler, Mussolini, and Stalin actually did to control music and who were the winners and the losers. For Hitler, it all seems to have centered around Wagner.

CHAPTER 5

Hitler, Wagner, and the Poison from Within

The shortest book on Richard Wagner, *Aspects of Wagner* (1968) by the late British philosopher Bryan Magee, which is both brilliant and succinct, has a chapter called "Jews—Not Least in Music." In it the author discusses Wagner's recognition that Jews would somehow dominate classical music. Magee offers a unique explanation for the extraordinary explosion of Jewish achievements in art, literature, science, philosophy, and music starting in the nineteenth century. He writes that it is not a question of Jews being superior as a race (which would turn anti-Semitism on its head and fall into the trap of inverted racism). Nor is the explanation that Jews have a unique intellectual tradition that suddenly flowered after centuries into the aforementioned fields. Instead, Magee writes:

> Originality in fundamentals is inimical to any closed, authoritarian culture, because such cultures do not and cannot allow their basic assumptions to be questioned. As Napoleon conquered Europe, he opened the ghettos of Europe, and when the ghettos were finally opened, the Jews had a . . . renaissance of their own, with all the same broad features (as in ancient Greece, the Renaissance, and Protestant Europe): the lapse of two or three generations between emancipation and the

peak achievement; the dissociation of the greatest creative geniuses from the closed religious and intellectual achievement; the lifelong struggle against institutional prejudice and personal resentment—and before the end, murder on an enormous scale, highly organized and state supported.

Seemingly before anyone else, Wagner saw it coming. He railed against his contemporary composers who controlled the Opéra in Paris—Fromental Halévy and Giacomo Meyerbeer, both Jews—and commended Felix Mendelssohn (born into a prominent Jewish family but raised without religion until being baptized at the age of seven) for his immense talent, while criticizing his total lack of profundity. At the time of Wagner's death in 1883, two great composers who were Jewish—Gustav Mahler and the other, still a boy, Arnold Schoenberg—would lead a wave of Jewish talent that would permeate the first half of twentieth-century classical music. Great German composers, instrumentalists, conductors, and singers who happened to be Jewish would confront how the German people—and the world—would define what made music "German." In 1933 there were a mere 400,000 German citizens who identified themselves as Jews. They were living in a country of 67 million.

What happens when a highly cultured country officially declares itself to be anti-Semitic—and Jews constitute much of its creative class? The answer is obvious: cultural suicide. Seventy-five years after the end of World War II, Germany and Austria (once it was annexed to the Third Reich) have simply never recovered.

Much has been written about what the Nazis called "degenerate art" and "degenerate music." The German word *entartet* was invented in the nineteenth century, and it is a repulsive word: *ent-* means "away from" and *art* means "type" or "kind." In its original form, *Entartung* was a term used by Max Nordau in an 1892 book of the same name, which attacked the excesses of Wagner and others (as well as anti-Semitism!) as examples of the degeneration of *fin de siècle* society. The Nazis appropriated the term for their own ends.

This strange word can be used to refer to anything at all that is outside borders or expectations. It evokes a repulsion because it implies that the object is a deformed thing, something with flaws. At the same time, it is vague enough to go beyond words such as "retarded," "malformed," and "sick."

Because art and music were considered so important in unifying the German Reich, the Nazis mounted two exhibitions to show Germans how disgusting and dangerous certain art and music can be. The first exhibition, in 1937, was for visual art (*Entartete Kunst*) that had been confiscated from museums and private owners and was first seen in Munich before being taken to various cities in Germany and then Austria. Hitler had decided, against Propaganda Minister Joseph Goebbels's desire to show the Reich as forward-looking and modern, that no modern art was to be seen in Germany. The Nazis were thorough in their bookkeeping and we know that 16,558 works were stolen from German citizens and institutions and over two million Germans attended the touring exhibition. Those artworks selected to be on display were then grouped in terms of various forms of degeneracy—"Insolent Mockery of the Divine," "An Insult to German Womanhood," "The Ideal: Cretin and Whore," "Revelation of the Jewish Racial Soul," and so forth.

In 1938, the Reich decided to mount another exhibition. This one, curated by Weimar's theater intendant, Hans Severus Ziegler, and first seen in Düsseldorf, was dedicated to music (*Entartete Musik*). Although it was on a smaller scale, it officially set out the Nazis' view on what it saw as dangerous—and officially forbidden—music. The difficulty was that the outlawed music had no consistent style, whereas the artworks displayed in the *Degenerate Art* exhibition were non-realistic and selected to show distorted visual images and "depraved" subject matter. Any music by a Jew or a Communist was outlawed. However, Jews and Communists, like the rest of Germany's composers, were writing in many musical styles, regardless of their ethnicity, religion, or political persuasion. The Lutheran Paul Hindemith and the Roman Catholic Ernst Krenek had also disturbed the leaders of the Third Reich and would also become artistic enemies of the state.

It was, therefore, incumbent upon the government to explain its rather confusing position to the German people. Musicologists who wished to maintain their positions at universities—which no longer allowed Jews to be professors, or indeed to teach—wrote thoroughly researched and argued academic articles that justified the damning of the music of Hindemith, Korngold, Weill, and Schoenberg, and supported the exclusion of Mendelssohn and Mahler, too. Trying to find common denominators in Hitler's aesthetic pronouncements when it came to music is not simple, because there weren't any.

Although he had fallen in love with Wagner's operas as a teenager, Hitler apparently showed less interest in classical music than most of us think. He liked Verdi's *Aida* and operettas—Franz Lehár's 1905 *Die Lustige Witwe* (The Merry Widow) being a personal favorite. Lehár lived until 1948 and supplied a grand overture to his *Widow* that was premiered by the Vienna Philharmonic in 1940, two years after Austria was annexed into the Third Reich. And while Hitler knew he *should* express a passionate interest in encouraging Germans to support their classical institutions (indeed, members of the Berlin Philharmonic were excused from military service, and he saw to it that Wagner's theater in Bayreuth was protected), he much preferred watching—and rewatching—his favorite Hollywood movies.

INVENTING THE ENEMY WITHIN

Hitler needed to bolster a sense of Germanness, and one of the ways to do it was to celebrate the universally accepted supremacy of German classical music. As already noted, the public for classical music was shrinking. Germans (and other Europeans) turned toward having more fun and excitement. In the cabarets and jazz clubs of their big cities, as well as on the radio, they heard music that was inspired by or emanated directly from the United States due to America's presence in the last years of World War I and afterward. However, even though Germans might not attend a concert of Beethoven, the German people were still fiercely proud of their "brand," as market research demonstrated.

In order to read the wishes of the Germans, the Nazis studied American polling techniques, which were understood to be the most advanced in the world. One person who helped her countrymen was the twenty-year-old Elisabeth Noelle, who was sent to the University of Missouri as a German exchange student from Berlin in 1937—much to the suspicion of fellow college students. She became a member of the Alpha chapter of the Gamma Alpha Chi sorority (founded at the university in 1920 and no longer in existence), which called itself "a national honorary advertising fraternity for women."

Returning to her native country, Noelle in 1940 wrote a thesis titled "Amerikanische Massenbefragungen über Politik und Presse" (American Mass Surveys on Politics and the Press) on public opinion polls, especially those by

George Gallup's American Institute of Public Opinion, which had been formed in 1935. She was subsequently accused of politicizing ambiguous data, publishing it, and then taking a poll to show how the fake data influenced the public's opinion. Her writings came to the attention of Goebbels, who put her to work for him. Thus, public policy and knowledge of how to read and control public opinion—learned from the United States—entered aesthetic decision-making in the Third Reich.[1]

It is well known that Germany had been insulted by the Treaty of Versailles that set the conditions for peace after World War I. The war had, after all, ended in an armistice, not in surrender. And yet Germany had been treated as the sole guilty party and severely punished. The Treaty of Versailles was signed on June 29, 1919, the fifth anniversary of the assassination of Archduke Ferdinand, formally ending the war. Arguably, it was also the first day of World War II insofar as it set in motion the environment of unpayable debt, public humiliation and rage that enabled Hitler to be seen as a champion of the German people and its culture. The German delegation was not even allowed to use the same exit as the other delegations at the signing ceremony at the Palace of Versailles. It took ninety-two years for Germany to pay off its war debts, with its last payment made on October 3, 2010, sixty-five years after World War II had ended and on the twentieth anniversary of German reunification.

If the German public valued its unassailable position as the country of classical music and was being humiliated from outside—while also needing a scapegoat from within—music had to play a crucial role in solidifying power for the Nazis.

Jazz was popular, but it was also linked with immorality and had a definitely "outsider" sound. It could therefore represent the German sense that its musical heritage (metaphorically representing the country of Germany) was under attack, and by racially inferior and dangerous foreigners from outside Germany. It was a drug and needed to be addressed by the government as an illegal substance.

The other poison came from within. The music of German Jews was deemed truly dangerous because some of it cleverly imitated beautiful and uplifting music as a way of infiltrating "True German Music" and taking over the country. It was not authentic. The "Wandering Jews" were a people without a true home. They survived through assimilation, and by stealing and profiting from the profound works of others—and they did it for money. "Degenerate music" could be experimental and modern, and it could be seductively old-fashioned and beautiful. It was to be destroyed because of the race of the artist who was committing either cultural adultery or cultural larceny.

This meant that the public *had to be told* what music was poisonous and what was not. Surely no one could tell that Korngold's magnificent achievements were evil and empty by listening to his glorious 1927 opera *Das Wunder der Heliane,* which owes a great debt to Strauss's 1917 opera *Die Frau ohne Schatten* (The Woman without a Shadow). *The Student Prince,* the tuneful Viennese-sounding operetta by the Jewish Sigmund Romberg (whose real name was Siegmund Rosenberg), was a hit in Berlin (as *Der Studentenprinz*) and was shut down in 1933.[2]

It would be more difficult, indeed impossible, to attack similar-sounding music of Johann Strauss and his son, Johann, Jr., especially after 1938, when Germany brought Austria into the Reich. The younger Strauss, who died in 1899, was known as the Waltz King. How could *The Blue Danube Waltz* and *Die Fledermaus* be banned? Instead, the Nazis simply erased the numerous Jewish aspects of the family's lineage (even taking a pair of scissors to the baptism registry entries) and never mentioned the fact that Strauss, Jr. married three times, twice to Jewish women. His stepdaughter, always under threat of deportation, married a high-ranking Nazi official, but was nonetheless made to renounce the Strauss inheritance and royalties.

Lehár emotionally admitted after the war that he was given a choice as to whether to save his Jewish wife or the librettist of many of his operettas, Fritz Löhner-Beda (born Bedřich Löwy). He chose his wife, and Löhner-Beda was killed at Auschwitz.

Much contemporary music and music theater was easy to put on the list, because it was unpopular and much of it was meant to shock and be provocative. Schoenberg was clearly of Jewish origin. His recent music was not liked by the public, given its reliance on dissonance and unpleasant texts. He and his followers (who were not Jewish) could be outlawed without an outcry from the masses. Other non-Jews, such as Hindemith, had also set edgy stories for the stage. In one opera, *Sancta Susanna* (1921), a nun, having observed two young people making love from her window, tears off the veil on an enormous crucifix in the chapel of the nunnery. Once discovered naked and in a state of transcendent sexual frenzy, she demands to be buried alive within its walls. In his 1929 comic opera *Neues vom Tage* (News of the Day) Hindemith put a naked soprano in a bathtub, singing of the joys of the municipal water system. Goebbels was not only not amused, he was outraged, and any thought of remaining in Germany became impossible for the composer, even though he had already distanced himself from his earlier works. (One of the multiple ironies of this story is that composers such as Hindemith and Schoenberg, who were being attacked before World War II for being radical, were subsequently attacked after the war for being conservative and therefore irrelevant.)

Music that was *entartet* represented a grab bag of styles and used pseudo-science, aesthetic theories, moral outrage, and outright lies to push the Nazis' political agenda. It is important to understand that the outlawed music had one other commonality—its compositional roots and the rigorous German training of its composers. Each composer whose music was deemed to be *entartet* had found fame and success, however, with very different "voices," and had been lauded with much publicity and international fame.

Richard Strauss, universally seen as Germany's greatest living composer, remained in place during the war. He was born in 1864 and died in 1949.[3] At first he accepted the position as president of the Reich's Music Bureau, which had been set up soon after the Nazis came to power in 1933 by Goebbels to promote "good German music" and act as a guild for composers. Strauss accepted this honorary position because he hoped he could do some good "and prevent worse misfortunes, if from now onwards, German musical life were going to be . . . 'reorganized' by amateurs and ignorant place-seekers." He used his fame and official position to fight for the rights of classical composers to receive larger royalties for their music and extend copyright protections.

Since popular music from America, as well as music for beer halls, cabarets, and German operettas, was preferred by the German masses, Strauss felt that classical composers needed a higher royalty rate to ensure the survival of "serious" German music—something he achieved through legislation. This meant that all music had to be registered for copyright as either *U-Musik* (*Unterhaltungsmusik,* or "entertainment music," that is, popular music) or *E-Musik* (*Ernste Musik,* or "serious music"). Thus, the split (and the royalty disparity) between serious and popular became a matter of law, imitated throughout the world, and initiated by classical music composers under the leadership of Strauss—and so it remains today.

Strauss was otherwise uninterested in politics. Useful to the Nazis for symbolic reasons, he was soon replaced. That his son Franz had married a Jew, and Strauss's grandchildren were defined as Jews, meant the elderly composer had to avoid risk and stay out of trouble, writing his pure and transparently pastel operas. He had taken a big risk in setting the Jewish Stefan Zweig's libretto for *Die Schweigsame Frau* (The Silent Woman) in 1935.

Only one classical work emerged from the Nazi period (1933–45) that succeeded globally: Carl Orff's *Carmina Burana*. An immediate success when it was first heard in 1937, it was embraced by the Nazis as proving to the world that new and great German works were being composed by pure Germans. (Orff is thought to have had some Jewish ancestry, but provided he was less than one-quarter Jewish, it would have been ignored by the Nazis.) In its own way, *Carmina Burana* is to World War II what Stravinsky's *Sacre* is to World War I.

Inexorable and unstoppable in its tribal brutality, *Carmina Burana* had the advantage of being easier than *Sacre* to perform and understand. Its immediately recognizable and monumental blocks of simple harmonies and repetitive rhythms, and its periods of exotic sensuality, made it more of a musical aphrodisiac of power, rather than the unpredictable and undomesticated animal that is *Sacre*. To this day it remains the only work composed in the Third Reich by a German composer that has entered the repertory. The other great "German" works would be written in other countries—primarily in the United States, but also in France and England—where the great classical music traditions of over two centuries were successfully transplanted and flourished.

CHAPTER 6

Stalin and Mussolini Make Music

Unlike Adolf Hitler, whose Germany had 4,700 newspapers, Joseph Stalin and Benito Mussolini controlled countries in which literacy was spotty at best. Music, however, could be understood whether or not a person could read.

Both Mussolini and Stalin were already in power in the 1920s, with Stalin surviving until 1953, well after World War II. Their influence on composers and the music that represented their regimes is quite different from Hitler's, whose reign was the shortest. What was the same, however, was their use of music to represent their governments, their political philosophies, and the countries they led. There was some precedent for this. Napoleon, for example, wanted new music to welcome him and his troops before entering a big city and even offered money for composition competitions to rally support for the French Republic in conquered lands.

In a letter to the inspectors of the Conservatoire in Paris dated October 17, 1797, Napoleon seemed to be channeling the ancient Greeks when he wrote, "Among all the fine arts music is the one that exercises the greatest influence upon the passions and is the one that the legislator should most encourage. A musical composition created by a master makes an unfailing appeal to the feelings and exerts a far greater influence than a good book on morals, which convinces one's reason but not one's habits."

Hitler, Mussolini, and Stalin had *stylistic* demands that would give an official sound to their regimes. Stalin's tastes in music remained a constant for three generations of composers because his legacy, unlike Hitler's and Mussolini's, was carried on even after his death, with varying degrees of control, through 1991, when the Soviet Union crumbled.

THE OFFICIAL MUSIC OF THE USSR

Unlike Germany and Italy, which had demonstrably lost World War II, Russia's government maintained its aesthetic policy as determined by Stalin in 1932, called "socialist realism"—music that was defiantly *not* experimental or futuristic. And the Soviets had two superstar composers living in Russia, Serge Prokofiev (from 1936 onward) and Dmitri Shostakovich, composing operas, ballets, concertos, symphonies, and film scores. At the end of World War II, Prokofiev, for example, had just completed his *Cinderella* ballet (1940–44) and was in the middle of composing the opera *War and Peace,* which he had started in 1942. He had just finished the composition of his great film score to Sergei Eisenstein's *Ivan the Terrible* (1945), and his enormously popular Fifth Symphony had been completed in the summer of 1944.

For the Soviets, the accusation of "formalism" (that is, the use of systems to create incomprehensible music) could result in the equivalent for a composer of a one-way ticket to Siberia: having your music—its publication, performances, and broadcasts—silenced. Mussolini was less strict, but after embracing the artistic philosophy of Italy's cutting-edge modernism—airplanes, muscular men, misogyny, and the noises of machines as musical art—he rejected the musical aspect of this aesthetic, and, it is fair to say, so did the Italian public. Hitler saw Schoenberg's system as part of a Jewish conspiracy to destroy German culture—the very opposite of Schoenberg's goal. Germany, Italy, and Russia, however, came to the same conclusion, though for different reasons. They silenced non-tonal and twelve-tone music along with anything that might be considered "experimental." In the United States, where a more subtly nationalistic music was lauded, Aaron Copland, William Schuman, Walter Piston, and others wrote in America's equivalent of socialist realism, Copland's *Appalachian Spring* being a particularly famous example. That would all change, as we shall see, in the post–World War II Cold War era.

The list of officially approved composers who were members of the Union of Soviet Composers is large, but their music, with the exception of Prokofiev's and Shostakovich's, remains rarely heard anywhere, including in Russia. The occasionally heard works of Dmitry Kabalevsky and Aram Khachaturian are small examples of the thousands of hours of music of many composers waiting, perhaps, to be discovered. Whether it is "good" or not can only be revealed by rummaging in the basements of Russian music archives—and then performing it.

And not just Russian archives. The Soviet Union included as many as fifteen countries: Armenia, Azerbaijan, Belorussia (now Belarus), Estonia, Georgia, Kazakhstan, Kirgiziya (now Kyrgyzstan), Latvia, Lithuania, Moldavia (now Moldova), Russia, Tajikistan, Turkmenistan, Ukraine, and Uzbekistan. The classical music of these former Soviet Republic members remains largely unknown for both political as well as aesthetic reasons. Recently, interest has been ignited in the music of Mieczysław Weinberg (1919–1996), a Pole who was a friend of Shostakovich. How many others are there?

Prokofiev and Shostakovich, however, managed to walk a fine line between approbation and annihilation. The early music of Prokofiev is harmonically dense, verging on non-tonal, but, compared to that of his contemporary Stravinsky, it is rhythmically more predictable and therefore more acceptable to the public. He also had a greater gift for melody, something that eluded Stravinsky, who made frequent use of other people's melodies.

And unlike Stravinsky, who kept moving westward and as far away from Moscow as he could, Prokofiev's successes in Paris and in America led him back to Russia, where he lived much of his life under the thumb of the Soviets. (No one could ever imagine in 1913, when both Stravinsky and Prokofiev were in Paris, that forty years later Prokofiev would die in Moscow on the same day as Stalin and Stravinsky would be a long-time resident of West Hollywood.)

Prokofiev's brutal and ferocious early music had made him famous, but when it fell out of favor in Europe and America, his style changed into something far simpler and more accessible. One of the possible reasons occasionally cited was his conversion to Christian Science. Another, perhaps, is that Prokofiev did what many youthful renegades from the early twentieth century did—he moved away from harmonic and rhythmic saturation once he had played out what composer Ned Rorem referred to as a "tantrum phase." That he and his family moved back to the Soviet Union in 1936 made his stylistic simplification absolutely essential under the various bosses who frequently hauled him before their committees to interrogate and humiliate him. Living in poverty at the end of his life, Prokofiev was persuaded to rewrite his last symphony, No. 7, and give it a "happy ending" so that he could receive the Stalin Prize of 100,000 rubles. He added the happy ending but was not awarded the prize. Instead, he was given the Lenin Prize in 1957, four years after his death.

Shostakovich's story is similar. Although his lifespan overlapped that of Prokofiev, he lived well into the Cold War, dying in 1975. In that sense his musical output more closely mirrored the historical times of Stravinsky, who died in 1971. That the West had Stravinsky and the East had Shostakovich as their Russian musical poster children makes for fascinating comparisons vis-à-vis politics and music.

Stravinsky was "free" to write whatever he wanted but was haunted by the expectation that he continue to be modern—the eternal enfant terrible attempting to maintain 1913 and, as he once said, "outlive [his] fame." Shostakovich, who was routinely trotted out to represent Soviet music, was also dragged in to be officially drubbed for not adhering to socialist realism, and thus lived on another kind of roller coaster from that of Stravinsky, the latter needing to be in the news by being current, edgy, and quotably amusing ("The only way to escape Hollywood is to live in it").

From the very beginning of his compositional career, Shostakovich showed a remarkable sense of humor. During a lunch we shared in 1971, Leopold Stokowski recalled discovering the young Shostakovich in a Moscow cabaret "after the Great Revolution and playing the funniest piano music I ever heard." Like Nino Rota's scores to Fellini films, Shostakovich's music was never very far from the circus, whether in operas, symphonies, or film scores. Unlike Rota, who used circus music as emblematic of fantasy and dreams, Shostakovich's evocation of the circus is sardonic and seems to represent his love/hate attitude toward being required to be entertaining—a clown, an acrobat, a dancing bear.

The monumental change in his musical language occurred after his opera

Lady Macbeth of the Mtsensk District premiered in 1934. It caused a sensation in Leningrad, as many iconoclastic works had done twenty years earlier in Paris and Vienna. Its music was a brilliant mixture of expressionist musical gestures that Stravinsky dismissed as "primitively realistic." There is no doubt as to how Shostakovich used Western musical symbolism to portray its sex scenes, including a descending trombone glissando to indicate erectile dysfunction. The libretto itself was not something Stalin's regime wished to see onstage, telling as it does the story of a frustrated wife, seduction, and graphic domestic violence involving whipping, strangulation, bludgeoning with a heavy candlestick, and murder by rat poison. Here is where Hitler, Mussolini, and Stalin—and most other people—would agree.

Texts like this were once fairly routine in expressionist dramas and operas, as in Weill's 1925 opera *Der Protagonist*—which told a story of incest and murder—and the aforementioned early operas of Hindemith. Béla Bartók's 1926 ballet *The Miraculous Mandarin,* which mostly survives today as an orchestral suite, has a scenario that is as obscene and racist as anything put on the ballet stage. Its story takes place in a whorehouse in a noisy city where a prostitute works with three tramps who rob and murder her clients. When a mysterious and wealthy Chinese man enters her room and begins to have sex with her, he is attacked—first suffocated with a pillow, then stabbed with a rusty sword, and then hanged on a hook. Since he will not die, the woman figures out what needs to happen. As he reaches orgasm, the mysterious green light emanating from his eyes goes out and he bleeds to death. Curtain. Even in anything-goes, pre-Hitler Weimar Germany, Bartók's *Miraculous Mandarin* was banned.

Shostakovich was made to understand that he was never again to write anything like *Lady Macbeth* if he wished to continue his life in the Soviet Union, and he famously withheld his new symphony (No. 4) from being premiered. He regrouped and composed his most famous and popular work, the Symphony No. 5. The triumph of this work is that it pleased not only the Soviet authorities but also audiences throughout the world ever since its premiere in 1937.

As with all languages, there can be ambiguities inherent in telling stories through music, especially when no words are being sung. Music has the ability to tell secrets, not only because of generally understood metaphors that have developed over the centuries, but also through embedding inner musical quotations others might not overtly hear, and also because of the possibility of parody and sarcasm. Music depends on interpretation in order to be performed, at which time it is simultaneously interpreted by the public (and the authorities) who are hearing it. Thus, the triumphant finale to Shostakovich's Fifth Symphony can be played as (1) a real triumph, (2) a vulgar parody of a triumph, or (3) something of both: vulgar enough to please the Soviet authorities and profoundly triumphant because the composer gave his political bosses what they wanted *and* also saved his own life—a multiple, simultaneous triumph. Shostakovich not only outlived Stalin, he outlived Soviet premier Nikita Khrushchev and died in his bed during the leadership of Leonid Brezhnev, after having composed another ten symphonies. That would constitute a triumph in anyone's book.

Would Shostakovich have survived after his *Lady Macbeth* if he had not changed his musical style and the subject matter of his texts? Probably not. If he had been transported to a democratic country, or if the Soviet Union had collapsed in 1935, and he had written more *Lady Macbeth*s, would we be playing his music today? Probably not. Leonard Bernstein once said to me that "every note Shosty wrote is worth hearing." The unanswered and unanswerable question that looms over "every note [Shostakovich] wrote," and all the beauty and drama of Prokofiev's output, is whether rejecting modernism actually gave us a number of masterpieces we would otherwise not have. It also begs the question of why certain artists transcend limitations and others cannot. Is it a mark of genius that the greatest ones do, and is that somehow the test of true genius, whether the limitation is Bach's little choir at Leipzig's St. Thomas Church or the fixed time code of a movie? Does the genius *need* limitations to achieve the masterpieces we cherish as the cornerstones of our civilization?

We cannot ever compare which terror was worse when we speak of the Third Reich, Stalin's Soviet Union, and Mussolini's Fascist Italy, even as the numbers of dead would lead us to give first place to the murderous Stalin. To this day estimates vary, but it is generally understood the Stalin killed tens of millions of his own citizens. However, when it comes to the destruction of an entire art form, those who ran Italy after Mussolini's death managed that feat. The Italians had, after all, invented opera in 1598. It is rare that any art form can be invented and given a birth date, but opera is one. Appropriately, perhaps, it was the Italians who then went ahead and terminated it in the years after World War II.

ITALIAN OPERA AS COLLATERAL DAMAGE

Puccini's *Turandot* remains one of the most interesting and mysterious operas ever written, in spite of what seems on the surface to be a simple fairy tale. The origin of its story is a wish-legend that emanated from Persia after the death of Timur (Tamerlane) in 1405, and his failure to recreate a Muslim Mongol Empire of Genghis Khan and restore China's Yuan Dynasty. (*Turan* is the Persian name for a region in Central Asia, and *dokhtar* is Persian for daughter.) For our purposes, it remains the very last Italian opera in the general repertory.

Left incomplete at the time of the Puccini's death in 1924, its world premiere took place on April 26, 1926 at Milan's Teatro alla Scala. Arturo Toscanini, who conducted the performance, stopped the performance in the middle of Act III, just at the point where Puccini's completed manuscript ends. Later performances made use of a short duet and finale composed by Franco Alfano, who had access to Puccini's sketches, in order to give the audience a conclusion to the opera. Toscanini had refused to play the Fascist hymn "Giovinezza" to start the performance and, as a result, Mussolini canceled his attendance for the glittering world premiere.

It would be accurate to say that *Turandot* is *now* part of the active repertory of opera houses. After its premieres in various countries, and well into the 1960s, it was more on the fringes of the repertory. Until then, Puccini's fame had rested on only three works written between 1895 and 1903: *La Bohème, Tosca,* and *Madama Butterfly.* There are various reasons for the return of *Turandot* to the active repertory, but that is not our concern here.[1]

Puccini died during the first years of Mussolini's power—before Il Duce made himself the undisputed dictator of a fascist state. In the early 1920s Italian opera was in a glorious period, with many composers finding a unique and brilliant way of telling stories that demanded great singing as well as a newly developed reliance on the orchestra as an equal partner in the musical drama. In previous periods, Italian opera rarely made use of the orchestra as a symphonic component to its storytelling, unlike German Romantic opera, in which it is a fundamental element. Puccini had been one of the first Italian composers to adopt Wagner's orchestral tone painting into Italian opera, while maintaining its dependence on beautiful and memorable melodies.

Generally speaking, the public has been led to categorize Italian operas from the early twentieth century until 1945 as either "verismo" or "post-verismo," the latter denomination being code for not being worthy of our interest. The word *verismo* roughly means "realism" (deriving from *vero,* "true") and refers to operas that tell dark stories of common people—not kings and queens— who get embroiled in passionate situations, usually ending in death. Verismo is said to have petered out around 1920, and anything composed after this rather vague moment is called post-verismo, or sometimes "post-Romantic" or "neo-Romantic." It might in fact refer to historical/political periods: "pre-Fascist" and "Fascist."

Here is a short list of some of the most successful Italian opera composers of the twentieth century, and you will see how most of them lived through the Fascist period and after. You will also see how many operas (almost all of which were successfully produced in their lifetimes) they composed: Italo Montemezzi (1875–1952), eight operas; Franco Alfano (1875–1954), twelve operas; Riccardo Zandonai (1883–1944), thirteen operas; Ermanno Wolf-Ferrari (1876–1948), fifteen operas; Pietro Mascagni (1863–1945), fifteen operas; Umberto Giordano (1867–1948), thirteen operas; Ottorino Respighi (1879–1936), nine operas; Nino Rota (1911–1979), eleven operas (as well as over 150 film scores, including *The Godfather* and *The Godfather II*). The Italian-born and American-trained Gian Carlo Menotti (1911–2007) wrote an astounding twenty-six operas, including two Pulitzer Prize winners and the first opera composed for television, *Amahl and the Night Visitors,* which has been seen by more people than any opera in history.

Of course, there is no way of knowing how viable most of these works are. The Italian public was already turning away from opera by the 1930s with the arrival of talking pictures—a situation akin to how Germans were losing interest in their classical music at the same time. What is obvious from perusing some of these scores and pirated recordings of an occasional performance, however, is that these operas "sing." They defy the simple category of verismo. They frequently tell stories based on great works of literature, and with dazzling orchestration. Imagine Respighi's *Pini di Roma* (Pines of Rome) with voices, if you will.

Respighi, it should be said, was responding to Mussolini's desire to build nationalism through imaginary recreations of the Roman Empire, especially in architecture and music. The Fascists determined that there was but one overarching cultural common denominator to unite Italians in the 1920s— ancient Rome, which brought civilization and culture through military conquest to the world. The rousing and extremely popular finale of the 1924 *Pines of Rome*, with its overwhelming musical depiction of a triumphant Roman legion, was very much a Fascist dream of Italian power. Respighi may not have joined the Fascist party, but, as author and scholar Harvey Sachs correctly points out, he did not need to. He was already composing exactly what Mussolini wanted. It remains a rare example of Italian orchestral music from this period that is in the repertory, along with its companion piece, *Fountains of Rome.*[2]

The music of these composers—and this is merely a partial list—had been performed all over Europe, especially in the opera houses of Italy, and broadcast on the radio. It perhaps goes without saying that except for a brief period in which a few Italian futurists flirted with noise and machine-made sounds in the first decades of the twentieth century, by the 1920s Italy mostly absented itself from the aesthetic wars of the French-Russian avant-garde and the Austro-German serialists. Italians wanted big-hearted, intellectually stimulating grand operas throughout the first half of the century, and, in the cases of Menotti and Rota, some Italians kept at it in the decades that followed.

The key to understanding why practically all of this music disappeared from our opera houses emerged from an interview with Menotti on March 7, 1999, at his New York apartment, excerpted below. At eighty-seven years of age, he was bright and provocative.

> [Menotti] had been trained [at the Curtis Institute of Music] in Philadelphia [beginning in 1928], at the suggestion of Maestro Toscanini who had little respect for the conservatories in Italy. He was thus both Italian and an outsider. In America, he heard Brahms and Tchaikovsky.
>
> "In Milano, we heard only Puccini, Mascagni, and Beethoven, and the orchestras were not very good. Suddenly, at age sixteen, I heard the

Philadelphia Orchestra! And I learned Schubert, who was practically unknown in Italy."

In the early 1940s, he was the most important young Italian-born opera composer in the world, having had two operas produced at the Metropolitan Opera House. Invited back to Italy, he disappointed the Minister of Culture by refusing to become a Fascist. And after the war, when it became fashionable to be a communist ("Even Visconti was a communist," he says with incredulity) and play only twelve-tone music, his music suddenly became a product of American Imperialism, scorned by [fellow Communists] Luigi Nono and Claudio Abbado.

"This was particularly sad, as Lenny [Bernstein], [Fausto] Cleva and I had given Abbado the Mitropoulos Conducting Award two years before." He speaks of this now with disappointment and irony.

The battle over his Pulitzer Prize–winning opera about a totalitarian state, *The Consul,* at the Maggio Musicale, is part of history now. Nono, who also was participating in the festival, had sent out a declaration inviting artists to protest Menotti's opera. The *cause célèbre* ended in Nono having to withdraw his own opera, when the chorus and orchestra came to the defense of Menotti. "His opera was called *Intolleranza* ["Intolerance"], if you can believe it!" Menotti says with a rueful tone to his voice.[3]

Thus, Menotti had handed me the clues to what had happened to Italian classical music during and after the war. Most of the composers mentioned earlier were members of the Fascist party. Italian fascism was based on a shared nationalism, on passion rather than intellect, on respect for tradition, and was totalitarian. Mussolini said in his *Dottrina del fascismo* (Doctrine of Fascism), first published in 1932, "Therefore, for the fascist, everything is in the state, and no human or spiritual thing exists, or has any sort of value, outside the state."

Every Italian opera house, publishing house, radio station—everything that had to do with supporting a composer and his music—was therefore linked to the state. Menotti had pointed to his lapel while talking to me in 1998 about joining the party. Apparently, the minister of culture had said, "We only need you to wear this pin." That lapel pin would have announced to the world that Menotti supported Mussolini and the government of Italy. Menotti, like Toscanini, refused.

Every composer who lived, worked, drank his espresso in the morning, and ate his pasta for lunch, and who was commissioned to write a new opera—and got it performed—was required to be a member—or at least a de facto supporter—of the Fascisti.

Not all Italian composers were. Montemezzi, for example, left Italy in 1939 to live in southern California, returning once the war was over. Mario Castelnuovo-Tedesco (1895–1968), who composed seven operas and numerous symphonic and instrumental works, was a descendant of a wealthy Jewish banking family that had been expelled from Spain in 1492. Unlike his Catholic Fascist colleagues, Castelnuovo's music was banned in 1938 when Mussolini issued his "Manifesto of Race" that declared Italians were Aryans and, since Jews were not, no Jew could be Italian. Suddenly, Castelnuovo's son, Pietro, was not allowed to attend public school. Emigrating to America and broken-hearted to leave his beloved country, he continued to compose. In a letter to his mentor, the composer Ildebrando Pizzetti, Castelnuovo wrote, "I cannot tell you how painful it is . . . to leave this country, my parents and so many dear friends!"[4] In Hollywood he also continued to teach. Among his students were André Previn, Henry Mancini, Jerry Goldsmith, John Williams, and Frank Sinatra's great arranger, Nelson Riddle. Mussolini's racial laws gave America Mario Castelnuovo-Tedesco. In return, Italy got one fewer Jewish family living in Florence.

Italy, opera, and World War II are not spoken about around the dinner table or at the artistic planning sessions of the Italian lyric theaters. Italians love their opera. Like Beethoven, Brahms, and Wagner for Germans, opera is an endless source of national pride for Italians. And so they quietly agreed to a deal after the cataclysmic ending of World War II. They could keep everything composed up to and including Puccini, and give up everything afterward that was redolent of the Fascist fantasy.

Harvey Sachs's 1987 book *Music in Fascist Italy* has yet to be translated into Italian, though his 2017 book *Toscanini: Musician of Conscience* has been. Over the years, there have been a number of updated productions of Puccini's *Tosca* that take place in Fascist Rome. It works quite well, but the irony that the music is by Puccini, who just barely escaped the post-Fascist purge by dying

in 1924—just before the Fascists took totalitarian control—escapes most people's knowledge. For Italians, the Fascist period is not a source of pride, especially since the entire point of Mussolini's fantasies was about Italian pride and
restoring the greatness of its past.

However, the violence and racism of the Fascists, the revenge of the Nazis
toward Italy when it attempted to pull out of the war in 1943, and the humiliation and starvation that ensued when Italy lost the war, created in the eyes
of the new Italian regime an understandable need to distance itself from all
things Fascist. The Communists who survived were released from jail and
became a powerful cultural force. The founder of the Italian Communist
party, Antonio Gramsci, who died before the war ended, had studied in Turin
when the big auto companies Fiat and Lancia were bringing poor, illiterate
workers to their factories from various regions of Italy, mostly Sicily. He was
clear about where Communists needed to focus their attention: education,
jurisprudence, and the arts. And so, working together with their political
enemies—the formerly outlawed Christian Democrats, the Socialists, and the
Reformists—the Communists cleaned the (opera) house of the stench that
was fascism.

Practically overnight, all that passionate, epic music depicting the glories
of ancient Rome, Italian culture—the collection of stories and traditions that
made Italians laugh and cry and swell with pride—all of that which smelled
and tasted of the folly that was Mussolini was now condemned to take a collective vow of silence.

It was hard to find anyone who admitted to having been a Fascist after
1943, when Italians naively thought the war was over—and when the king fired
Mussolini and Italy signed an armistice. People were cheering in the streets
and throwing their pictures of their Duce out the windows. What they did
not know was that their government had quietly left Rome, leaving the city
to whatever destiny might await. The Allies had other priorities, and so the
Nazis got there first, rounding up an estimated one million Italians during the
next months, sending them to concentration camps, into the mines, or hanging them in the piazzas.

In setting up some sense of a new normal in music, post-war Italy did
much as Germany and Austria did—it went "back to before" and to the last
Italian composer left standing—Puccini—more or less untouched by the Fas-

cist period, one who had died on an operating table in Brussels on November 29, 1924. He had barely squeaked by, having met with Mussolini twice in the year before his death and written a few letters supporting the Fascists—but luckily, all before Mussolini had made himself a dictator. One might wonder what would have happened if Puccini had not contracted throat cancer but instead had lived another ten years, probably becoming the official composer of the regime—a fate that then befell Mascagni. Would we be arguing for "discovering" his operas in these pages had he lived into the 1940s? Perhaps his early fame would have insured his place in our repertory. In a curious way, Puccini's tragic death resulting from an experimental radiation therapy saved him from the compromising fate met by most of his contemporaries.

With the banishing of all Italian operas composed during the Fascist regime—and that includes operas composed before 1922 by composers who lived well into and after the war—something had to become the "source" of new music for Italy's many orchestras and opera houses, and it could not sound anything like what had been a continuous stream of melody and passion that even predated the invention of an art form called "opera" more than four centuries ago.

But, if Italy could no longer play the operas of any composer implicated in the Fascist era, what new music could it play, even as it had hundreds of years of old music to perform time and time again? (And what of Germany and the former Austro-Hungarian Empire?)

The answers would have been complex enough without something new emerging within months of the cessation of hostilities—another war, a "cold" war, where music was once again a pawn in the chess game of politics. It would become a game of defeat, humiliation, rage, and rebuilding. In the new game, the losers would become victors overnight because as the previous war was winding down and Allied victory was imminent in Europe, it became clear to the United States government that our enemies had to be transformed into powerful friends as soon as possible. In this rapidly changing environment, our essential ally in defeating the Axis Powers, the Soviet Union, was emerging as an even greater threat to the United States than the Nazis and the Italian Fascists ever were. The Russians still see themselves as having sacrificed the most to win the war for the Allies. America lost 405,000 lives, whereas the Soviet Union lost 27 million. This new war pitted the Christian West against the godless and ruthless East, defining Russia not in terms of its profound European heritage but rather as a soulless monster bent on destroying all of Western civilization.

Music was once again called in to join the battle, putting on a new suit of armor and uniting all freedom-loving people in a musical language that no longer expressed separate ethnicities. Henceforth, French, German, Italian, English, and American intellectuals would speak the same musical language, share the same grammar, and, inspired by freedom of expression, rout the heathen Slavs, once and for all—whether you listened to the music or not.

CHAPTER 7

⊶⟨∞⟩⊷

The Miracle of a Second Exodus

While so much attention has been given to the experiments of the early twentieth century, something else happened during the World War II period that inadvertently kept the continuum of thousands of years of musical development alive, even as a small group of composers were working hard to break with it.

Hitler was making it impossible for Jewish composers and musicians to work in Germany in 1933, and Propaganda Minister Joseph Goebbels was organizing new ways to promulgate "good German music"—with Wagner as a prime source of inspiration. The doors were closing fast for Jewish composers in Germany and its ever-expanding Third Reich precisely as they were opening for a new medium that immediately needed composers to write great dramatic orchestral music on a Wagnerian scale: the talking pictures of Hollywood.

JEWISH COMPOSERS—AND WAGNER'S THEORIES—TRIUMPH

Wagner's nineteenth-century dream of music drama that was both intimate and epic in scale, would transcend the limitations of theatrical design, and achieve the absolute synchronization of music with gesture was becoming a reality in Los Angeles, California. Motion pictures would of course shift Wagner's balance between music and image, but by 1933 American engineers would solve the challenge of talking pictures with an orchestral accompaniment and make Wagner's most complicated stage requirements possible.

On the one hand, Wagner's stage descriptions appear to be an intimate play of emotions—something like a screenplay—as in this short section at the end of the second scene in Act I of *Die Walküre:*

> Sieglinde stands awhile, undecided and thoughtful. [8 bars of music] She turns slowly and with hesitating steps towards the storeroom. [8 bars of music] There she again pauses and remains standing, lost in thought, with half averted face. [12 bars of music] With quiet resolution she opens the cupboard, fills a drinking horn, and shakes some spices into it from a box. [6 bars of music] She then turns her eyes on Siegmund so as to meet his gaze, which he keeps unceasingly fixed on her. [4 bars of music] She perceives Hunding watching them and turns immediately to the bedchamber. [2 bars of music] On the steps she turns once more, looks yearningly at Siegmund and indicates with her eyes, persistently and with eloquent earnestness, a particular spot on the ash-tree's trunk. [12 bars of music] Hunding starts and drives her from the room with a violent gesture. [2 bars of music] With a last look at Siegmund, she goes into the bed chamber, and closes the door after her. [4 bars of music]

Significantly, the musical elements that underscore this scene are specific motifs associated with woe, love, the magic sword, and Sieglinde's husband, Hunding. And while Wagner's stage descriptions can tell his singers precisely what the composer expected when they were *not* singing—where to look, how to stand, how to listen—he also created stage requirements that would be impossible to achieve more than 150 years after he imagined them—except in the movies—as he does here in the transition into the last scene of Act III of *Siegfried:*

> With one stroke he hews the spear in two pieces from which a flash of lightning shoots up towards the rocky heights, where the ever-brightening flames become visible. A loud thunderclap, which quickly dies

away, accompanies the stroke. The pieces of the spear fall at the Wan-
derer's feet. He quietly picks them up. The growing brightness of the
clouds, which continually sink lower, meets Siegfried's sight. He puts
his horn to his lips and plunges into the waving fire which, flowing
down from the heights, spreads over the foreground. Siegfried, who is
soon out of sight, seems to be ascending the mountain . . .

Although motion pictures were invented in the last years of the nineteenth
century, technological developments in the early twentieth century transformed a curiosity into an art form that proved to be revolutionary. Music
was always part of the experience with silent movies. It masked the sound of
the projector and had the curious ability to make the visual storytelling seem
organic. It made the constant use of editing and cutting from various points
of view within a scene appear to be seamless.

De During World War I, the American phone company AT&T, and its man-
ufacturing subsidiary Western Electric, developed a system of recording and
sound reproduction that used amplifiers made from vacuum tubes and electronic, horn-shaped loudspeakers. With this technology, recorded music and
sound could be heard in large theaters for the first time. After the war various
companies made other technological improvements, so that by 1930 every film
company was making talking pictures, and by 1933, with the release of *King
Kong,* composer Max Steiner (1888–1971) demonstrated to even the most re-
sistant film producer that a full symphonic score could turn a silly movie that
starred a very fake-looking miniature monkey puppet into a terrifying fantasy
that could entertain millions of people and make a lot of money. The new
horn loudspeaker would also be an important component for large political
rallies throughout the world, where thousands could hear the voices of those
seeking and demanding power.

For many young composers, this was an alternative avant-garde, based not
on style but on technology. They could write music that would be eternally
fixed in its performance and its functionality, something that had never happened before. Music had always depended on performers to interpret it. And
while some people thought the experiments with tonality and rhythm were the
cutting edge of new music, others saw a brand-new way of creating music and
drama in sound film as even more exciting. According to Helen Korngold, it

was also about control. Referring to her father-in-law in 2020, she recalled, "He was a maestro and controlled everything in the house, including re-organizing every object in his music room after the maid had moved them. With movies, his music and its performance were under his direct supervision."

At the same time, Steiner, the son of a wealthy Jewish Viennese family, would also prove that the compositional techniques Wagner had perfected in *The Ring of the Nibelung* would continue to be developed by Austro-German-trained composers and their American students, all of whom—with hardly an exception—were defined as Jews by the Third Reich, though most were non-religious and some grew up in homes that had converted to Christianity in earlier years. "We saw ourselves as Germans," goes the oft-quoted phrase. "It was Hitler who made us Jews." The first generation to compose for Hollywood sound films were "degenerates," their names entered on Hitler's list of dangerous composers of illegal music.

Composing for the cinema was not considered to be a second-tier job for a composer, though it could be an entry-level one. The film studio was just another commissioning agent for new music. In the Soviet Union, for example, it was not considered a mark of lowering one's standards, as Prokofiev and Shostakovich persuasively demonstrated. In Great Britain, composers like Arthur Bliss and William Walton were fully accepted for their film music as well as symphonies and concertos. Bliss was appointed Master of the Queen's Musick in 1953, and Walton composed the coronation marches for both King George VI in 1937 and Queen Elizabeth II in 1953. As we shall see, only the World War II refugee composers who succeeded in Hollywood would find their "serious" reputations destroyed by their association with—and their enormous success in—the new medium once, in the post-war years, it was determined that writing music for Hollywood was intrinsically bad (while composing music for Soviet, British, Italian, and French films was good).

MOVIES AND MUSIC

It was during the twentieth century that movies became a worldwide phenomenon—the ultimate collaborative medium for storytelling, one that made use of historical models as well as emerging technologies: visual, aural, and, ultimately, immersive. Just as earlier composers had found a life in the church, the theater, and subsequently in the concert halls and grand opera houses of the ever-growing urban centers, movies became a new source of music in the twentieth century. It is no wonder that so much young, creative energy turned away from the traditional classical music venues to write for and co-create movies. Equally important was the fact that everyone went to the movies: classical music aficionados as well as those who never went to a concert or to the opera.

Motion pictures became a reality during the 1890s through the genius of a number of photographers, chemists, and inventors, though two French brothers with an apt last name, Auguste and Louis Lumière, brought the new invention to a large public beginning with the screening of ten short films in Paris on December 28, 1895. Once it was determined that movies could tell stories, music was added, played on a piano, an organ, or sometimes by an orchestra. By the late 1920s, music was recorded and synchronized onto the film—and there it has remained ever since.

At first, the music was improvised. Then books of classical music themes as well as new ones, categorized according to emotions, were sold to the pianists and organists who found jobs in this new market. And soon enough, full original scores were being composed specifically for important "silent" films.

While a living theatrical tradition was proceeding in the great theaters in the cities of Europe and America, this new medium, which had vast potential for unprecedented intimacy and grandeur, could also tell its stories anywhere there was a darkened room, a screen, and electricity. Not surprisingly, a number of famous composers who wrote for the new medium, among them Camille Saint-Saëns, Pietro Mascagni, and Richard Strauss, were opera composers.

It was new and it was exciting. As already noted, writing for this new medium must have carried with it the same frisson that attracted young composers to the possibility of writing experimental music during more or less the same period. Writing music for the cinema, however, opened up tremendous challenges and possibilities for composers with talent, and instead of a private club with a few hundred members to hear your new music, there was the potential of an enormous, worldwide audience for your work.

One of the crucial pieces in the puzzle of twentieth-century classical music is the place assigned to movie music, or, if one wants to be careful and avoid fake pejoratives associated with the word "movie," music for the cinema. Once the technology advanced so that music, image, and the singing and speaking voice could be synchronized—in the early 1930s—the music was composed by those trained in the most demanding and prestigious conservatories of Europe and, to a lesser extent, America. It was the greatest emerging platform for young composers.

What interests us is not what makes movie music different, but what connects it to the very heart of all music. It is not particularly useful to describe movie music as a genre because film is simply a delivery system for music, and the music it delivers is as varied as music itself. However, if one wants to categorize music in terms of where it was originally meant to be heard—a concert hall, an opera house, a theater—then can we talk about movie music as a separate entity. The problem with that line of categorization inevitably gets us into arguments such as whether Gershwin's *Porgy and Bess* is an opera or a musical, whether Stravinsky's *Le Sacre du printemps* is ballet music, or whether Mendelssohn's incidental music for *A Midsummer Night's Dream* was ever meant to be heard in a concert hall.

One of the results of the twentieth century's preoccupation with strict requirements of modernity in new classical music was that many composers preferred to find artistic freedom in the unlikeliest place in the arts: commercial cinema. In spite of the requirements of timings and of multiple bosses (and the total lack of job security), it was/is in the movies that many found a home. And a composer never had to worry about a bad review because usually he would be ignored in the press by serious music critics. It was only at the annual Oscar ceremony that there was honor and notoriety to be found, the composers' names proclaimed for all to hear. Otherwise, they worked in relative anonymity—which was quite different from contemporary classical composers, whose names were promulgated on their scores and in concert programs and recordings.

What is often described as "movie music" or "Hollywood" music is a certain *style* of orchestral music that was being written at the time that sound films were invented, that is, the classical music of the late 1920s and 1930s. Strauss, as already noted, was very much alive and writing tuneful and complex tonal operas, as were many Italian, Russian, German, and Austrian composers of symphonic and operatic music, such as Korngold, Rachmaninoff,

Puccini, Prokofiev, and Respighi. It is a style of music brought directly to the Hollywood studios by Europeans. To those who attended concerts, it was simply *music*. It was what was taught in the conservatories of Europe, Russia, and America, and there is nothing particularly remarkable or separate about it as a style. As with any style, what should be remarkable is what an artist does within it: how it is tweaked, balanced, made unique in some way, transcending its implicit limitations and doing whatever job it is meant to do.

Equally important to this narrative is that with the aging of the first generation of European-trained Hollywood composers, their hugely Romantic music morphed into a much leaner style of movie music, composed primarily by the American-born-and-trained musicians who were, nevertheless, mentored by their European idols. These include Elmer Bernstein (studied with Aaron Copland, Roger Sessions, and Juilliard's Henrietta Michelson), Jerry Goldsmith (studied at the University of Southern California with Miklós Rózsa, and with refugee master teacher Mario Castelnuovo-Tedesco), Bernard Herrmann (studied at New York University and Juilliard), Leonard Rosenman (studied with Schoenberg, Sessions, and Luigi Dallapiccola), and Alex North (studied at the Curtis Institute, Juilliard, and the Moscow Conservatory). Meanwhile, the elder statesmen of film scoring were themselves evolving in the normal way, adapting to their new environment and responding to music they were hearing through recordings, broadcasts, and from their colleagues— world music ("ethnic" music), popular music, jazz, concert music, and the avant-garde.

During the twentieth century, some composers accepted the concept of separate styles for concert music and film music. John Williams's DNA is difficult to find in his concertos, much to the surprise of many of his fans. Williams embraces an amorphous non-tonal language free of the exuberant melodic gift he shows in his beloved film scores. Ennio Morricone had the same view. When he began conducting concerts of his music, the first half was devoted to his experimental avant-garde compositions. The second half of the program was excerpts from his film scores. The public soon knew what to expect and started showing up after the intermission. When I asked Morricone why he composed in two styles, he responded "out of respect for the genres." In other words, concert music (or "absolute" music, that is, music that is not "about" anything) was non-tonal and film music was still based on big melodies and dramatic development that help tell a story and describe place and time.

The overall question regarding the viability of any dramatic music is whether the style (or musical language itself) has enough variety and flexibility to tell many kinds of stories or set the listener on complex emotional journeys. Music that developed in Europe has shown a remarkable capacity to *represent* things to its listeners. It describes emotional states. Around 1600, for example, books of new musical compositions inevitably began with a foreword containing passionate arguments by composers such as Claudio Monteverdi and Giulio Caccini as to how best to express emotion through music and poetry. European music was never a neutral aural canvas. Centuries after the Greeks first wrote about this essential aspect of music, audiences in Europe responded to a new symphony by Haydn by naming it after what they "saw" as a result of what they heard. And so there are symphonies by Haydn with nicknames like "The Hen" or "The Clock."

As instrumental music became more descriptive, composers began openly "telling stories" and giving their works specific titles—not the nicknames audiences appended to their works. In the nineteenth century, Hector Berlioz created dramatic symphonies, and Franz Liszt invented a new term for stand-alone musical works (with a title) that told a story in one movement. His "symphonic poems" were a clear demonstration of the ability of music to tell a story without words, scenery, or, indeed, a theater. The theater was in the audience's mind.

In addition to symphonic works, operas, and ballets, there was a significant classical music tradition, beginning as far back as Haydn, to accompany spoken plays. These productions, like operas, began with an overture to set the tale in motion. There was music to accompany scenic changes and to create the mood, and there was music played beneath spoken dialogue. These sections were called melodramas.

Music for straight plays—comic, tragic, epic, and intimate—was composed by just about every major classical composer we all know, including Haydn, Schubert, Beethoven, Tchaikovsky, Strauss, Korngold, Prokofiev, Sibelius, Shostakovich, Debussy, and, in 1948, Pierre Boulez, who wrote music for a radio play by René Char. Mendelssohn's *A Midsummer Night's Dream*,

Beethoven's *Egmont,* and Schubert's *Rosamunde* were never intended to be played in a concert hall, where we hear them today (usually merely their overtures).

What made dramatic music for a movie different from all of the above was that the music and its performance were one entity, like so-called electronic music, which was also developing in the first half of the twentieth century. A composer could use his genius for sculpting emotion at precisely the moment when a visual action took place. This was not in and of itself unique to movies. After all, dramatic ballets had choreography and music synchronized from start to finish. And, as said previously, the singers in a Wagner opera moved precisely with certain musical gestures that were described in the music— music and action were one and the same. However, with film there would be total control, achieving an optimal and repeatable result—a collaboration of action and music in an ideal visual setting.

Each year brought improved technologies and greater challenges, but also greater rewards. Composers who had mathematical ability, such as Korngold, could enjoy determining exactly how many bars of music would be needed at a certain tempo to achieve an accompaniment to a section of film passing through a projector at twenty-four frames per second. And just like other composers who were attracted to the arithmetical and mathematical applica- tions used in twelve-tone composition, film composers could also enjoy the sheer fun—and daunting challenge—of writing to a strict template of time and intention. The great composers fulfill the requirements and transcend them—and make their music sound organic and inevitable.[1]

In the early days of synchronization (1927–32), Hollywood's executives and directors thought that the only use for music would be for films in which there were songs and dances. The studios raided Broadway for composers, lyricists, and arrangers. Richard Rodgers and Lorenz Hart, George and Ira Gershwin, Cole Porter, Jerome Kern, Oscar Hammerstein II, Harold Arlen, and Irving Berlin were all called to the West Coast.

However, the idea of playing music under dialogue in a dramatic scene— known as underscoring—was not a consideration for most filmmakers. In- deed, it was thought that orchestral music would compete with the spoken scene and confuse the audience. Why was there an orchestra playing just off camera in the desert or on the ocean? Whether any of the Hollywood executives had ever experienced a spoken play with an orchestra in the pit is unknown, but even if they had, the "realism" of the screen would lead them to conclude that music would only add confusion to a dramatic scene in a movie.

In 1932, composer Max Steiner, the music director of RKO Pictures, was asked by producer David O. Selznick to perform the experiment of underscoring a dramatic film, based on a story by the then-famous American author Fannie Hurst called *Night Bell*. Steiner knew well from his youth in Vienna about the power of music to impart a larger meaning to spoken text. He also knew how music worked in the epic operas of Wagner. And he knew how Wagner's theories of memory and musical motifs worked to tell stories over long periods of time. He had grown up in the world of epic dramas, great symphonies, and brilliant performances of the music of his time, including the operettas of Johann Strauss, Jr. that his grandfather had produced. The young Steiner, like Korngold, was familiar with both "kinds" of Strausses: Richard and Johann, Jr. (who were not related). He had tried unsuccessfully to persuade his bosses at RKO to let him underscore dramatic films, and not limit music to the "All singing! All dancing!" musicals.

With the arrival of David O. Selznick in November 1931 as RKO's new studio chief, Steiner found a kindred spirit. According to Steven C. Smith, author of *Music by Max Steiner*,[2] Selznick loved attending silent movies accompanied by orchestral music as a child, and the first film he greenlit was the Hurst film. Significantly, it was renamed *Symphony of Six Million* and its script states upfront that "the entire film is to be accompanied by a symphonic underscoring." Throughout the script, indications of musical underscoring specified an imagined and historically unprecedented cinematic collaboration of spoken text, visual image, and music. "Felix is in the sunlight . . . as he raises his eyes to the light, the very picture of a man reborn, the underscoring music rises to a climactic finale."

Steiner began composing as the daily rushes came in and before the film was anywhere near finished. The experience would change his life and, arguably, the course of symphonic music forevermore. *Symphony of Six Million* is a melodramatic potboiler about a young Jewish surgeon who abandons his family and ghetto neighborhood in Manhattan's Lower East Side to become a successful doctor for the rich and famous on Park Avenue. When his father requires emergency surgery on a brain tumor, his mother begs him to perform the operation ("Don't ask me to do it, Ma!"). He relents ("God will guide your fingers, my son!"), and his father dies on the operating table. The death scene of Gregory Ratoff, with its close-ups of scalpels, blood pressure machines, and furtive glances, made the greatest point for the use of music. No one thought twice about hearing an orchestra play during scenes in a hospital. Music and silence held the audience's attention and the world noticed.[3]

Released a few months before Hitler became chancellor of Germany in 1933, *Symphony of Six Million* was an enormous critical success, with Steiner's underscoring noted in the reviews. For his next film, *Bird of Paradise,* Selznick wrote to Steiner, "For my money, you can start on the first frame and finish on the last." Author Smith did the math. "Only two of the film's 82 minutes are without score."

Soon, every Hollywood studio was busy creating and expanding their music departments—each of which employed its own symphony orchestra. By 1940, Warner Bros. was releasing fifty motion pictures in a fifty-two-week period—all of which had new music. A war raged in Europe and Hollywood's composers were desperately working to get their European families out, while in a new country and in a city filled with sunlight and the scent of orange groves, the refugee composers wrote music—German music.

Steiner went on to compose over 300 orchestral film scores, some lasting only a few minutes (main title, a few transitions, and end title) and some lasting well over an hour (with *Gone with the Wind* from 1939 lasting three hours—longer than *Das Rheingold*). Steiner absolutely knew the source of his art. "The idea originated with Wagner. If Wagner had lived in this century he would have been the Number One film composer."

Just as Wagner had composed a theme for Siegfried and another for his sword, Steiner composed unique motives for Tara, Mammie, and Melanie. He knew exactly how to use the audience's memories to create a sense of time, recollection, and pathos, just as Wagner did in the myriad musical quotations in his funeral music for Siegfried in *Götterdämmerung*.

Steiner, for example, first announces "Tara's Theme" at the very start of the main title to *Gone with the Wind.* The words "Gone with the Wind" pass from right to left, and the melody, which is based on the rhythm of those words, is implanted in the viewer's mind. Approximately ten minutes later, the melody is linked to the plantation, Tara, and the land, when Scarlett O'Hara's father tells her of its importance. The melody, returning for the first time in the drama and played on the English horn, underscores his speech. When he has finished, the full orchestra plays the heroic melody for a mere twenty seconds as the camera pulls back to reveal a father and daughter in silhouette, beside a mighty oak tree and surrounded by the verdant land. The music has continued the father's emotions much as Wagner makes his greatest statements *after* a character has stopped singing.

The Tara theme is not heard again for over an hour, when Scarlett returns to her home after the devastation of the Civil War. Little snippets of the theme, again linked to the plangent sound of an English horn, are interspersed with melodic memories of the happier pre-war days, while the basic musical palette is of complex and morose Wagnerian chromaticism. Scarlett's mother is dead, Tara has been pillaged, and her father has gone quietly mad. Only when she turns her sadness into a determination to do whatever it takes ("As God is my witness, I'll never be hungry again!") does the theme return to its first iteration heard in the main title an hour and half before. The effect of Steiner's use of Wagner's principles is electric and seals the heroic conclusion of the first half of the film.

Other film composers created unique themes for Errol Flynn's Robin Hood, for Gregory Peck's psychological condition in *Spellbound,* for Boris Karloff's Frankenstein's monster and his bride (Elsa Lanchester), as well as for Gloria Swanson's fading silent screen star in *Sunset Boulevard.* Steiner and his European contemporaries had experienced firsthand the effectiveness of Wagner's synchronization technique in aligning music to gesture in the opera house and applied it to their scoring—even though their characters were speaking and not singing. Korngold, who had composed five operas in Vienna, referred to his film scores for Warner Bros. as "operas without singing" and called Puccini's *Tosca* "the greatest film score ever written."

In this sense, Wagner's great achievement in creating coherence in dramatic music can be seen as the direct antecedent of writing film music. This is what Steiner meant: it can set a mood, define a character, and illuminate the structure of a narrative that is told over a significant period of emotional and actual time, with every physical gesture and scenic demand in a synchrony of sound and image to tell its story.

Thus, beginning in 1933—and because of the immense success of Steiner's use of German orchestral traditions of underscoring dramas and operas—an entire industry that required new symphonic music beckoned. European-trained Jewish wunderkinds heard the call and took a chance at survival for themselves and their immediate families in a new country, thousands of miles away from their homes:

—From Hungary, a child prodigy who could read music before he could read words, Miklós Rózsa, who was a straight-A student at Leipzig's demanding conservatory, would emigrate and compose ninety-eight film scores, including *Spellbound, Double Indemnity, Ben-Hur,* and *El Cid,* along with orchestral and chamber works for the concert hall.

—From Germany, the twenty-seven-year-old Franz Waxman—rigorously trained in Dresden, who earned money upon graduation by working in a bank while moonlighting as a jazz musician in Berlin—came to America with his friend Billy Wilder and composed *The Bride of Frankenstein* in 1935. Waxman was immediately appointed head of music at Universal Studios. He would go on to compose 150 scores for the movies, including his two back-to-back Oscar winners for *Sunset Boulevard* and *A Place in the Sun.* It was Waxman's ability to mix jazz with the harmonic world of Mahler and Strauss that made him the perfect composer to portray Grace Kelly (*Rear Window*), Katherine Hepburn (*Philadelphia Story*), and Elizabeth Taylor (*A Place in the Sun*).

—In St. Petersburg, the brilliant Dimitri Tiomkin was studying piano with Felix Blumenfeld—who was also Vladimir Horowitz's teacher—and composition with Russia's greatest professor of composition, Alexander Glazunov—who also taught Shostakovich and mentored Prokofiev—when he discovered American popular music. One night at a student hangout just off campus, the seventeen-year-old Tiomkin came across a page of a contemporary American song printed in a magazine—the 1911 hit "Alexander's Ragtime Band." He knew he had to find a way out of Russia, toward the source of this new and vital music. He could not have known at that time about Irving Berlin, who was born in Siberia, came to New York

City as a five-year-old in 1893, and assumed an invented name because his real one, Israel Baline, was misheard on the telephone by
a music publisher. Tiomkin spent time in Berlin, where he studied
with its greatest composition teacher, the Italian futurist Ferruccio
Busoni, and went to Paris, where he played the solo part in the
European premiere of George Gershwin's Piano Concerto (with
Gershwin in the audience) at the Opéra in 1928.

Tiomkin's first significant Hollywood film score was for *Alice in
Wonderland* (1933). He would win four Academy Awards for his
scores and his songs (along with 22 nominations). It is perhaps a
little-known irony that while another Slavic-American Jew, Aaron
Copland (whose parents came from Lithuania) was composing
"fake" cowboy ballets in New York (*Rodeo, Billy the Kid*), the Russian Jew Tiomkin was composing "fake" cowboy music for John
Wayne movies such as *Red River,* along with *High Noon* and the
theme from *Rawhide,* on the West Coast. (Asked why he was so
good at invoking the vast spaces of the American West since he had
no experience with it as a Russian, he famously said, "A steppe is a
steppe.")

—From Poland came another wunderkind: Bronisław Kaper, who
studied composition at the Warsaw Conservatory. In Berlin he
befriended the Austrian Walter Jurmann, and together they jour-
neyed to America, where they wrote songs such as "San Francisco
(Open Your Golden Gate)" and the songs for the Marx Brothers'
A Night at the Opera and *A Day at the Races.* Kaper would win an
Academy Award for *Lili* and compose the music for *Mutiny on the
Bounty* and *Auntie Mame.*

—From Vienna came Erich Wolfgang Korngold, perhaps the most
lauded of all. Fascinated by the new medium of sound pictures,
Korngold at first spent half of the year in Vienna, composing his
concert and theater works—even as his music was being banned
in Germany—and winters in Hollywood, which also improved the
health of his younger son, George, who suffered from recurring
lung ailments. In 1938, when he was in Los Angeles, he learned that

Hitler had commanded Austria's chancellor, Kurt Schuschnigg, to visit him. Schuschnigg was presented with an ultimatum, to hand over power to Austrian Nazis, and informed that the annexation of Austria (the *Anschluss*) was an inevitability. The Korngolds could not return home, and the challenge was to get his parents and their older son, Ernst, out before the borders closed. Ernst and his grandparents got the last train out of Vienna, which was so crowded the teenager had to sit on the lap of a Nazi soldier. Once in Los Angeles, Ernst attended North Hollywood High School, where he graduated as valedictorian and subsequently joined the Marines.

These Jewish composers, who rose to the very top of their classes in the greatest conservatories of Europe, would all make use of Wagner's leitmotif technique and the Wagnerian discovery of the power of memory in telling long-form music dramas and comedies. The greatest irony is that they not only brought Wagnerian aesthetics to the non-opera-going public, they also "taught" the world classical European music—its symbols and its lexicon—while expanding it in their individual ways. No one ever objected to the fact that Steiner's score to *Gone with the Wind* is a Wagnerian tone poem that occasionally quotes a few famous popular melodies from the American South. It is simply heard as music. As Leonard Bernstein once said, "Millions more people heard their music than ever would have, had they composed chamber music, a symphony or an opera."[4]

THE THEATER OF THE MIND

Wagner and Wagnerism did not emerge in a vacuum, of course. Given the writings of our Greek forefathers, music has always had a narrative propensity and an ability to link itself to physical objects, emotions, and other senses. Did composers in the pre-cinema era who were not specifically writing for the stage expect the listener to provide a narrative understanding when experiencing their music? If so, was there an interpretation that was generally understood or was it a personal translation . . . or both? The German musicologist Anno Mungen is a leading academic investigating "pre-film music" in Europe and the United States. Mungen's research has discovered enlightening information in the books and newspaper advertisements of the nineteenth century linking instrumental music to visual imagery.[5]

For example, in February 1812, the Vienna premiere of Beethoven's Fifth Piano Concerto (the "Emperor") was performed in the Hoftheater accompanied by two *tableaux vivants*.[6] (Or is it the other way around: two *tableaux vivants* were seen accompanied by Beethoven's Fifth Piano Concerto?) Beethoven's student Carl Czerny was the soloist, and Beethoven was very much alive and certainly present. For the first movement, a *tableau vivant* of Raphael's *Queen of Sheba Paying Homage to Solomon* was depicted by living actors, frozen in position.

Later, Poussin's *Swooning of Esther* was presented. We cannot be sure that the music and the images were performed simultaneously, but the fact that the music was framed by visual art is important to our understanding of the affect of Beethoven's music in his own time. The Beethoven concerto has only one break in it, and the second and third movements are played without interruption. This could lead to the possibility that the two paintings were seen *during* the performance, with the pause used to re-set the stage.

By 1870 there had been several attempts to illustrate Beethoven's symphonies in Düsseldorf, Wuppertal, and London. (Remember that Walt Disney did much the same the thing—and to general derision by "purists"—seventy years later with Beethoven's "Pastoral" Symphony in *Fantasia*.) Original music for *tableaux vivants* was composed by Otto Nicolai, Fanny Mendelssohn, Giacomo Meyerbeer, Leoš Janáček, Jean Sibelius, and Richard Strauss. Strauss's four pieces composed for the 1892 wedding of Grand Duke Carl Alexander to accompany *tableaux vivants* were subsequently played in the concert hall (1897), thereby demonstrating Strauss's opinion that the music could work with or without the images. Some of this music was then recycled for scenes in his 1925 silent film score to *Der Rosenkavalier*, all of which shows a fluidity in function and purpose by the composer himself.

In the early nineteenth century, a popular form of visual entertainment in the great cities and courts were dioramas, with a cinema-like screen in a dark room showing an imaginary place accompanied by sounds and music, like grating glaciers in a view of the Alps, or an interior of a basilica accompanied by organ music. "Pleoramas" were moving panoramas. Here, the changing imagery might be of a trip down the Rhine, in which the audience sat in a

stationary boat while painted, moving scenes on either side—unrolled by synchronized operators—gave the impression of a journey. This was accompanied by horn calls. Wagner would certainly have been aware of this audio-
visual entertainment when he composed Siegfried's "Rhine Journey" for his
Götterdämmerung (Twilight of the Gods).

It should be noted that this kind of entertainment can still be experienced
today in Disneyland's "Star Tours—The Adventures Continue" and in Laguna
Beach, California—just south of the original Disneyland Park—at the annual
Pageant of the Masters, which presents a series of *tableaux vivants* accompanied by a live, original orchestral accompaniment. This old European tradition, transplanted to southern California in 1933, probably goes unnoticed by
those who disdain Disney theme parks and think of the pageant as merely an
example of southern California kitsch. If it is kitsch, then it is old European
kitsch, otherwise known as its traditional culture.

Even more important is how Europeans defined the word *picture* in the
nineteenth century. First of all, it was not just an optical phenomenon. It was
a product of one's imagination that was the result of certain means, such as
color and perspective, but also sounds and smells. Thus it is possible to consider the possibility that people *heard* pictures when they experienced a Beethoven symphony and that, equally important, Beethoven intended them to.

His "Pastoral" Symphony (1808) is an overt declaration of his visual inten-
sion. (Vivaldi had done much the same thing in his *Four Seasons,* composed
around 1717.) Beethoven breaks open the symphonic form by giving visual
descriptions of each movement—much as he did in terms of musical structure with his Fifth Symphony, which used a rhythmic motif that runs through
its score and thereby breaks the wall between movements, and his Ninth Symphony, which added voices to affix explicit poetic images to reinforce its implicit meaning.

We know that there are descriptions of Schumann's Second Symphony
from the mid-nineteenth century that describe it as a novel, but one based
on feelings rather than words (the German word being *Gefühlsnovelle*). And
so it is just possible that musicologists, led by Mungen's important work,
will come to the conclusion that there is no such thing as non-descriptive or
non-narrative music in Western culture because there was always a series of
images, emotional and pictorial, going on in people's minds when they heard

symphonies, sonatas, and string quartets. The retired great opera coach/accompanist Susanna Lemberskaya was instructed by the faculty at the conservatory in Kyiv (Kiev) to "make up your own story" for every piano sonata you learned so that when you played it, it was a personal narrative you were "telling."

Perhaps, then, movies can be seen as an expression of what music was already doing in people's minds, rather than movie music being a musical response to or description of the visual and dramatic elements of a film. Anyone who has had the privilege of conducting Mahler's Third Symphony cannot but "see" things when a team of snare drums plays a military marching rhythm that fades away, as if into the distance, and suddenly, in a totally different tempo, eight French horns surprisingly intone the recapitulation of the opening heroic theme, played *fortissimo*. It is what the movies call a cross-fade, but it could not have been achieved in movies in 1895 when Mahler imagined and composed it, because movies had only just been invented.

With this understanding of the meaning of *picture*, we can better comprehend the genius of Puccini in his choice of words to describe the four acts of the opera *La Bohème* (1896). Based on a book of short "scenes from the bohemian [that is, poor student] life," each act of the opera is called a *quadro*, or picture. At the end of Quadro Terzo (Act III), Puccini indicates that the curtain begins to fall slowly during the last forty-five seconds (typically, a curtain falls in five to seven seconds). Mimì and Rodolfo are alone as the snow begins to fall. Mimì sings, "*Vorrei che eterno durasse il verno!*" (If only winter would last forever), and the curtain begins to fall slowly, as the two reunited lovers continue to sing. A curtain in a nineteenth-century opera house did not fall from above, like a guillotine. It closed from above and the sides, creating an ever-reduced frame through which the audience could view the stage. In other words, it was the closest thing to a close-up. Two stagehands would walk upstage of the curtain, guiding the edges of the enormously heavy curtains that were being operated by other stagehands in the wings, and with the final two chords of the act, Ta-DAH, they closed the tabs precisely with the music.[7]

Mahler, Debussy, Sibelius, Puccini, and Strauss—theirs was the contemporary music being created during the era when the Lumière brothers took their Cinématographe Lumière on tour to Bombay (now Mumbai), London, Montreal, New York, and Buenos Aires. Classical music and the resultant moving images created in the minds of its listeners would soon be linked in the new visual medium that would carry the language of Europe's classical music out of the concert halls and opera houses and into every corner of the world.

A generation later, the world was proceeding inexorably toward a second world war. The newly appointed chancellor of Germany, Adolf Hitler, would soon install the latest sound film projection equipment in his Berlin office and at his residence in Berchtesgaden, where he could show the latest movies from Hollywood. America and Germany were not yet at war, and Hollywood's studios had thousands of European employees who oversaw the promulgation of its films. While Hitler was enjoying late-night screenings of *King Kong,* with its score by the Jew Max Steiner,[8] Stalin had Prokofiev to score the Soviets' greatest films, and in 1937 Mussolini was producing movies in the largest film studio in Europe, the newly created "Cinema City" (Cinecittà) in Rome.

CHAPTER 8

A New War, an Old Avant-Garde

After the cessation of hostilities in 1945, European and American classical music leaders and curators, those expressing and determining what should be commissioned and presented, and what the public should be listening to, faced a recurring twentieth-century question: "Where do we go from here?" To that question was implicitly added, "Where have we just been?"

After a generation of political upheavals in which music was employed as a symbolic representation of political ideology, these questions became uniquely problematic. This time, the question did pertain to the general public because it related to *everyone's* behavior and identity, both during the war and now, in its aftermath. This was true whether or not the politicians or the captains of industry or the "average" person attended concerts and operas. It was not a trivial question. Governments in the newly liberated countries, using public funds, would re-establish their orchestras, opera houses, and radio stations. It was, therefore, a matter of who we are now, not who we were or who we once wanted to be. What music do Germans give themselves permission to listen to in Berlin in 1946? What opera can La Scala present to its public in Milan while a defeated Italy is creating a new constitution in Rome?

The previously expounded polemics and directives of the World War I era as to what constituted art music up to that point in twentieth-century

history—the various avant-garde movements—had not resulted in a generation of accepted new repertory. In addition, other kinds of classical music the
general populace wanted to hear—the non-avant-garde Italian operas, the symphonies composed in exile—were, more than anything, painful reminders of
things best forgotten. For European intellectuals, including but not limited
to German and Italian music critics and professors, there was also a sense of
panic to find justifications for what they had said and published in all those
complicit and now compromising classes, speeches, and academic papers.

European university professors under the former Third Reich who re-
tained their academic positions after the war found new ways to maintain a
consistent position toward the "degenerate" composers. With the rejection
of the American music of Hindemith, Korngold, Weill, and Schoenberg, the
Germans, who led post-war intellectual criticism, effectively removed the still-
beating heart of their musical legacy from the concert hall. It was the *coup de
grâce*. An entire generation of music was eliminated by the passionate feelings
of the vanquished—articulated in the most authoritative voices of "experts"
and subsequently by the victors who respected their opinions and needed their
support in the new war with a new enemy—Soviet communism.

A simple solution was found that involved a tacit agreement between the
masses and the masters: Do not play *any of it*. The "Nazi" music *and* the
entartete Musik the Nazis banned fell into the same convenient category
of inconvenient music. This was especially awkward since Weill, Hindemith,
Korngold, and Schoenberg had music to share with Europe. Would Europe
listen? Italy's now-compromised composers, as well as those who had "abandoned" their homeland and survived in America, were all thrown into the
same dump: Pizzetti and Menotti; Mascagni and Castelnuovo-Tedesco. Thus,
the net trawled the musical waters and cleansed the world of the music it now
preferred not to hear. How this was done, and continues to be done, is something worth exploring, as we shall see.

The audience, as always, chose what it wanted to hear. The democratiz-
ing of music had come with the radio, the phonograph, and the talking (and
singing) pictures. The classical repertory that Europe liked before the war was
the repertory it was grateful to hear again, even from compromised performers, who were generally given a pass. New interpreters soon emerged and new
technologies made for new discoveries of old masterpieces, all of which made

performing pre-war music safe from recent complications. Beethoven's Ninth Symphony and a new production of Verdi's *Aida* could open the seasons in Berlin and Milan, and the CEOs of Krupp and Mercedes as well as the president of the Italian Republic and the mayor of Milan, alongside the glamorous movie stars and fashion models, the general populace, and the press, could show up without giving even a whiff of commentary about the recent war.

Wagner, however, was a particular challenge. In post-war Bayreuth, Wagner's British-born—and defiantly unapologetic—daughter-in-law Winifred, who had welcomed Adolf Hitler and his financial support of the Wagner festival, made for a difficult legacy to erase. The composer's two grandsons and one of his two granddaughters, along with the American governing overseers, had to figure out a way to cleanse recent history from the eyes and ears of a public that was still craving to see and hear the master's operas performed in the opera house built to his specifications in 1876.

Granddaughter Friedelind Wagner and her brothers were given legal responsibility for the festival after the war, even though their pro-Nazi mother was still alive. Wieland and Wolfgang Wagner each had 33 percent, and Friedelind was granted 34 percent. The reason for her symbolic 1 percent advantage was that Friedelind had left Germany in 1940 and broadcast speeches in London against Hitler. ("If Hitler really understood my grandfather's operas, he would ban them, too," she said.) It was Arturo Toscanini who helped bring her to the United States, where she became an American citizen. At the "New Bayreuth," which opened in 1951, Friedelind ran a school for young artists, many of whom were American. That helped mitigate some of the recent past.

What Wieland and Wolfgang did was probably more important, with Wolfgang taking responsibility for much of the administration and both directing and supervising its productions. All the old scenery from the Nazi era, which had maintained the traditions of the original nineteenth-century designs, had either been destroyed during the war or needed to be, since it carried too many recent memories. Instead, the brothers developed a new way of staging the Wagner operas that discarded more than the scenery. It discarded the staging, too. Wieland had studied architecture and was inspired by the futurist architects of pre-war Europe to create starkly timeless images that were projected on a gigantic, curved cyclorama. The stage area was a mysterious, raised platform in the shape of an ellipse that was slightly tilted toward the audience and appeared to float in space. Because the Wagners had little money for scenery, they put all their resources into state-of-the-art lighting and projection systems.

Then Wieland, an immensely talented director, stripped Wagner's synchronizing gestures from his productions. Singers related to each other on the disk with little or no three-dimensional scenery or props. A scene from his 1965 production of *Götterdämmerung* between Brünnhilde and her sister Waltraute resembled something like a sumo wrestling match, with each countering the other's moves. The famous "Ride of the Valkyries" presented the eight demi-goddesses standing in place while more than twenty projectors made the sky appear to be moving in surprising and vertigo-inducing cloud formations.

At first, the music was conducted by men who had performed for the Nazis—Hans Knappertsbusch, Karl Böhm, and Herbert von Karajan—all of whom could trace their interpretations back to Wagner himself. The theater reopened on July 29, 1951, with something truly safe: Beethoven's Ninth Symphony conducted by Hitler's favorite maestro, the mesmeric Wilhelm Furtwängler. After that, Wieland presented his radical production of *Parsifal,* which was still in the repertory in 1966, the year he died. Unlike in 1951, when the work was conducted by Knappertsbusch, in 1966 it was under the musical direction of none other than Pierre Boulez, the leader of the post-war European avant-garde.

By 1966, Boulez had become the most articulate, influential, and one might say lethal musician to emerge from the rubble of World War II. Through his appearances at modern-music festivals, speeches, and occasional incendiary articles, Boulez, the composer and opinion maker, had already become the arch-modernist intellectual spokesman of Europe's dogmatic serialists when he agreed to take on conducting the Romantic music of Wagner. A happy Wieland publicly announced that he had finally found an interpreter of his grandfather's music who fit his vision for New Bayreuth.

Boulez erased the great roiling ebb and flow of the performance tradition that Wagner himself had invented, and instead gave a cool and meticulously prepared account of the scores. When asked in 1974 whether Bayreuth maintained the original markings in its set of orchestral materials, he looked surprised and disinterested. "No, the parts are simply replaced with new ones." And so, Bayreuth was de-Nazified, tradition-bound Germans could occasionally boo with impunity (in the dark), and the radical modernists were given permission to cheer what they saw and heard. And while Wieland was alive, there was no more exciting place for a Wagnerian to be. Everyone, it seemed, was served.

Meanwhile, popular forms of music—in broadcasts, recorded performances, and live performances of big bands in dance halls and jazz clubs—once again satisfied Europe's and America's desire for new music that was tuneful, exciting, memorable, and fun. New symphonic scores were being composed by Americans who followed Wagner's theories and composed them for the movies. That they were immigrants was mostly unknown to audiences, since Americans had many types of family names. Did anyone imagine that Franz Waxman was Franz Wachsmann when his music accompanied movies that starred Henry Fonda, Katherine Hepburn, and Cary Grant?

At war's end, new repertory had been composed by the four previously mentioned titans of Austro-German music. In Los Angeles, Schoenberg continued to compose strictly twelve-tone works, but also ventured into writing intricate and beautiful tonal compositions, including a violin concerto, a piano concerto, orchestra variations, a chamber symphony, and a suite for string orchestra. In New Haven, Connecticut, Hindemith completed five symphonies, two operas, an epic requiem mass, and many chamber works and sonatas. In Los Angeles, Korngold composed more than a dozen enormous scores to Warner Bros. films—comprising more than thirty hours of symphonic music—and once Hitler was dead, he wrote for the concert hall, completing a violin concerto, a four-movement symphonic serenade, and a grand symphony. In New York City, Weill completed an epic-scaled Bible play, an opera, five musicals, a folk-opera for radio, a pageant, and art songs. His Broadway musicals explored important political and social conditions such as apartheid, mental illness, age discrimination, war, American racism, and sexual hypocrisy. German music, it would seem, was doing just fine in America.

The idea that "modernism" was the only path forward for post-war European and American classical music was not generally accepted by composers who kept on writing, and were not willing or able to change their styles to accommodate the pressures that were coalescing against them. Of course, their music changed and developed in extraordinary and unique ways in their adopted countries. They and many others let the public determine success or failure, much as Giuseppe Verdi did in the nineteenth century. He judged the value of his operas by their level of success with an audience, nothing more, never blaming the public for not understanding his latest opera. After Wagner had published his books and essays on opera, drama, art and revolution, and the future of music, Verdi was asked by a journalist if he, too, had a theory on theater. "Yes," the maestro is reported to have said. "The theater should be full."

The twentieth century proved to be a golden age of popular song, especially love songs, and the source of much of it was America. For a century frequently described as modern, to contrast it with the so-called Romantic nineteenth century, the twentieth century saw a passionate outpouring of love—and the other powerful emotions that come along with it.

The challenge persisted, however, in finding the style of music one could call "modern"—the predetermined prescription for the twentieth century that never seemed to go away. This concept had new relevance for those who wanted to *represent* the new democratic western Europe and its eager-to-please liberator, America, in *high art* music. As mentioned earlier, a solution, at least for the Americans, who had both the money and the political goal of establishing a democratic Europe, was for the music to demonstrate a strictly delineated concept of freedom of expression, and thereby distinguish itself from the Soviet's official and unapologetically anti-avant-garde musical language. Freedom *from* sounding like the recently composed—and sweepingly attractive—music of Europe and America was also important to the young European survivors of their parents' war, all of whom were innocent victims of its violence, its deprivation, and, perhaps more profoundly, the humiliating loss from a catastrophe they hardly understood in the first place.

What kind of new classical music should be officially supported by the West? What voice should fill America's and Britain's concert halls and opera houses, as well as those concert halls and opera houses in a brave new continental western Europe, where significant monies derived from the American government and private U.S. foundations were supporting new European art and music? The Allies, after all, had made a commitment to rebuild the decimated cultural infrastructure of Germany. What should all the German, French, Italian, Danish, British, etc. radio orchestras be playing in 1945? 1955? 1965? America, after all, was financing much of the reconstruction of Europe.

In retrospect, of course, this was a totalitarian concept—a universally approved language for all new music—promoted by the very people who had been fighting totalitarianism.

As we have said, Stalin's Soviet Union maintained its policy regarding contemporary music. Russia, too, had won the war. Italy, France, and the German-speaking countries, however, had a big—and complicated—job ahead of them.

A SOLUTION EMERGES: THE RETURN OF THE AVANT-GARDE

Avant-garde is a military term. It refers to a group of highly trained soldiers who advance ahead of the others (the main-guard and the rearguard) to seek out the enemy. But if you look up the word *avant-garde* in terms of art, you will find yourself in a forest of definitions, some of which directly contradict each other.

At its start in the early 1900s, the avant-garde movement that became codified and published as a call to action in Marinetti's *Futurist Manifesto* of 1909 seems to have been fueled by a hatred of capitalism and mass markets. As a result, instead of rejoicing in the influence the movement was having on other artists and the public (the main-guard and the rearguard), the avant-garde artist was meant to reject influence altogether—as if such a thing were possible. In addition, the movement defined any art that it *might* have influenced as being derivative and therefore fake or kitsch.

The avant-garde also emerged out of a concept of futurism—in which new is better than old—and a general opposition to mainstream concepts of art and music was central to its beliefs. Thus, once the avant-garde's external manifestation—its voice, as it were—was accepted, it was either abandoned or denigrated as no longer being truthful. In its hermetically sealed definition, it could only exist as a group of leaders of a club that no one can join because it no longer exists. Of course, the circular logic of this philosophy is exposed when one attempts to define newness and oldness.

The word *obscene* comes from the Latin *obscena,* meaning offstage. The holy altar of the theater, as determined by the Greeks and Romans, would never permit certain actions to be seen by an audience. To solve the dilemma of telling stories that involved objectionable acts, the Greeks had invented the role of the "Messenger"—the actor who reports that the queen has hanged herself, and so forth. The audience was required to imagine these things but never actually see them.

The avant-garde in art likes to tweak society's ideas of what is art, as well as what is objectionable. In 2014, for example, a sale of four paintings made from pigeon droppings on white canvas (created by the artist Dan Colen) sold for $545,000 in New York City. In 2017, advertisements promoting a retrospective of erotically explicit images by the expressionist painter Egon Schiele (1890–1918) were banned from appearing on the sides of buses in Vienna and London.

With the embrace of the pre–World War I avant-garde within the artistic communities of western Europe and America in the 1960s, composers took its founding principles to their logical, and some might say absurd, conclusions. You could spend hours imagining new musical works that achieved most of what you read in the above paragraphs. Then, following this logic, you could decide it might be more appropriate to write a book *about* these works without ever actually composing or performing them. Then, once this book of recipes was planned, there was no need to publish a book of recipes for this musical/happening/installation/performance art because, after all, it had already been thought of and experienced in the artist's brain.[1]

In short, what is generally understood by the term *avant-garde* has a few central characteristics:

—It challenges accepted judgments.
—It is revolutionary in that it wants to effect radical change.
—By its very existence, it forces us to rethink pre-existing conditions.
—It is perceived as lively, exciting, new, and linked to intelligence and
    youth.

All of the above continually seeped into the language of European and American musical thought throughout the twentieth century, mostly lying dormant after World War I and the Great Depression, only to be brought back after 1945. The dramatic and overt influence the avant-garde had, however, was on other people who attempted to join the club: smart, articulate, and sometimes pharmaceutically stimulated people who were determined to keep this concept of eternal newness and youthfulness alive—and separate.

After all, how else does one define newness other than by its separateness? This would explain the appropriation of the phrase "contemporary music" to mean much less than "music of its time." The phrase is only applied to music that is part of something viewed as a cutting-edge movement.

A concert of contemporary music therefore could not include tonal music of the twentieth century because it is music that was eliminated from the data pool. In 2019, André Previn recalled that Boulez told him that as long as he was music director of the New York Philharmonic (1971–77), he would "protect it from Shostakovich." "You're kidding, Pierre," Previn said. He was not. One thing the avant-garde composers and supporters did not have was a sense of humor about their art, with its many militant-sounding manifestos. There is one exception—Humphrey Searle. The British Searle, who had studied composition with Schoenberg's most ascetic Viennese student, Anton Webern, and who promoted serial composition on the BBC in the years after the war, served as president of the International Society for Contemporary Music from 1947 to 1949.

When the post-war European avant-garde composers were being sponsored in concerts that excited many—and enraged many more—this rare voice of humor emerged at a 1958 concert masterminded by the Berlin-born satirist and cartoonist Gerard Hoffnung, and none of Searle's compositions was funnier than his irreverent parody of twelve-tone music titled *Punkt Contrapunkt*.

Amid the laughter and satire at London's Royal Festival Hall that evening, one can divine a certain British concern for this invasion from the continent a mere decade after the war had ended. The British had been extraordinarily forgiving and welcoming of German musicians after the war and took a profound interest in what was going on with the youthful non-tonal masters and the lessons they wished to teach their British colleagues. The imaginary composer whose music was receiving its "British premiere" was one Bruno Heinz Jaja—a mash-up on the names of Bruno Maderna, Karlheinz Stockhausen, and Luigi Nono, all living avant-garde composers.

The two very German-sounding "professors" (Hoffnung and scriptwriter John Amis) began their lecture as follows:

Musik began when Arnold Schoenberg has invented the tone row. [Laughter] Before twelve-tone, composing was chaos absolute! Haydn,

Mozart, Beethoven—all has been superficial. Schlagers! Or as you like to say, "flagellated cream" . . .

Now to perform the music of Jaja in England brings a problem already, for here you are not *ganz organisiert.* You do not have the electronic *Machinewerks.*

In Germany, we make it other. In Germany every self-respecting young composer carries no more the pen, or the forking tune [applause] . . . but the mathematical slide rule and the spanner.

Musik paper is out of date. Graph paper is essential now, and every good German composer is ready to put his spanner in the works . . . [Huge laughter]

Each note is dependent on the next. Each note is like a little, polished diamond, as Igor Stravinsky has once said. Of course, Stravinsky has only said this after, *Gott sei Dank,* he has stopped writing his old tonal muck. [Laughter]

Kitsch! Ja, kitsch! Jaja, unlike Stravinsky, has never been guilty of composing harmony in all his life. [Laughter] Jaja is pure, absolute twelve-tone.

The fallacies of the ultra-modernists were right there to be seen in this lethal parody—especially their dependency on very conservative musical concepts such as thematic variation and climax (old German musical ideas, after all). In attempting to distance themselves from older music, however, the pseudo-professors explained that anything that functioned like tonal music must have the prefix "quasi" before it. It was not really acting like the dead tonal system. It was merely similar to it.

What Hoffnung and Amis called a "quasi-development" and "what seems like a quasi-recapitulation" were actual terms used in analyzing twelve-tone and serial composition during that period. In the case of this fake piece, the climax ("so 'quasi-lyrical' as to be 'quasi-emotional'") is three bars of silence. The central bar of silence, we are told, is in three-quarter time (waltz time) and gives the whole work a "quasi-Viennese flavour." And, as if that wasn't absurd enough, "the silence makes a crescendo." Wonderful and funny, except for those who were not laughing and who were taking this very, very seriously indeed.

The United States also had its own musical avant-garde, and none of its members had more influence than John Cage, a student of Schoenberg. His unique puckish humor, coupled with his brilliance, made him a darling outsider. Indeed, he seemed to exist outside of the Outside. And, oddly enough, he became something of a household name. Like Charles Ives, who embraced the chance overlapping of music in our lives, finding joy in hearing marching bands playing different tunes as they pass you by at a parade, or replicating the amateur musician playing "mistakes" in his music, Cage opened Euro-American music to the influences of ancient non-European music and ideas. Ives was not played much during his lifetime, but Cage was very much present in intellectual circles.

Cage's passionate embrace of Indian philosophy, Zen Buddhism, and the Chinese *Book of Changes,* the *I Ching,* meant that his ideas, if not his music, filtered into the consciousness of composers and listeners at the highest echelons of classical music. That he collaborated with the great dancer/choreographer Merce Cunningham meant there was a dramatic "face" to his music. More important, he encouraged people to listen to the sounds around them: traffic, a toy piano, or the fidgeting of an audience waiting for something to happen—as in his famous silent piece known as *4'33".* Indeed, within the universe of John Cage, there was no such thing as silence and there was no such thing as noise.

The March 15, 1943 issue of *Life Magazine* featured a story about Cage called "Percussion Concert—Band Bangs Things to Make Music." It reported on a concert at the Museum of Modern Art in New York City that had taken place the previous February 7. It described Cage as "patient and humorous," adding that "Cage believes that when people today get to understand and like his music, which is produced by banging one object with another, they will find new beauty in everyday modern life, which is full of noises made by objects banging against each other."[2]

What is particularly fascinating about the article in this hugely popular magazine is its historical justification for Cage's experimentation. "Percussion music goes back to man's primitive days when untutored savages took aesthetic delight in hitting crude drums or hollow logs." Significantly, it also described the audience at Cage's concert as "very highbrow."

As if that were not enough, Cage also proposed and created what is sometimes called "chance music" or aleatoric music. This flew directly in the face of the *ganz organisiert* faction, in which every element of a composition—its series of notes, its dynamics, its note-lengths, and the attack qualities of each note—was controlled by various formulae. What Cage was suggesting was the exact opposite. "Choose whatever note you want from this group and play it any way you want until you are asked to stop."

Whereas Europe's young avant-gardists Boulez, Iannis Xenakis, and Stockhausen had originally promoted this American maverick and enjoyed his "disorder" among so much of their music's preoccupation with order, he ultimately went too far. Cage was expelled from school. As devout structuralists, chance music implicitly negated all they stood for. However, one could argue that Cage's ideas of chance were truly new to classical music, whereas structure, whether tonal or non-tonal, was not.

Above all, one must ask if a listener can hear the difference between the resultant sounds from an "indeterminate" piece by Cage for a symphony orchestra and a totally determined piece for the same size ensemble by, say, the much-lauded Elliott Carter or Milton Babbitt. In his *Atlas Eclipticalis,* Cage took maps of the stars and printed the five-line staff one normally sees in printed music over small groups of them. Each player is instructed to use whatever clef is normal for his or her instrument and play the notes in a chosen area (or constellation), but only those notes, and in any order, loudness, or duration, until the conductor moves his or her hands, at which point the player moves to another constellation. The conductor's gestures are like a clock, rather than the normal gestures one makes in conducting notated music—whether by Bach or Boulez. The conductor must move at least twice as slowly as a clock's second hand.

The result, assuming the orchestra players take it seriously, is a kind of feathery sound, not unlike the music of other avant-garde compositions that are specifically notated to give individual orchestra players unique lines of music determined by complex arithmetical and sometimes mathematical calculations.

And therein lies an important point: total saturation of harmonic textures, imperceptible internal rhythms, a sense of stasis, and simultaneous complexity achieve much the same aural result no matter how they are created. Cage and his European colleagues arrived at a place where the sounds of chaotic chance music equaled the resultant sounds of totally controlled music of immense complexity. In later years this music would be called a "soundscape" or "spectral music." It is still viewed as modern, even though its sounds were first heard in the 1940s and then almost without exception in the 1960s, with the music of Stockhausen, György Ligeti, and Krzysztof Penderecki. It is the music many people find absolutely insufferable after two or three minutes. A significant number of music lovers have been taught—and believe—they just aren't smart enough or trained enough to understand it.

One of the most enlightening and, for some, devastating musical experiments of the twentieth century took place during Leonard Bernstein's very last televised Young People's Concert on March 26, 1972. The program—the fifty-third in the series—was called "Holst: *The Planets.*" Since Gustav Holst never wrote a movement for Pluto (even though he was alive when it was discovered in 1930), Bernstein and the New York Philharmonic improvised a movement that he called "Pluto: The Unpredictable." "We have no prearranged signals, and we here onstage are going to be just as surprised as you at the mysterious sounds we will be making. In other words, you are going to hear a piece that doesn't exist yet and will never be performed again." The children in the audience laugh.

For the next three minutes, Bernstein makes gestures to the orchestra, which, it should be said, had played many new works under Bernstein's leadership since he became the orchestra's music director in 1958. Therefore, the vocabulary of the serialists, the avant-garde, and the expressionists of the early twentieth century was well known to the players. Without a note written for anyone to read or an instruction as to what and how to play, the Philharmonic plays an absolutely authentic piece of new music—and it is new in every sense of that word. Except for its rather obvious ending, it is doubtful that anyone who did not know the conditions for the creation of this piece could tell how it was created, but would simply hear it as another work from the twentieth century in the international school of post–World War II modernism.

If you look at the score of Ligeti's *Atmosphères*, which became famous because of its use in Stanley Kubrick's 1968 film *2001: A Space Odyssey*, you will see that every player in the orchestra has a different part. Within the string section, players are asked to change notes in a series of slightly shifting moments of attack in which no one moves at precisely the same time.

John Williams achieved a similar sound world in his music to *Close Encounters of the Third Kind* by giving the string players instructions (in a John Cage way) to choose a note and change it (within certain parameters) as they will. The resultant sound is exactly the same as Ligeti's. John Adams's high-octane minimalism is given its dangerous energy when the composer changes beating patterns and bar lengths from measure to measure, whereas Williams's score to *AI: Artificial Intelligence* achieves much the same result by using regular beating patterns and bar lengths in which the changes of harmonies fall on surprising beats within the bars. In other words, the bars are even in Williams and the music is syncopated against it. These are notational issues, not issues of how something sounds.

Cage also created a genre of performance art known as "happenings." Today, we call it performance art, as if it were something new. He said things like "Consider everything an experiment," and the Ives-like "Nothing you play is a mistake." He just encouraged us to listen and provoked us to think about the world of sound that surrounds us. That, it would seem, is an eternal gift from a true avant-gardist.

------··◄◦❀◦►··------

CHAPTER 9

A Cold War Defines Contemporary Music

Adolf Hitler committed suicide on April 30, 1945. After one final battle, the Red Army raised the Soviet flag over Berlin's Reichstag on May 2. Six weeks later, on July 17, Prime Minister Winston Churchill, President Harry Truman, and Soviet leader Joseph Stalin met in nearby (and Soviet controlled) Potsdam at the Cecilienhof palace—just far enough away from the stench of dead bodies, starvation, rubble, and smoke—to determine the future of Europe. The "Big Three" met for thirteen sessions every afternoon at 5:00 p.m. for an hour or two, followed by a banquet dinner, entertainment, and the singing of jubilant songs.

In an attempt not to repeat the errors of the Treaty of Versailles after World War I, Germany was divided into four zones occupied by France, Great Britain, the United States, and the Soviet Union. Berlin, which was in the middle of East Germany, would itself be carved up into four sectors. Early in the morning of August 13, 1961, with East Berlin hemorrhaging approximately 1,000 of its citizens to the West every day, East German soldiers began building what would become the six-foot-high, ninety-six-mile-long concrete Berlin Wall—which would stand until November 9, 1989.

The Potsdam Conference managed to keep Europe free of another hot war, but it also gave the Soviet Union de facto control over Poland, Bulgaria,

Hungary, Czechoslovakia, Romania, and Albania—all of which became satellite "republics" under Stalin's control.

Thus the scene was set for the *Quo vadis?* (Where are you going?) moment for new classical music in Europe. You may ask why classical music took on this question, whereas popular music just kept bringing new love songs, lively dances, and joy to the world. Popular music cannot easily be controlled: too many people want to hear it. Because of a uniquely twentieth-century *use* of "art" music—that of its being an official marketing device of the state—new classical music was once again required to respond and lead. The goal was music that represented a united, intellectual, freedom-loving—and dispassionately organized—Europe.

As happened throughout the post–World War II period, a dynamic alliance was forged within the community of composers, this time among the Austro-German non-tonal composers, led by Karlheinz Stockhausen; the French avant-garde, led by Pierre Boulez; and the Italian Communist intellectuals, led by Luigi Nono. The life of Nono's older colleague Luigi Dallapiccola demonstrates the challenges facing any serious composer who lived through the war years, starting as it does with his pro-Fascist youth, his anti-Fascist response to Italy's 1938 racial laws, and his post-war music composed in the free democratic Italian Republic. That Dallapiccola's musical style moved from the profound influences of Wagner and Debussy with *Volo di notte* (Night Flight; 1938) to the chromatic expressionistic styles of the pre-war Vienna avant-garde, the 1944 *Il Prigioniero* (The Prisoner), and finally, his twelve-tone opera *Ulisse* (Ulysses; 1968)—critically acclaimed and almost never produced—can almost be seen as an emblematic journey of classical music in the free West of the last century.

As stated earlier, the Italian Marxist philosopher Antonio Gramsci had said that once the Fascists were defeated, Italian Communists should focus on three elements to gain power: education, jurisprudence (which interprets laws, rather than makes them), and the arts. This is precisely what they did. The language of the Italian avant-garde, rejected by Mussolini, became the official language of post-war Italian classical music.

Completing this Italian group were Bruno Maderna, who had joined the anti-Fascist partisans near the end of the war—and subsequently became a Communist in 1952—and his fellow Communist Luciano Berio, who studied with Dallapiccola in the United States and who was the most experimental, composing with electronic sound generators and manipulating acoustic sounds electronically.

New Italian music would break with the past and only look forward. A difficult period—one that arguably saw the last flowering of Italian opera—was, as previously noted, erased. No serious young Italian composer could easily find a teacher or a conservatory in Italy that would support picking up the artistic pieces. Some Italian composers, such as Gian Francesco Malipiero, even dared to excoriate those Italians who had left the country during the war, seeing himself and the others who stayed as the true martyrs. ("Homesickness for one's country is certainly a serious form of suffering for those in exile, but bombings, revolutions, hunger, etc., etc., don't make life very pleasant.") He then pointed a finger at America for not welcoming him and his music. "What has happened to hospitality these days?"

Any contemporary work that attempted to present (in musical terms) continuity with Italy's operatic legacy was seen as crypto-Fascist and condemned, especially if it was presented in Italian opera houses, which were—and still are—given massive (though shrinking) subsidies by their government. Critics, who support the intellectual and complex musical style that proliferated after the war, would only write scathing reviews if any of these works was given a major new production. As a result, hundreds of scores sit in the archives of Italian publishing houses, awaiting some future time when they can be heard without prejudice. Perhaps we are about to enter that period. Perhaps it is too late.

Only Nino Rota, who, like just about every Italian composer of the twentieth century, made a living teaching within the Italian conservatory system, broke through Italy's officially approved "new" musical world. In his two years at Philadelphia's Curtis Institute in the early 1930s, he studied with two traditionalist immigrants: Fritz Reiner (conducting) and Rosario Scalero (composition). (Scalero's other composition students included Gian Carlo Menotti, Samuel Barber, and Marc Blitzstein.) Rota composed operas, oratorios, and many works that languish outside of the classical canon, due, in part, to his unwillingness to conform to the twelve-tone and serial procedures used by his colleagues. However, the filmmakers Federico Fellini, Franco Zeffirelli, and Francis Ford Coppola encouraged his Italian music to live unimpaired by political aesthetics. Public policy be damned! The private citizen who had begun to abandon the opera houses before World War II spoke with a loud democratic voice. In search of beauty, the private citizen went to the movies and responded to Italy's post-war musical modernity with a hearty *"Basta!"*

If one looks for a continuous line of Italian melody in the post-war years, it sang in the popular songs and the film scores heard throughout the world—having escaped the watchful eye of those who wrote about serious music in the "free" West. Since it was popular, the theory went, it must be easy to write, making it of no intellectual interest. But in spite of the Cold War's requirements for Italian classical music, there were beloved orchestral film scores by Rota and Ennio Morricone, alongside the latter's stylistically opposite and unloved concert works, and, in New York and Spoleto, Italy, there was Gian Carlo Menotti, increasingly condemned with each successive work by those who rejected his "old-fashioned" musical language.

Ultimately, Menotti could not bear to read the *New York Times* every morning expressing what it deemed to be good and what it damned with negativity or worse—silence. He escaped to a castle in Scotland appropriately called "Yester House," where he died at the age of ninety-six, in the seventh year of the twenty-first century.

AMERICA JOINS THE NEW-MUSIC WAR

For America, which had a brief period of government-supported art (the Works Progress Administration from 1939 to 1943), determining and supporting new music for a hoped-for democratic Europe was a bit more complicated. In the 1930s, Aaron Copland, Virgil Thomson, and others were determined to "solve the problem" of finding a uniquely American classical musical voice—one that was, curiously enough, distinct from, and perhaps an overt rejection of, Gershwin's African-American–inspired ragtime/jazz adaptations in his symphonic works and his one opera, *Porgy and Bess*. This new American classical voice could not sound like echoes of Brahms and Dvořák. And for Copland, it also erased any sense of his immediate heritage, that of being born in America's quintessential melting pot, Brooklyn, the son of two conservative Jewish immigrants from Lithuania.

Copland and his colleagues succeeded brilliantly. The world soon came to embrace the classical American sound of *Billy the Kid, Rodeo,* and *Appalachian Spring,* and an entire American school emerged. The dilemma in the post–World War II era was how to take a leadership role vis-à-vis young Europeans who distinctly did not want music to represent a country or an ethnicity, even as America had just found its classical voice.[1]

Larger goals took precedence, and the DNA of the U.S. government is everywhere to be found in the *sub rosa* support for certain kinds of music, art, and literature in the post-war era. This makes perfect sense, considering the perceived and probably real stakes. America was fighting for freedom everywhere, but the looming shadow of a Soviet takeover of Europe, especially West Germany and Italy, was, in the words of Secretary of State John Foster Dulles, "not only the gravest threat ever faced by the United States, but the gravest threat that has ever faced what we call Western civilization, or indeed any civilization which was dominated by a spiritual faith."

The Communists were avowed atheists—something that both horrified and challenged America to its core. On February 1, 1953, after his inauguration as president, Dwight Eisenhower was baptized into the Presbyterian Church. It would be during his administration that "under God" was added to the Pledge of Allegiance and a brand new and official motto of the United States of America, which had prided itself on a separation of church and state, "In God We Trust"—replacing *"E pluribus unum,"* first used in 1776—was engraved on the dollar bill, without a single member of Congress voting against its adoption in 1956.

Like all musicians, classical composers always needed to look for work or a steady job. Sometimes this was composing to the specifications of the king or the church. Sometimes it was writing a concerto for oneself, performing it, and collecting receipts at the door—and therefore depending on commercial public support. In the 1950s and 1960s, it was European governments and their support for its arts that were doing the hiring, the commissioning, and the performing of new classical music—underwritten by the United States, with a mixture of overt and covert financing: Voice of America, Radio Free Europe, and the U.S. Information Agency were openly known as arms of the United States government, but there was also the secretive CIA, large private foundations such as the Ford and Fairfield Foundations, and the "privately supported" Congress for Cultural Freedom—which had offices in thirty-five countries funneling CIA monies into this new war.

It was a war that did not make use of armies. President Eisenhower, John Foster Dulles, and Dulles's brother Allen, who headed the CIA, knew that America could support and topple governments without sending in troops. This was an era in which secret infiltration was essential in winning over skeptical intellectual Europeans—including the recent enemies, now essential allies—all without the American public's knowledge.

Along with good and generous people in America who saw it as their patriotic duty to fight censorship and repression in a world that seemed to be closing in on all sides, there were inevitably those who saw a way to profit from the situation and adjusted their aesthetics accordingly. And in both camps there was enough gray area to embrace this new, intellectually challenging music coming from a young generation of articulate composers in western Europe.

It goes without saying that many of the European Jews who had fled to the United States before the war were leftists. Many were indeed Communists because they believed in communism's philosophy of protecting the rights of workers and sharing profits from their collective labor. And many stopped being Communists once Stalin emerged as the monster he was. That still left the former Communists and left-leaning naturalized citizens suspect after the war was over. The Soviet Communists had been our ally during much of World War II and now were our enemy. It was a good cover for anti-Semites never to say anything about America's internal enemies as being Jewish. Rather, Americans would be taught to support all activities that would root out subversive artists and writers who might be, or had been, Communists or Communist sympathizers.

It also meant that certain ex-Nazis who were rabidly anti-Communist needed to be hired to fight the global threat to the West. Thus the tables were turning fast as to who was a desirable American citizen and who was not. The old question of whether a glass is half empty or half full became "How shall we describe this person: a Nazi (who is passionately anti-Communist) or a passionate anti-Communist (who was once a Nazi)?"

When America was celebrating the fiftieth anniversary of the moon landing on July 16, 2019, very few people noted that much of the underlying technology—indeed, the scientists who brought that technology to America and led the "space race" against the Soviets—emerged from the Nazis' secret military rocket program, built on the backs of an estimated 20,000 Soviet, Polish, Italian, and French prisoners who died at the Mittelbau-Dora concentration camp ("the highest death rate in the entire concentration camp system"), working as slaves to build and test the V-2 rocket (*Vergeltungswaffe 2*— "Retaliation/Vengeance Weapon 2") that killed 4,000 civilians in London, Antwerp, Paris, and other European cities. Political comedians in America during the Cold War, such as Tom Lehrer and Mort Sahl, famously parodied the émigré space engineer Wernher von Braun's claim that he was only interested in space travel ("I aim at the stars but sometimes I hit London"), but the world in 2019 did not seem to care. *Untersturmführer* von Braun and 1,600 other former Nazi engineers and scientists—all American citizens—had aided America in its "giant leap for mankind."

And so another perfectly understandable, ironic, and odious bond was implicitly created between former Nazis and freedom-loving Americans, with both sharing a hatred for the Soviets who were encroaching westward into Europe and into the Americas, while the Chinese Communists were supporting North Korea's invasion of South Korea in 1950, creating a very real war— and less than five years after World War II had theoretically ended.

In April 1966, the *New York Times* began a series of articles on the CIA that shocked many. It told the story of how the agency had been acting throughout the world as a covert sponsor of U.S. "citizen groups" engaged in Cold War propaganda, including the Congress for Cultural Freedom. The CCF had presented itself as a private organization that was supported principally by the Fairfield Foundation, a philanthropic organization (incorporated in 1952) that was funded by the very rich Julius Fleischmann, who acted as its president. Fleischmann was a well-known patron of the arts who served on the board of the Metropolitan Opera and who had ties to arts organizations in London and Monte Carlo. He was also a CIA operative.

America had hurled invective upon the Soviets for having its cultural commissars and a blatantly obvious factory of lies—the Communist Party newspaper was called *Pravda*, or "Truth." Propaganda was something the Nazis and the Soviets did. The United States was free and would never stoop so low. Within six months, however, that fiction had been irretrievably blown with more articles in the *Times* and other publications, culminating in the revelation that the programs of the U.S. National Students' Association were financed covertly by the CIA. The scandal that ensued, which has fueled much-needed studies on the cultural side of the Cold War, cast a pall on all the many astounding things achieved not only in cultural understanding but also in the proliferation and establishment of a truly international vision of a postwar style of music, art, and intellectual discourse.

For fifteen years the Congress for Cultural Freedom, under the tireless leadership of the Russian-born composer Nicolas Nabokov, had fought a cultural cold war to win over the intelligentsia of Europe and Asia. Nabokov, a White Russian with a political score to settle with his native country, developed the idea of creating spectacular festivals of new music and art in Paris, Berlin, Milan, Brussels, Tokyo, Venice, and Rome that brought American performers and creators, along with their European and Asian counterparts, into the very heart of the war's wreckage, confronting and confounding the skeptics who were suspicious of America and dismissive of its cultural bona fides. His first festival, called "Masterpieces of the Twentieth Century," took place in Paris in 1952. Nabokov brought the Boston Symphony to play great works that remained outlawed in the Soviet Union.

He achieved two goals. One was to show the unquestioned excellence of American musicians and the grand, vital tradition of the performing arts in the United States. (It was easy for Europeans to forget that the New York Philharmonic and the Vienna Philharmonic had been founded in the same year, 1842.) The other was to demonstrate the fundamental importance of universal freedom of expression, which Nabokov achieved by including artists and music from all over the world, even by the USSR's Shostakovich and Prokofiev.[2] That Pierre Monteux conducted *Le Sacre du printemps* thirty-nine years after having led its premiere at the Théâtre des Champs-Élysées in 1913—and with Stravinsky in the audience—was just one of Nabokov's triumphant ideas, ideas that helped overcome the anti-Americanism of the cynical, condescending French intellectuals, many of whom were Communists or Communist sympathizers. George Balanchine's New York City Ballet, brought to Paris by the festival, accomplished much the same thing. An all-Black opera troupe performed *Four Saints in Three Acts* by Virgil Thomson and Gertrude Stein. There were productions of Benjamin Britten's newly composed opera

Billy Budd, conducted by the composer, and Alban Berg's 1925 *Wozzeck,* conducted by Karl Böhm—both operas seen for the first time in Paris. Schoenberg's expressionist monodrama *Erwartung* and Stravinsky's *Oedipus Rex* were two more brilliant elements of this first festival under the auspices of the Congress for Cultural Freedom. There would be many more, including a "Black and White" festival in Berlin that explored the influence of African art on Western art. When one thinks of the Nazi position on "Negro elements" in art and music, this was a direct rebuttal to the official racism in the former capital of National Socialism.

Even the touring of great African-American musicians to Europe and, later, to the USSR was a counteroffensive to the Russian claim—a correct one, mind you—that in America our Black population was treated badly. We sent Ella Fitzgerald, Duke Ellington, Louis Armstrong, and a tour of *Porgy and Bess* with Leontyne Price and William Warfield (which *Pravda* predictably excoriated) to every major European city.

What makes all of this so extraordinary is that without the CIA funding, none of these initiatives could have taken place. Nabokov insisted to his dying day that he was never required to follow a covert party line. In fact, many members of the U.S. Congress had little belief that a cultural cold war would have any impact at all on the serious political situation confronting America and Western civilization in the face of Soviet aggression. Some were enraged that Nabokov had hijacked the original propaganda purpose of the CCF. However, former ambassador to the Soviet Union and historian George Kennan said in the aftermath of the discovery of the U.S. government's secret activities and the scandal that followed, "[The United States] has no ministry of culture, and the C.I.A. was obliged to do what it could to try to fill the gap. It should be praised for having done so, and not criticized."[3]

What is certainly true is that Nabokov hated what had become of his native Russia and what was being done to artists there. The CIA did not have to coach him on that. What is also true, and can be found in his writing, is that Nabokov was a strong proponent of the "new." While he was hardly an unquestioning supporter of the avant-garde, he wrote and spoke frequently and passionately against music that sounded old-fashioned to him. He likened any new Western music that did not embrace modernism as somehow similar to the music that Soviet composers like Prokofiev and Shostakovich were being pressured to write. In other words, he was feeding the very perceptions that we are meant to accept today regarding the value of dissonance and rhythmic complexity as appropriate in the second half of the twentieth century.

The avant-garde also represented *political* freedom. Nabokov saw the simplification of Russian classical music as a sad reminder of the negative effects of totalitarianism, calling Prokofiev's beloved *Romeo and Juliet* "full of trivial and obvious themes, conventional harmonies, and a general artificial simplicity," and Shostakovich's most enduring work, his Fifth Symphony, as "reminiscent of nineteenth-century music."[4]

What lurks in Nabokov's passionate defense of freedom is his belief in an elite class that not only leads the arts but is essential to understanding and evaluating it. That the Russians, who had initiated a brilliant avant-garde, had settled into something quite tame, in Nabokov's view, was the result of emigration and the destruction of the Russian intelligentsia after the Great Revolution and Stalin's murderous purges. The now defunct Russian upper class, he wrote, had "set the tone of cultural life of the nation, because it alone could understand and encourage the work of the pioneers in the arts." Thus, complex modernity was not only an expression of freedom, it could only be understood by a highly educated aristocracy, and not the common man.

Since the *New York Times* series on the CIA's covert activities in sponsoring a network of "[money] passing foundations" in the late 1960s and early 1970s, there have been hundreds of books—spy thrillers, plays, movies, and so on—about this period, officially named "the Cold War" by Bernard Baruch in 1947 and said to have ended with the fall of the Berlin Wall and the dissolution of the Soviet Union in 1991. In the twenty-first century, as more and more files continue to be declassified and the seemingly insatiable interest in World War II has expanded, we have learned of the complexities of postwar politics and how, among other things, the United States was in fact a haven for thousands of Nazis—scientists, doctors, and less famous citizens formerly active in the Third Reich's enormous apparatus—in order, as already noted, to build defenses against the one area where Nazis and Americans could find common ground—a shared hatred of communism.

Is it too much to consider how that hatred relates to music and the officially supported aesthetics of its—and our—time?

A MUSICAL AESTHETIC FOR A FREE WEST

Music had once again become the plaything of politicians, intellectuals—some of whom needed to distance themselves from their previous writings on music during the Nazi and Fascist eras—and those who saw an opening for advancement. From the start, an important question remained in the de-Nazification process: Was there such a thing as a Nazi music?[5] In fact, while there may not have been Nazi music, there were definitely Nazi composers and apparently, from a stylistic point of view, there was definitely *anti-Nazi* music, at least for the American military. Those knowledgeable in music and with a vague idea of what constituted "degenerate" drew up their list of criteria for judging the culpability of European musicians after the war. It is worth stating once again that if a German composer could prove that he was writing modern-sounding (especially serial) music *during* the war, it was corroborating evidence that he was anti-Nazi and a part of the resistance movement.

The French, it could be added, had picked up the remnants of the "noise" music of the futurists and, using a new device that the Nazis had invented—the tape recorder—created the avant-garde electronic music known as *musique concrète* that made use of sounds recorded and edited together at the National Radio Station (Radiodiffusion Nationale), which, during the war, had functioned as a center for the French Resistance movement against the Nazis, and thus linked the modernist movement in music with the Resistance.

Italian Communists, unlike Soviet Communists, uniformly supported non-tonal music as anti-Fascist. In the months after the Allied liberation, Italian opera houses reopened and performed new but traditional works by Pizzetti and Malipiero, but that all came to a screeching halt as a new government and a democratic constitution were enacted. West Germans took the same path, whereas East Germans, who were Communists, absolutely did not.

Of course, as we have said, everyone knew what constituted Soviet Communist music because it was officially judged and promoted as early as 1932 by the Soviet government. Could we now listen to Shostakovich *as music,* or had it always been propaganda—or a secret demonstration *against* Soviet authority, while pretending to be pro-Soviet? (Indeed, how do we listen to it today?) The American premiere of Shostakovich's Seventh Symphony ("Leningrad"), which was said to represent the Russian resistance to the German invasion, was conducted by the openly anti-Fascist Arturo Toscanini and broadcast live from New York City on national American radio on July 19, 1942. And, as a head-spinning reminder, 1942 was soon after Russia, which had started out in 1939 signing a nonaggression pact with Germany, had become America's ally—and before it became the enemy of the West in 1947.

How did the West pit "our" Russians (Stravinsky, Balanchine and his New York City Ballet, and all those ballet stars who would come to our shores, including Mikhail Baryshnikov and Natalia Makarova, not to mention superstar cellist Mstislav Rostropovich) against "their" Russians (Shostakovich, Prokofiev, the Bolshoi Ballet)? It did not help the Soviets that no major Western artist left America to live in the Soviet Union, and the German Communist state—ironically known as the German Democratic Republic—had to build a wall to prevent the citizens of East Berlin from fleeing into the West. According to Frederick Kempe, in his book *Berlin 1961*, in the first four months of 1953, 122,000 East Germans fled Communist East Berlin into West Berlin—twice the rate of the previous year. With East Germany about to lose its population and implode, and America fighting for Christian values and Western civilization, both sides of the Iron Curtain were on the brink of another hot war by 1961.

All of the above once again required music to act as an official marketing device, a meta-metaphor of political ideologies. In other words, a certain style of music *was* the state.

The answer—the only answer—for the West was to resurrect the avant-garde experiments that had petered out decades before but still had their adherents. The old processes that attempted to control the chaos of non-tonal music, developed just after World War I, came roaring back, and this time they were not for members of a private society. They became officially supported by governments, private funding, and opinion makers. It was as if the West skipped from 1923 in Vienna to 1945 without missing a beat.

The newly minted new music erased an awkward and contentious phase (World War II), and it pleased the intellectuals because it was very intellectual. Every article about this music, usually written by the composers themselves, was full of technical terminology and mathematical references that were dazzling and intimidating, using what Ernest Hemingway derisively called "ten-dollar words."[6] It pleased the politicians because it sounded like the music Hitler, Mussolini, and Stalin hated. It pleased many of the young, discontented, and smart musician-children of the ruins because they could express what they believed to be an appropriate response distilled from the iconoclastic pre–World War I artistic movements while taming the beast with new mathematical controls and justifications. It was non-ethnic, refuting the nationalistic music that had been developing since the nineteenth century. Its only problem was that audiences did not particularly want to hear it.

There were two answers to that complaint: First, that all the great composers of the past wrote "ahead" of their time (this is certainly not true; otherwise Bach, Handel, Mozart, and most composers you have heard of would have made a living as waiters and bell boys, while composing on their days off); and second (which was quite pleasing to the intellectuals), that the public is just not smart enough to understand the new music because they, unlike us, don't *know* anything about music.

This might help explain the greatest mystery of all: Why wasn't all the music banned by Hitler not instantly embraced, indeed officially supported, after the war? Germany had lost the war and America was busy winning the hearts and minds of Europeans by supporting its arts, which included subsidies to restore concert halls, opera houses, and radio stations. And even if we find a measure of understanding as to why the Italians needed to prove they were no longer Fascists and therefore simply erased an entire generation of successful composers of operas, why were those Italians who emigrated and/or were successful in America treated with the same disdain? Were there "gentlemen's agreements" made with the state-run theaters and opera houses, not to mention the academies and conservatories of Europe, in the post-war period? Was this merely the zeitgeist and had European classical music, like some long-awaited affirmation of the 1909 *Futurist Manifesto,* collapsed in 1945, its course finally run?

In a way, this is the conclusion one has to arrive at if we accept current aesthetic pronouncements that the vast majority of classical music composed by the survivors of the war—tonal and uniquely personal—was simply old and irrelevant. The music of a wounded and complex world that was picking up the pieces from decades of European wars had to look forward and sound fresh and, well, new. There is also the argument that every art form and art movement has its ending built into its creation, like all carbon-based life forms. All the public funding in the world cannot bring back Dutch and Flemish painting, Broadway's Golden Age, or the Russian novel. Perhaps, then, even though the war accelerated the demise of epic, tonal music, it was, after 1945, once and for all irretrievably dead.

If that is the case, an equally important question in reviewing the second half of the twentieth century is, what music *replaced* the condemned repertory—once it was determined that the music classified as degenerate would not be welcomed back and all the Italian operas of the post-Puccini period (1924–45) would be equally jettisoned?

We know the answer—none. No repertory replaced the irreplaceable ones in the concert hall. Instead, a few composers, such as Mahler, Rachmaninoff, and Gershwin—who had been marginalized or dismissed by classical music experts—were gradually welcomed into the canon of classical music. Although there are exceptions (the operas of Benjamin Britten, for example), there is a general void that skips from the 1920s to the latest world premiere. In 2001, film director Baz Luhrmann "had the inspired notion that [popular music] is to our age what the arias of grand opera were to an earlier age."[7] That "earlier age" was the pre-modernist age. Indeed, classical music lovers might be hard pressed to name their favorite beloved works from the 1950s, 1960s, 1970s, 1980s, and 1990s. The music that remains in our collective consciousness comes from what we have been led to believe was the disposable (popular) music of a half-century. It is a Broadway show, *West Side Story,* that represents 1957 to the world and not Xenakis's *Pithoprakta,* Stockhausen's *Klavierstück XI,* or Nono's *Varianti.*

The state-supported Italian opera houses temporarily found new repertory in a series of operas that sang in the new voice, such as Stockhausen's *Samstag aus Licht* (Saturday from Light), produced by La Scala in 1984. If one looks up that great theater's officially published online history, it jumps from the world premieres of Verdi's *Falstaff* (1893) and *Turandot* (1926) to its major renovation in 2004 and its recent music directors, Claudio Abbado and Riccardo Muti, as if nothing happened in between. The new operas in the Italian opera houses have been few and have not, as of yet, demonstrated any viability whatsoever. However, new productions of old operas have become the lifeblood of these lyric theaters, and new productions of little-known operas from Italy's past, such as Gaspare Spontini's 1805 *La Vestale* (The Vestal Virgin), act as ersatz new operas since no living member of the audience has ever heard them before.

In the case of Germany, the story is all the more confounding because there were two Germanys from 1949 until 1989. Is there any German commonality between the official tonal music of Communist East Germany and the official non-tonal and serial music of democratic West Germany? Or is it just easier to erase the whole complicated corpus of Germany's Cold War music? And since so many of Europe's greatest composers were American citizens at the time, what actually constitutes post-war German music anyway? Is it "American" Schoenberg or just "Schoenberg"? Is it "American Hindemith" or just "Hindemith"? As for Weill, there was absolutely a conclusion that there was a German Weill and an American Weill, not only because of a development in his style, but because his later texts were in English, which exaggerated the difference from his German-texted musical theater. Do we feel the same way about Handel (1685–1759), a German who wrote Italian operas in London and then switched to English texts for his oratorios? Did he write German music, Italian music, and, finally, English music?

In Los Angeles, the controversy over the Schoenberg family's sending all their father's manuscripts, scores, photos, and memorabilia back to Vienna in 1996 is an important and telling story in that they felt that more would be done for his music in Vienna than in his adopted home, and they were correct. The spelling of his name reverted from its American version—Schoenberg—to its original version—Schönberg. Vienna's Arnold Schönberg Center is a model institution that preserves the music and encourages performances, for which all musicians are grateful. However, the opening concert in March 1998 with the Vienna Philharmonic and Giuseppe Sinopoli included only works composed before the composer came to America.[8] And when it comes to the émigré composers who succeeded in Hollywood, the so-called aesthetic assessments became truly poisonous. They are, without exception, men without countries.

The decade after the end of World War II was a crucial period in setting the course for classical music and its institutions. Neutered of its overt emotionality and expanded through the advanced control theories of a brilliant and idiosyncratic Austrian student of Schoenberg, Anton Webern, the avant-garde was alive and well supported. Rarely performed in his day and ours, Webern's highly condensed and minutely controlled musical utterances became the eye of the needle through which all post–World War II contemporary music had to pass in order to be accepted. Like so many official composers of the non-tonal twentieth century, Webern's name has all but dropped from public consciousness.

Born in Vienna in 1883, Anton Webern was shot and killed in Mittersill, Austria, by an American soldier when, it was claimed, he stepped off his porch after curfew to put out a cigar on September 15, 1945. His death was tragic, but the event also had an air of martyrdom that elicited suppressed rage at the ignorance of the occupying Americans. How dare Private First Class Norwood Bell murder the great Austrian composer after the war ended? Consumed with guilt, Bell would die an alcoholic ten years later in North Carolina.

Some returning American GIs who were classical musicians showed a fascination with this new music. With the increased governmental support of the sciences in the aftermath of the Soviets' successful launching of the *Sputnik* satellite in 1957, American universities were awash in grants that supported computer centers and electronics. Savvy universities opened electronic music centers and taught courses in computer music. It was all the rage in the 1960s. It also employed a lot of people who taught composition and music theory and who lived off the largesse of a closed and protected system for composition, unprecedented even for the Greeks of ancient Athens. You might think this was the most enlightened period in music history, one that would endow the world with generations of sublime new music.

The new post-war serial music contained the DNA of the old avant-garde, but it had been genetically re-engineered. Its pictorial and poetic lineage, derived from the nightmares of expressionism—murder, rape, and mental and emotional illness that were the texts of the experimental music of the 1920s and 1930s—was generally removed from the new "new" music. No more wandering in a dark forest looking for lost lovers under a blood-red moon. The music was intellectualized and demonstrably free of any associations outside of the process of notes moving through time. The titles alone indicate the new aesthetic: *Kontakte* (Contacts), *Pli selon pli* (Fold by Fold), *Stabiles for Orchestra, Gruppen* (Groups), and the aforementioned *Helicopter String Quartet.*

What ultimately emerged was something truly new: an institutionally supported avant-garde. Pierre Boulez, its eternal firebrand, probably led or advised more classical music institutions than anyone in history.[9] On Boulez's ninetieth birthday (March 26, 2015), American radio host John Schaefer broadcast and subsequently posted an interview on his *Soundcheck* with the composer-conductor about the maestro's top ten classical works from the twentieth century. In an aside, here's what Boulez significantly said:

> Our century is supposed to be the fastest, the quickest, the one which reacts instantly and likes progress—and sometimes in music, you find it's the slowest of all centuries. If you compare with Wagner, take *Tristan und Isolde* for instance, around 1860—ninety years later, that's 1950, Wagner is no longer a problem. I don't want to criticize my century, but the process of absorbing what is composed during this century is a very slow process, much too slow for me.

Perhaps there is an underlying truth here: maybe "his" century was a meticulously constructed solar system, while the actual century was a gloriously messy universe. However, the very concept of a never-ending iconoclastic movement should be a discussion point not just among philosophers and art historians but also among the public. Everyone wants to see and hear new things. But while people in the nineteenth century looked forward to the next score by Wagner or the next symphony by Brahms, today the excitement of new music generally comes from places other than an opera house or a concert hall. Those who support an eternal avant-garde will understandably try to encourage enthusiasm for the new music they like. While that is fair enough, it has not managed to convince a wider public—as noted by Boulez himself—even as it sustains those composers blessed with the approbation of the trinity of contemporary classical music: The Donor—The Critic—The Institution. When the donor is the government, politics and power once again enter the equation. This trinity leaves out something quite significant: the audience.

We can find profound interest in the early twentieth century's experiments, like Alexander Scriabin's color keyboard or Charles Ives's cosmic haze (created by overlapping multiple folk tunes, hymns, and band music). However, it seems that nothing has changed in many decades when one reads a review (with a photograph) in the *New York Times* of a festival of new music in New York City in 2015 by Corinna da Fonseca-Wollheim, which contains the following:

> In Megan Grace Breuger's "Liaison," a dancer—the darkly expressive Melanie Aceto, who also choreographed the piece—is tethered to a grand piano, with fishing lines attached to her wrists and ankles looped, via a pulley system, around the instrument's strings. By straining, arching and jumping against her restraints Ms. Aceto created metallic shimmers and rumbles inside the piano. Several times, she approached the keys raising her hands as if to strike them, but a force seemed to forbid it, leaving her twisting and writhing—a human marionette at the mercy of an inanimate instrument.[10]

Reading this, one cannot but marvel at how similar this description is to an untitled work composed by a student at Yale a half-century earlier for a highly resilient rubber ball and a grand piano, for which this writer received an A. It is also reminiscent of Luigi Russolo's 1913 noise orchestra in pre–World War I Italy.

John Cage taught us that *nothing* is a justifiable choice in music. Sometimes the best music is silence. Knowing when to underscore a scene in a film is as important as when not to provide any music at all. (See, for example, *Ben-Hur,* in which the chariot race—ten minutes long—is presented without a note but is bookended with huge military marches.) And silence is the single most powerful tool in live performance of classical music. It has the effect of "collecting" the public and getting its attention. It makes loud have meaning. And as one approaches total silence, one realizes that it can never be achieved because the background simply becomes the foreground.

At a recent performance of *Parsifal* at the Metropolitan Opera, the dynamic palette was so great that the quiet passages exposed the outdated heating and air conditioning equipment. Every now and then Wagner's music became the accompaniment to the ventilation system of the fifty-year-old auditorium. Music must be louder than the ambient noise that fills our lives—even noise that calls itself music must be louder than ambient noise in the room in order to register.

The problem with music that is perceived as noise is that we humans navigate our lives by filtering it out. Our brains can only process about 110 bits of information per second, according to the distinguished professor of psychology Mihaly Csikszentmihalyi. It takes sixty of those bits to decode speech alone, so we survive by ignoring noise in order to perceive important information. We are social animals and we actually *need* to send and receive information in order to live. Removing the ability to communicate with other humans is a torture reserved for the most heinous of criminals in prisons. For this reason, solitary confinement is considered the "most inhumane" of tortures. Sirens, alarms, and the dissonant "bonk" that sounds when we attempt an action on our computer that does not work, all tell us something is wrong. It is a sound we flee. It warns us. It is not neutral.

Nobel laureate Frank Wilczek has written that scientists define *noise* as describing "any kind of fluctuation that has an element of randomness. Noise contrasts with signal, which is valuable because it conveys sought-after information. Separating interesting signals from obscuring noise is a big part of the art of experimental science and statistics. Sometimes, however, the noise is the signal."[11] Indeed, it is this very randomness within our bodies—a "jumbled activation of injured nerves"—that is involved in what we experience as pain from wounds and inflammation.

The same definition is applicable to music. Here, for example, is an excerpt from a positive review of contemporary music that is described by a sympathetic critic in terms of noise:

> When the guitarists Fred Frith and Les Cline played their first public duet on Saturday night at Subculture, it didn't always sound like guitar music. It sounded at times like a sanitation truck's trash compactor, like an orchestra tuning up, like a brawl between flocks of geese, like a creaky water pump, like a collapsing carillon and like a slowed-down train wreck. That's the beauty of the Alternative Guitar Summit, which is now a regular part of the New York Guitar Festival.[12]

Creating this kind of music is not only confrontational, it also runs counter to the way we communicate—otherwise we could not ride in a train and successfully read a book or have a conversation in a noisy restaurant. In 1863, the German physician and physicist Hermann von Helmholtz published his *On the Sensations of Tone as a Physiological Basis for the Theory of Music,* in which he attempted a scientific explanation for our human sense of consonance and dissonance based on the clashing of the overtones of the various pitches in a chord. It was not a matter of aesthetics, but rather of what he called "psycho-physiology." In other words, it is how we humans are built.

Not all contemporary classical music of the second half of the twentieth century was what most people would call noisy, though they might call it incoherent. Because its general aesthetic was an anti-aesthetic—that is, not tonal and not sounding like a continuity of the past—much of this music registers as being goalless, even when it is light and translucent, like works by Christian Wolff, Morton Feldman, and others. The dramatic/musical process appears random—or non-existent—to the listener because there is no perceivable harmonic or melodic direction. A recent headline about visual art inspired by science fiction proclaimed, "In Space, Everyone's an Alien." It is not surprising that Ligeti's *Atmosphères* seemed so apt in Kubrick's *2001: A Space Odyssey*. It was not ironic or amusing, as was the filmmaker's use of "The Blue Danube Waltz" for an elegant space docking. The Ligeti work, which has no melody, no pulse, and is based mostly on very quiet simultaneous events (what used to be called "chords") in which every note within the spectrum of instrumental music is being played at the same time, fully expressed what being in outer space might "feel" like.

Creating art that abjures comprehensibility is not only unsociable, it runs counter to the way humans hear and process sounds. Perhaps therein lies its fascination and its eternal otherness—which is different from calling it "new" or "contemporary." It is neither.

MUSIC OF THE FUTURE?

As listeners, we are always hoping to discover and experience a new voice. Without any preconceived notions of how the next great opera, string quartet, or symphonic work will sound, we long for something great. It will be new and it will be old, but which aspect of it is the one thing or the other cannot be predicted, and only when greatness is perceived can we "place" it. No one could have predicted, for example, that Lin-Manuel Miranda would create the epoch-defining work of musical theater of the second decade of the twenty-first century that is *Hamilton*, but he did. And it will last.

Popularly supported music is not an American plot to make lots of meaningless music on Henry Ford's assembly line, no matter what the enraged and influential German, Theodor Adorno, expressed in the middle of the last century: that music of value is the music that is fundamentally not popular. The reason there was so much music coming out of Tin Pan Alley, Broadway, Hollywood, and the urban centers of the world was that millions of people wanted to hear it, in spite of all the wars, the politics, and the philosophies. It is the music that has remained while the experimental works have not. As the Austrian-American refugee composer Ernst Toch wrote, "The true nature of art, which comes from religious depth and naiveté, is both un-teachable and un-learnable. This is what makes great art neither modern nor old-fashioned but timeless. . . . The continued rejection of modern music comes not from our unquestioned lack of respect for it, but from our inability to love it."[13]

People resemble plants: we express positive phototropism. We want light. Our feet are pulled downward toward the center of the earth by gravity and our dreams lift us skyward. Surrealism, dadaism, expressionism, futurism, brutalism—they all take us to strange and interesting places, usually in the form of a work of visual art delimited by a frame and hanging on a real wall or standing in the middle of a museum gallery. You can step away from it whenever you choose.

Music, the invisible art, makes that far more difficult. Under its influence and in its presence, we become not unlike Dorothy Gale, Alice Liddell, Peter Pan's Lost Boys, and the alien botanist who calls himself "E.T.": explorers, wanderers, and imaginary children. We want to go on our adventures, but no matter how circuitous the journey, how bizarre the environments, how fantastic the sounds, we all need to return home at the end. Acknowledging this need is a central component of classical music.

CHAPTER 10

Creating History and Erasing History

The history of German classical music is generally explained as a line of influence and progress. Music history—the scholarly pursuit known as musicology—was invented by the Germans in the late nineteenth century. How could this new field of study "make sense" of 2,000 years of music? Was there a process—evolutionary or a series of revolutions—or was it just a lot of music that seemed to change every now and then? Was there a "reason" for those changes? Is there a story in this history?

It makes sense that the German intellectuals who created a structure for music history were seemingly inspired by two contemporary models to "explain" it in terms of a process. One is what is called the Hegelian dialectic. It refers to the work of the German philosopher Georg Wilhelm Friedrich Hegel (1770–1831), and in its simplest form it means that something (called *thesis*) meets its opposite (*antithesis*) and combines or argues/fights to create something new and better (*synthesis*). This is thought to be a reasonable tool in understanding the history of music.

The other model is loosely based on the work of Charles Darwin (1809–1882), the English naturalist and geologist, and his theory of evolution, which by the 1870s had been generally accepted as a reasonable explanation of how carbon-based life forms developed. Like Hegel's cosmology, social Darwinism (a phrase proposed by one of his followers, Herbert Spencer) was used in music history as a way of describing, justifying, and eliminating data so as to demonstrate not only the "survival of the fittest" but also the triumph of more complex (life) forms. In other words, like comparing an ape to a human, more complicated is "better."

Thus, according to this model, new and interesting music developed through a process of ever-increasing harmonic—and to a lesser degree, rhythmic—complexity, with extremely rare periods of simplification. That is to say, new and important music is more complicated than the music of a previous time period.

This historic progression also assumes a line of direct influence. It is important for the younger composer to know the older composer's work, understand and support it, and then move onward, having absorbed all that the master had to say. The student then creates new music that accepts some of the master's teaching, rejects other aspects of it, and adds new elements of his own. Thus: a combination of Hegel's philosophy of the dialectic achieving a new synthesis, and Darwin's theory of evolution in which a more complex life form supersedes a simpler one and is deemed "the fittest."

We can use Beethoven (1770–1827) as an example. He knew the music of Haydn (1732–1809)—the man who developed what we call "a symphony" and composed 108 of them. Beethoven took a few lessons from Haydn in 1792 and then wrote music that was bigger and more complex than anything Haydn ever dreamed of. Those facts neatly explain the process and demonstrate the efficacy of the model.

In describing this process in the twentieth century, the paradigm became more confrontational and emotional, so that the younger composer was depicted as embracing and then overtly rejecting the older one—sometimes with words and deeds. This might be an aesthetic application of Sigmund Freud's early twentieth-century theories of the unconscious projected onto the relationship between the apprentice and the sorcerer: a kind of Oedipal Necessity.

Whereas Mahler revered and never overtly rejected Wagner, the younger Debussy found it necessary to openly reject and make fun of Wagner, whom he had previously worshipped. (He referred to Wagner's use of the leitmotif as a "*carte de visite*," or visiting card, for his operatic characters.) Stravinsky at first embraced Debussy as a mentor and then violently rejected his aesthetic. Stravinsky then attempted to outrun the youngsters by changing his style throughout the rest of his long career—and thereby subvert the historical model. This resulted in the young Pierre Boulez and his fellow students disrupting concerts in Paris of the neoclassical music of Stravinsky, who was once a hero but was now a traitor *because* his music had become simpler. (The ever-changing Stravinsky then turned the whole process on its head by embracing the theories of his arch-nemesis, Schoenberg, and his twelve-tone/serial system late in life, satisfying both the all-powerful serialists and the shade of Freud, since he waited until Schoenberg, his Los Angeles neighbor, had died.)

The young Elliott Carter was taken under the wing of Charles Ives, but subsequently attacked Ives's reputation by suggesting in 1987 that Ives had doctored his scores to make them more modern than they originally were. Chronology—an essential component of the futurist model—trumped any intrinsic or timeless value of Ives's music.

The concept of a linear progression of influence—and supersessionism—worked well for understanding how the music of Haydn and Mozart (which seemingly got more and more complicated as they grew older) led to the musical language of Beethoven, and from Beethoven to both Brahms and Wagner, after which the line splits as we enter the twentieth century. It also works with Italian opera: from the simpler harmonic style of Rossini to the more complex music of Bellini and Donizetti, to the even more complex operas of Verdi and then Puccini. In Verdi's case, when musicologists finally cast their eyes on non-German music (and on opera), each of his operas was generally judged as being better than the one preceding it. *Aida* (1871), *Otello* (1887), and *Falstaff* (1893) were far more interesting than, say, *Rigoletto* (1851) and *La Traviata* (1853). Thus, we can travel comfortably from the 1820s to the 1920s and have it all explained neatly, with only Verdi's *Les Vêpres siciliennes* (1855) and Puccini's *La Rondine* (1916) dismissed as old-fashioned throwbacks—which they are not—in the otherwise inexorable march of progress.

As this general teaching model goes, the early twentieth century began with Wagner's profound influence on Strauss and Mahler, leaving Brahms behind as a conservative dead end. He did not represent the future, or even modernity, and did not influence anyone of importance except perhaps Dvořák and Elgar. Strauss, also seen as a conservative who came to reject complexity, was subsequently left behind, but Mahler, with his genre-breaking pictorial/ autobiographical symphonies of unprecedented length and his daring use of intimate chamber music sections within enormous orchestrations, was seen to lead directly to Schoenberg—who then attempted to rescue Brahms by calling him a "progressive." It also helped that Mahler died in 1911, whereas Strauss lived until 1949, making his late music inconvenient since it did not fulfill the requirements of the model.

After World War II, when, as already stated, Schoenberg did not consistently write ever more complex music, he—like Stravinsky—was summarily discarded by the European avant-garde, with Boulez leading the Darwinian excommunication ceremony. Schoenberg had regressed and disappointed, living among Hollywood stars (the child actress Shirley Temple lived across the street). As already stated, Schoenberg's recently deceased (September 15, 1945) and ascetic student, Anton Webern, who composed remarkably short and highly structured music, replaced Schoenberg to become the inspiration for all subsequent serial and non-tonal composers. A relatively obscure composer, Webern became the godfather of a half-century of serious classical music, which, if you did not experience those years, seems hard to believe.

Since twelve-tone serialism was the only music admitted into the field of "contemporary music," the Darwin-Hegel model was employed to evaluate music up to the last years of the twentieth century, admitting only ever more complex music, much of which was generated by mathematical formulae and computer-generated manipulations of pitch, dynamics, rhythm, and timbres.

Somewhere in the last quarter of the twentieth century, another experimental music started to be heard that upended the historical model that had previously functioned so well in describing the two centuries that preceded it. It was music that felt totally fresh, rejecting the chromatic juggernaut that had dominated every aspect of classical music throughout the century. This new movement, which had a spiritual antecedent in the experimental works of Cage, replaced complex harmonies with a style of utter surface simplicity and repetition. It made use of a few, consonant harmonies—like those chords on a child's first keyboard instrument—divorced from the rules of tonal function, repeated endlessly in subtly morphing rhythmic patterns over incredibly long spans of time.

This new style also seemed to relate to certain minimalist artists of the period, such as Richard Serra and Frank Stella, as well as steady-state music of non-European cultures. For some, it was just endless patterns that went nowhere and was somewhat akin to wallpaper. For others it was the cleansing balm that music desperately needed. This musical style is known as minimalism, and the Greek gods Orpheus and Morpheus duked it out with the classical music public, since some adored it and others thought it to be the most insufferably boring music ever composed.

The historical model, however, was now inoperative to "explain" this new music, assuming it was considered to be music. Predictably, many of the aging avant-garde rejected it. By that point in the twentieth century, the old and trusted futurist paradigm had already thrown out so much music that there seemed little reason not to drag the annoying "doodle-doodle" of minimalism into the trash. Carter went on record to liken minimalism to Hitler's speeches, and Boulez, who was never without an opinion, referred to it (as quoted in the *Chicago Tribune*) as "kiwi fruit."

By the twenty-first century, minimalists such as Philip Glass, Steve Reich, and John Adams had become famous and popular enough to challenge the model that had justified the serial/twelve-tone avant-garde as being the inevitable flowering of a direct line of so-called revolutionaries: Beethoven and Wagner:

Haydn—Mozart—Beethoven—Wagner—Mahler—Schoenberg/ Webern—Boulez (followed by all the serial composers of the era).

An alternative model crosses the Rhine, replaces Mahler with Debussy, and carries forward with:

Wagner—Debussy—(early) Stravinsky—Messiaen—Boulez (and all the serial composers of the era).

However, it can be argued that, if there is indeed a "line" of influence, one that accounts for the most heard symphonic music in history, that line would look something like: Wagner—Strauss/Mahler—Korngold/Steiner (Waxman, Tiomkin, Rózsa)—John Williams (Elmer Bernstein, Alex North, Bernard Herrmann, Jerry Goldsmith)—Howard Shore, Danny Elfman, Hans Zimmer, Alexandre Desplat, Nobuo Uematsu, Ramin Djawadi, and so on. More simply put:

> Wagner—Strauss/Mahler—refugees in Hollywood—their living successors (meaning music for films, television, and video games).

The avant-garde and its experiments are left as influences on the model, along with jazz, Soviet socialist realism, and the absorption of "world music" in the last century.

Another logical question should follow. If the music that was removed from the repertory of opera houses and concert halls is so important and was so beloved, how could it have been removed for so many years without a trace? If Rózsa was so good that his concert music was being played by the greatest orchestras in the world and conducted by such maestros as Bruno Walter, Georg Solti, and Leonard Bernstein (on his debut concert with the New York Philharmonic in 1944), why has his concert music disappeared from the active repertory? After all, the New York Philharmonic did not play another note of his music for half a century (until 1995)—and has not done so since. Why did Korngold's 1927 opera *Das Wunder der Heliane* wait until 2019 to be performed in the United States, and not by a major opera company? Why did it take until 1990—forty years after his death—for the first complete recording of any of Kurt Weill's American works to be made (the 1947 *Street Scene* on Decca)? Why has the Los Angeles Philharmonic, which commissioned Schoenberg to write his Suite for String Orchestra in 1934, not played the work since 1935—not once?

Given the turbulent emotions of the post–World War II era, European music professors, classical music presenters, and writers found a way to maintain a consistent point of view that also supported the public's need to erase the reminders of the tragedy that had just befallen them. A methodology emerged to "prove" the collectively held point—that of not performing the music that was entwined with World War II. That methodology centered upon creating aesthetic criteria to justify the expulsion of the offending legacy from performance.

Music is uniquely vulnerable because of its lack of corporeality. Unlike the hunt for art looted by the Nazis, the music stolen from our repertory cannot be "returned" to us unless it is played. The manuscript of Mahler's Second

Symphony in the composer's hand sold at Sotheby's in 2016 for £4.5 million. But, as the symphony is in the public domain, what is a performance worth? It has little or no commercial value. And when it comes to the artistic value of any piece of music, we simply cannot have an opinion about it unless we hear it.

We often read or hear that certain composers or certain musical works are no longer performed because of a natural process of selection that has gone on for centuries. They have been forgotten "for a reason," as the ambiguous condemnation goes. And when a writer negatively reviews a work that has been reborn in a modern performance, the above theory seems to be proven.

At the same time, we know about the rediscovery of Johann Sebastian Bach, whose music was unknown to most music lovers for more than a half-century after his death in 1750. In 1829, the twenty-year-old Felix Mendelssohn fulfilled a dream he had had five years prior, when his grandmother gifted him with a copyist's complete score of Bach's *St. Matthew Passion*, considered now to be one of the greatest compositions in the history of music. It is safe to say that no living person had heard it in 1829. The performance Mendelssohn conducted in Berlin led to a re-establishment of Bach, who is now considered a founding father of classical music. In my lifetime, the symphonies of Mahler have gone from the fringes of the standard repertory to its very heart, due principally to the championing of this repertory—in concerts, recordings, and broadcasts—by Leonard Bernstein beginning in the 1960s, and its overwhelming acceptance by the public.

If restoring repertory is dependent on playing it, removing it is not particularly difficult, especially if the public is inadvertently complicit and decades pass without younger generations to hear and re-evaluate it. Here are some of the ways to achieve this goal:

- Create criteria that support the preferred music; define any category of music to be dismissed as being out of the field; describe the smaller field as if it were a general field.
- Use concepts and modifiers such as "new," "modern," "modernist," "challenging," "contemporary," "bracing," and "uncompromising" as if they were generally held positive characteristics and apply them to the music to be admitted. Note: In the case of *contemporary*, the

meaning of the word is redefined to mean music of a certain style, not music of our (or its) time. Also, the use of value-neutral words can be given powerfully negative connotations when combined with the above-mentioned criteria, such as "Hollywood."[1]

- In certain cases, write or speak in a way that intimidates people and makes them think they might not know enough to disagree. This aligns itself with the concept that popular music is intrinsically simplistic and a sign of lowered artistic standards.[2]

- Unlike sports, where you win by crossing the finish line first or by having the highest score—unless you are a golfer—music is susceptible to personal, general, and persuasive opinion. If you were not present at a performance or cannot access what the music actually sounds like, you can only trust (or question) the printed opinions of commentators who describe a piece of music or its performance by using similes and metaphors to support the criteria mentioned above.

- With the creation of a group that is "the Other," people will assume that its constituent elements—the composers and performing artists— all shared a neutral commonality. Using their animosities toward each other is a powerful rhetorical device to demolish the outsider group you created in the first place.[3]

- Regarding the music that has anything to do with the period of World War II, the field of study and opinion is best supervised by Europeans who, in the words of the late German conductor Kurt Masur, "experienced the war," and not by Americans "who have merely read about it."

THE CRITERION GAME

As Neal Gabler pointed out in his 1988 book *An Empire of Their Own*, "Hollywood was founded . . . by Eastern European Jews, . . . was supervised by a second generation of Jews, . . . and when sound movies commandeered the industry, Hollywood was invaded by a battalion of Jewish writers, . . . talent agencies [run] by Jews, Jewish lawyers and doctors. Above all, Jews produced the movies."

Gabler persuasively argues that it was the founding fathers of Hollywood, who had escaped the pogroms and shtetls of eastern Europe, who not only believed in the American dream, but created it for all the world to see on the silver screen. This fundamental starting point of a global art and entertainment phenomenon is mostly forgotten, but it is important to our story, as are the attitudes toward Hollywood and anything touched by it—such as its music.

The denigration of Hollywood became an international free-for-all in the decades after World War II. Hollywood began to be accused of stealing from and corrupting high culture, one of the main points made previously by the Third Reich toward its Jewish artists.

King Ludwig II of Bavaria, Wagner's patron, employed a *theatrical designer* to create the famous "fairytale castle," Neuschwanstein (1869–86), which is a make-believe version of a castle built many centuries before. Its function was fantasy. Today it is the architectural symbol of Bavaria and is used in marketing Germany itself. It is, of course, one of thousands of nineteenth-century Romantic fakes that evoke the same imaginary world as Walt Disney's Sleeping Beauty's Castle (which is based on Neuschwanstein), and surely those lovable Romantic counterfeits are not seen as corrupting European culture. They *are,* as already noted, a major component of European culture, and 1.4 million people visit the castle every year.

As for Hollywood's misusing and simplifying the classics, here's what the *New York Albion* of April 24, 1850, said regarding the New York premiere of Verdi's version of Shakespeare's *Macbeth:* "We felt certain that the subject was too grand for Verdi's mental capacity, and we soon found out that he was floundering about helplessly in his endeavors to reach its level." The *Tribune* echoed this with, "We cannot see without prejudice a softened and sentimental *Macbeth.*"

One hundred and forty-six years later, Paul Goldberger wrote in the *New York Times* regarding Disney's version of Victor Hugo's *The Hunchback of Notre Dame:* "It pretends to a level of profundity while corrupting the very aspects of high culture it claims kinship with."[4] It is fundamentally the same review but with different names. And it should be asked: Who among us has actually read *Notre-Dame de Paris* by Victor Hugo? Perhaps it is also worth knowing that one of the reasons Hugo wrote the novel was to encourage the people of Paris to stop defacing and destroying their old buildings, replacing them with modern architecture (the stained-glass windows of Notre-Dame were annoyingly dark and were being replaced with clear glass).

The impact of Disney's 1994 film *The Lion King* alone has surely been tremendous, with a score of pop songs composed by two Englishmen, Elton John and Tim Rice, presented comfortably next to symphonic underscoring by the German Hans Zimmer and the African Lebo M. The 1997 Broadway version, originally playing in a derelict theater that was renovated and restored by the same excoriated Disney organization, has undoubtedly changed theatrical expectations throughout the world because millions of children, dazzled by the assimilation of world theatrics and puppetry, under the direction of a woman, Julie Taymor, and at the service of a story told mostly by people of color, are already growing up and will always remember their first brilliant live theatrical experience.

The sustainability of this musical theater work was once again redoubled in 2019 with yet another film version, with its songs and voices performed by some of the most beloved and famous actors and singers of the era. What will the children create who attend each of these versions, carrying on a human tradition of telling great stories with music, art, and movement—the very thing the Greeks celebrated? Italians re-invented it when they called it "opera," and then Broadway and Hollywood brought musical storytelling into yet another century and to a global audience, translating the text and lyrics of *The Lion King* into six indigenous African languages, and producing complete stage productions in Japanese, German, Korean, French, Dutch, Mandarin, and Spanish.

Like the classical music of other refugee and non-avant-garde composers, a set of requirements emerged that removed all Hollywood music from consideration as viable art. However, if we apply the criteria used against the refugee and tonal composers of the last century—both Hollywood and non-Hollywood—to the legacy all music lovers agree to be the core classical music repertory, something illuminating emerges. Today, it may feel like we are over the aesthetic battles of the twentieth century, but wars may be said to end, and yet hostilities linger for generations after the last bullet is fired. For someone who lived through the second half of the last century, as I did, it is important perhaps to review how certain ideas crept into how we were meant to evaluate classical music.

Tonal music said all there was to say and ran out of ideas ca. 1910.

This idea was ever-present in the second half of the twentieth century and was a powerful "tool" in music criticism. Invoking this criterion across the board would eliminate the symphonic scores of Sibelius, Prokofiev, Shostakovich, Vaughan Williams, Copland, Rachmaninoff, Rózsa, Gershwin, Britten, and late Schoenberg; the operas of Puccini, Strauss, and Korngold; thousands of hours of orchestral music, much of it for films; a great deal of chamber music; and thousands of brilliant new songs composed after 1910. Then Hamlet would have indeed been right: the rest *is* silence.

The general public does not understand atonal, minimalist, and electronic music.

While this, too, is no longer overtly used as an explanation for a personal response to complex contemporary music, many people frankly feel intimidated by the next "world premiere." It is therefore useful to be reminded of the complex scores to *Planet of the Apes, Close Encounters of the Third Kind, A.I., Rebel without a Cause, Psycho, Forbidden Planet, The Hours,* and other films. Electronic music, for instance, is ever-present in television soundtracks. "Sound design" refers to the creation of aural environments in plays, motion pictures, and television, and it uses electronic music as a basic tool in dramatic music's lexicon. Minimalist music is one of the most prevalent styles in film scores when action is being underscored, and it has become a default sound in energetic television commercials. Non-tonal music has been part of film music's lexicon of meaning since underscoring first emerged in the 1930s, and heavy metal and contemporary jazz will frequently travel into non-tonal sequences. The public—both individually and collectively—absolutely understands all of these styles of music, but also chooses what to listen to and for how long.

Refugee composers (such as Hindemith, Schoenberg, Bartók, and Weill)
lost their connection to their homelands and, as a result,
could not find artistic footing in their adopted country.

Composers have always traveled and resettled. Georg Friedrich Händel became George Frideric Handel in London, where the German-born composer successfully wrote commercial and successful *Italian* operas, tailored for his British audience. Weill, Hindemith, and Schoenberg were no longer writing for Germanic audiences in America. What do we make of the famous (and quintessentially French) can-can of Jacques Offenbach, who was born Jacob Offenbach in Cologne, Prussia (now Germany), and whose heritage was anything but Parisian? Wagner composed much music in exile. Mozart toured just about everywhere to compose and perform his own music. Prokofiev lived in Paris, the United States, and the Soviet Union. Rachmaninoff died in Beverly Hills.

Some composers never found their footing outside of their native land, and that will always remain a tragedy of the last century. That said, others wrote a great amount of music in various styles. Whether the music composed in America is "good" music can only be determined by hearing it.

Film music (Hollywood music) is not real music
because it must be composed to strict timings.

There are unique requirements for scoring a film, of course, but it is worth remembering that Tchaikovsky wrote *The Sleeping Beauty* to a specific matrix of measures and beats created by the choreographer, Marius Petipa. (See also *The Nutcracker.*) When ballet music did not have a pre-existing matrix, the scores were routinely changed by the choreographers and administrators in significant ways. (See *Swan Lake, Romeo and Juliet,* and Leonard Bernstein's *Dybbuk.*) Also, note that all serial music is written to follow many self-imposed rules, which sometimes involve a pre-arranged matrix.

Film composers "write music by the yard."

There is nothing wrong with having the facility to compose quickly, provided a composer writes music people want to hear. Vivaldi, Telemann, Mozart, and Bach all wrote hundreds of compositions. Haydn composed over 100 symphonies, and Palestrina 105 masses. The image of Hollywood composers providing music on a conveyor belt is another way of saying they have deadlines that cannot be postponed. Also note that Charles Dickens was paid by the word, and he wrote lots of them.

Kurt Weill sold out to Broadway (that is, commercial theater).

This was an omnipresent attack on Weill and his brilliant American career, which has mercifully been quelled. Verdi, Rossini, and Handel all composed for the commercial theater, and depended on popularity (ticket sales) for their income. Weill was writing for the Broadway theater, not the Theater am Nollendorfplatz. All composers write to make a living unless they are wealthy or have another job (see Charles Ives and Elliott Carter). Many highly praised composers in the second half of the twentieth century were tenured professors, who had job security and pensions and felt no responsibility to cater to an audience. Theirs, too, can be seen as form of commercial music. Bach's letters are almost entirely about wanting more money. Another way of looking at Weill is to admire his courage in eschewing the protection of a university position in America and casting his lot with the popular success or failure of his new musical theater works written in a foreign country and in a foreign language.

Hollywood composers "Mickey-Mouse" their
music to fit gestures, rather than write natural music.

Wagner, as has already been pointed out, composed his operas with the staging written into the scores, and required his singers' gestures to be synchronized with the music. Puccini and Menotti did much the same thing. During his last American tour in 1938, Prokofiev spent time with Walt Disney to discuss how music was synchronized to film in Hollywood so he could take that technology back to the Soviet Union, where he and Shostakovich composed film scores. Ballet music is also composed for visual synchronization and the requirements of choreographers. Regarding composing music to specific movements of a character (represented in the compound verb "to Mickey-Mouse" music): it would be more appropriate to say that Hollywood "Wagnerized" its characters (Mickey Mouse included), since Wagner had demonstrated the effectiveness of this technique in the nineteenth century. "Mickey-Mousing" is a musical technique that has always existed but has been accorded a belittling name for a craft that takes imagination and skill.

Hollywood composers stole their music from the classical masters of the past.

"Stealing from" is a pejorative way of saying "being influenced by" or "inspired by." For decades after World War II, it was a common practice to insult film composers as hacks, thereby separating film music from the "real thing." Today's violinists all learn Erich Wolfgang Korngold's Violin Concerto and are not thinking of an either-or world of movie music versus classical music. This logic might profitably be followed by eliminating exclusively "film music" concerts and playing concert music alongside music composed for films, thereby creating a vital musical conversation. On July 28, 1995, the *New York Times* published a five-and-a-half-inch obituary for Miklós Rózsa under the headline "Composer of Classically Tinged Film Scores," implying that Rózsa sprinkled classical fairy dust on his scores. That same edition of the paper devoted two pages to Karlheinz Stockhausen's brand-new *Helicopter String Quartet,* including multiple photographs. Movie music comes in every possible style, size, and shape. It is not a style. It is a delivery system.

Within the core repertory of classical music, it is worth noting that Johann Sebastian Bach was accused by his detractors of stealing music from Dieterich Buxtehude; Rachmaninoff, of stealing from Tchaikovsky; Verdi of stealing from himself; and Puccini of stealing from just about everyone.[5]

Schoenberg suffered in America because Americans did not understand,
nor did they play, his music the way Europeans did.

Actually, data show that Americans treated Schoenberg very similarly to the way Europeans did. Schoenberg had to make a living in Berlin as a teacher (he complained about it there, too) and certainly there were, as already noted, noisy demonstrations that greeted his music in Vienna and Berlin, even though he had become famous there.

Schoenberg was known and performed in the United States before he emigrated in 1933, and he was treated with enormous respect—with the University of California Los Angeles breaking its own rules to grant him an extra five years of employment after he had passed the mandatory retirement age.

Germans have written that none of Schoenberg's American students ever became famous composers, as a way of showing how frustrating his life must have been in the United States. John Cage, among many "classical" composers who studied with him in America, was as influential as any composer in the twentieth century, along with many more who went on to teach and share their experiences within American society.

In fact, many of Hollywood's composers and arrangers studied privately with Schoenberg, as among them George Gershwin, Alfred Newman (head of the music department of Twentieth Century Fox), David Raksin (*Laura* and *The Bad and the Beautiful*), master orchestrator Edward Powell (over 100 film scores, including *The Robe, Carousel,* and *The King and I*), Franz Waxman (master composer who was also a conductor and brought premieres of new works by Britten, Stravinsky, and Shostakovich to the West Coast), and Leonard Rosenman (*Rebel without a Cause, East of Eden, Star Trek IV*). Moreover, his classes also included many young women whose influence has yet to be properly evaluated.

Schoenberg lived, raised his family, and wrote music in Los Angeles until his death in 1951. He owned a house in Brentwood and had enough money to donate to various charities, including regular CARE packages to Europe.[6] He developed a complex and beautiful late style of tonal music along with composing a number of twelve-tone works, and became interested in many things other than composing music—his Jewish identity and matters pertaining to it, pottery, painting, tennis, and even table tennis.

While in America, Schoenberg wrote a fairy tale called *Die Prinzessin* (The Princess) and would entertain his children with stories of "Little Arnold." His daughter Nuria wrote in 2018 that Little Arnold's adventures (when his mother left him home alone) included "going to China on his tricycle." He made up stories of resistance fighters who saluted each other with "Unheil, Hitler!" Who has the right to decide how Schoenberg should have lived? "We lived a very happy life," his youngest son, Lawrence, said in 2015.

Film music is not meant to be heard.

In its prime function—to underscore dramatic scenes and comment on them to forward the drama—film music can exist within the spectrum of overt perception and covert functionality. However, like any music that is good enough to transcend its original purpose, much good film music can be played and appreciated as concert music. While it is true that not all film music is meant to be heard, it is always meant to be perceived. Within the context of carrying the narrative forward, this music is no less important than recitatives in Mozart operas.

Suggest the above cliché—that film music is not meant to be heard—to any record company that releases soundtrack albums and compare the sales figures to those of contemporary classical music that is "meant to be heard." Also, check the playlists of classical music radio stations for music composed between 1930 and today, and see what shows up. Classical concert programming still excludes scores composed for Hollywood films from live performance without a film being screened, but curiously includes film music by Soviet (Prokofiev) and British (Walton) composers.

Hollywood producers and studio executives are/were culturally illiterate.

See, for example, Serge Diaghilev's self-description as "a charlatan." While it is true that most of the founding studio heads would not have known a quarter note from a trombone, they did know what they wanted from their music departments and they were instinctively right—which is not to say that every movie they produced was great. The assumption that only someone who has been thoroughly instructed into the jargon of music can "understand" it is comforting to some, but untrue.

The Paris Opéra, under the leadership of the now-forgotten Alphonse Royer, a playwright turned impresario, required both Verdi and Wagner to rewrite their operas to appeal to Parisian tastes—and they did. This is the same meddling with so-called artistic freedom that is an indictment of Hollywood. Verdi turned *Il Trovatore* into *Le Trouvère,* adding the requisite ballet, a longer ending, and many other required changes. Wagner rewrote his *Tannhaüser,* adding a required ballet for the Parisians. Wagner called Royer "ridiculous." Sam Goldwyn was also ridiculous, and we enjoy making fun of his phrases such as "Include me out" and "I don't think anyone should write their autobiography until after they are dead." And yet, both men were right about their audiences. They each ran successful commercial businesses—the Paris Opéra and Metro-Goldwyn-Mayer. See also Prince Anton Esterházy, whose father had set up Haydn as his court composer, and who disbanded the music division of the house. In 1717, the duke of Saxe-Weimar, Wilhelm Ernst, had Bach incarcerated for insubordination. These powerful men did not live in Holly-wood. Brilliant people make mistakes. Stupid people are sometimes in charge and make the right decisions. Geniuses tend to survive.

CRIME AND PUNISHMENT

Performing music that was deemed to be unworthy was something most serious musicians avoided. During the twentieth century and the first decade of the twenty-first, any artist guilty of this transgression might suffer mightily for lowering his/her standards by playing to the mob. It took a certain amount of courage for Riccardo Muti to record an album of film music by his former teacher, Nino Rota. Simon Rattle is another rare example of an internation-ally admired maestro who brought film music—on special occasions—to the Berlin Philharmonic, as has his successor, Kirill Petrenko.

However, if one looks at the conductors who grew up in Los Angeles, some of whom worked in the film industry (André Previn), others whose fam-ilies played in studio orchestras (Leonard Slatkin), and others such as Zubin Mehta, Lawrence Foster, and Michael Tilson Thomas, there was little cham-pioning of their local heritage at the podium. (Previn made an exception with Korngold, but clearly wanted little to do with Hollywood once he left it with his four Academy Awards.) An article from the 1990s in Los Angeles once wrote about my work in restoring and performing film music as "career suicide."

After I conducted a program of extended symphonic poems from classic films with the Detroit Symphony, its then music director, Neeme Järvi, said, "You must come back and conduct some *real* music next time." Kurt Masur was thoughtful at a New York restaurant shortly after my debut with his New York Philharmonic: "Oh yes, you're the conductor of *film* music." And at the Atlanta Symphony, a patron asked to borrow my wife's program. When she saw its contents, she angrily handed the program back and said, "We just came back from a strike and I didn't come here to be entertained!"

Finally, we must leave room for the made-up criterion, as musicologist Mal-colm Gillies did with his impressive concept of "American guilt" for America's supposed failure to support the great composers who came to the United

States fleeing the Holocaust. In addition, we can read in academic journals that Hindemith wrote too many (therefore meaningless and repetitive) works while living in New Haven and that Schoenberg did not write enough music in Los Angeles (in other words, that living in America made him unhappy). Ernst Krenek, who seems to have been a fairly dyspeptic man judging from what he said and wrote, felt his music was not played enough in America. What composer, we might ask, has ever been content with the number of performances he or she has gotten? (When Tchaikovsky came to New York, he complained that his music was played less in Moscow than in New York City. "I am much more of a big shot here than in Europe," he wrote on May 2, 1891.)[7]

INTERPRETING THE REVIEWERS, NOT THE REVIEWS

Oscar Wilde wrote that criticism "is the only civilized form of autobiography," and indeed one of the ways we can understand what a critic is saying is to read their words in terms of Wilde's perception. The late Pierre Boulez is of central importance in this text for a number of reasons, and perhaps more than anything, it was his function as an outspoken and exclusionist music critic in the second half of the twentieth century. Though he did not write for a newspaper, what he wrote in journals and said in public, and his unquestioned Olympian position as an adjudicator and inspiration to many students as well as arts administrators, made him the most important voice in twentieth-century classical music. Even as many readers may wonder who Boulez was and why his name keeps returning in this book, it is not merely that he and his opinions were quoted as fact, but that his students and devout advocates—now in their late middle age—are held up as living models of the exciting, the new, and the authoritative.

When he was young, Boulez called for the destruction of opera houses—though late in his life, his supporters described his words as symbolic and not "real." In 2001, the Swiss police arrested him and "dragged him from his bed and informed him he was on their list of terrorist suspects [because] in the 1960s Mr. Boulez said opera houses should be blown up, comments which the Swiss felt made him a potential security threat."[8] He and his fellow students had caused disruptions during other composers' concerts (something the Nazis also did before Boulez was attending concerts) and accused his colleagues whose music he did not like of being "stuck in a pit of liquid manure." He once wrote an angry letter to Nicolas Nabokov, after the 1954 Festival of Contemporary Music in Rome, suggesting that the next event be a conference "on the role of the condom in the twentieth century," which would be in "better taste."[9]

When Boulez was invited to speak at American universities in the early 1960s, he was quoted by composer Mel Powell as saying, "You have no composers here in America." He then smiled and added with Gallic wit, while referring to a rival: "Not even a Henze."[10] And much to Powell's amazement, we accepted that assessment. "Pierre never invited any of us to bring our music to France."

As an aging man, Boulez became ever more charming, less vulgar, and equally effective in his opinions. In spite of conducting music he officially had scorned—Brahms, Mendelssohn, and others—his obituaries referred to him as "uncompromising," which is patently absurd. As any musician who has partnered with a soloist knows, the very act of making music is a compromise. For all Boulez's talk of structures and objectivity, an open-minded listener will probably find his music to be complex, sensual, and distant. It, like all criticism, is autobiographical. You might like it or be fascinated by it—and still reject Boulez's opinions of other composers.

PLEASE DO NOT LIKE MY RECORD

As the twentieth century dissolves further into the past, it is perhaps useful to focus on one example of the kind of critical writing that appeared rather consistently in magazines, journals, and newspapers during the Cold War period. None is more telling than the program notes that accompanied one of the most important record series of that era.

When the great record producer and president of Columbia Records, Goddard Lieberson—who gave us original-cast albums of *My Fair Lady* and *West Side Story,* as well as everything Igor Stravinsky had written and was writing—released Volume VII in a series called *The Music of Arnold Schoenberg,* it was an essential purchase for those who loved classical music and could, for the first time, hear newly recorded music of this twentieth-century master.

The liner notes that accompanied LP sets always helped to inspire and educate the person who purchased them. Pianist Glenn Gould's notes in Volume VII for his performance, with the Juilliard Quartet and actor John Horton, of the *Ode to Napoleon Bonaparte* (one of Schoenberg's "American" works) ends with:

> But, overall, one has the impression of an advocate willing to rest his case solely upon that most tangential of motives—the twelve-tone row—and a row which, in this case, is neither particularly interesting in itself nor manipulated with an invention sufficient to link the revelation of its motivic secrets with the spontaneous growth and unification of the structure.

Those words seemed to be aimed at me, who in 1968 was a Ph.D. candidate in music theory and had just paid $7.38 of my hard-earned scholarship stipend for this recording. But, as if this were not enough, George Rochberg, chairman of the music department of the University of Pennsylvania, wrote about Schoenberg's American *Variations on a Recitative:*

> It is not really important whether this is a "tonal" work or not. Nevertheless, since it is often assigned the key of D-minor, let us examine this for a moment. If making constant reference to a given pitch locus, D in this case, makes a work "tonal," then Op. 40 is unquestionably tonal and in D. But if it takes more than constant reiteration of a pitch, melodically and harmonically, and more than chromatic motion to that pitch and away from it, then Op. 40 is not "tonal." What, then, is it? The answer for the present is: I do not know. . . . However this music is taken, it is undeniably a work by Arnold Schoenberg— and like the String Trio it is music of "cruelty."

By this point, it seemed unclear if I had just made a terrible mistake. Then came the final note (also by Rochberg) on Schoenberg's magnificent Theme and Variations, Op. 43b, a work that is hated more than any of his by the writers who wanted Schoenberg to be someone else.

> The *Theme and Variations,* Op. 43b, for orchestra, need not occupy too much of our attention here. Where the musical impulses of Op. 40

and Op. 45 appear to be deeply personal, the same does not appear to be true of Op. 43b. In fact, there is a curious awkwardness to the work, suggestive of a strong degree of self-consciousness in the building of the theme itself and in the carrying out of the variation plan. Perhaps this was the result of a limited personal commitment to the writing of a work intended, as was the original version of Op. 43b, for the ubiquitous American school band. The electric charge, which crackles in the best Schoenberg, is missing here.

This came from the company that released the recording, not a critic reviewing it. Were customers being dared to like that last piece or being encouraged to take an axe to the vinyl? One notes the deep problem both Gould and Rochberg had with a composer who had not done what they wanted him to do. He did not get more and more complex, non-tonal, non-developmental, anti-emotional, or use structures that controlled more than a series of pitches, the way Webern and his followers had done. What were these two experts, hired by Columbia Records, to do with the Schoenberg "problem"?

They both fell in line with what Boulez wrote, in a breathtaking act of cruelty, just months after Schoenberg died in 1951: "ARNOLD SCHOEN-BERG EST MORT" (yes, in capital letters). And the reason Arnold Schoen-berg was "dead" to Boulez, and therefore dead to all those with an understanding of the inexorable march of ever more controlled, unemotional, and non-tonal music, was that the Father of Atonality did not follow through on the implications of the twelve-tone system he had invented in 1921 and unveiled in 1923. ("Any musician who has not felt the necessity of the twelve-tone language is of no use," Boulez wrote—and that includes the man who invented it.) Schoenberg and his life in America, as opposed to Vienna and Berlin, with all its achievements were to be erased from the concert hall and history, much to our loss.

VOICES FROM THE YOUNGER GENERATION

By the dawn of the twenty-first century, after much work had been done to bring back some of the "degenerate" music through recordings, articles, and performances, younger critics still felt empowered to continue the attack on composers who did not adhere to the tenets of modernism. However, this does not prepare one for the level of hate engendered by some of the music outlawed by Hitler.

The 2007 British premiere of Korngold's *Das Wunder der Heliane* by the London Philharmonic Orchestra under the direction of Vladimir Jurowski was described by Rupert Christiansen in London's *Daily Telegraph* as "unmitigated codswallop." "Dreadfully overheated and over-loud, the prolix first act has a slavering and maudlin sensuality that gave me the creeps. . . . I felt slightly sick when it was all over and had to lie down in a darkened room."

That same morning (November 28, 2007), Michael Tanner's review in the *Spectator* stated that the performance was "an evening of disgust and revulsion" and "fully merit[ed] the description 'degenerate,' which has had to be abandoned since the Nazis used it as a category. But they weren't wrong that there is such a thing as degenerate art, and there is no more blatant example of it than *Heliane.*" Later on, the critic described the score as "unrelieved musical inflammation, with frequent burstings of the boil and deluges of musical pus before the next one starts accumulating."

In 2007. Two of London's serious music critics. Not a blog. Not a Tweet.

In 1935, the *Times* of London reviewed the British premiere of Kurt Weill's musical satire *A Kingdom for a Cow.*[11] The unidentified critic wrote, "It is not stated whether [Weill's] recent departure from Germany was occasioned by his partiality for politically tendentious satirical texts like this one or for the kind of music he writes, but the music would be the German authorities' most valid justification." That same year, the American composer and esteemed critic Virgil Thomson wrote a review of the world premiere of George Gershwin's *Porgy and Bess,* stating, "At best it is a piquant but highly unsavory stirring-up together of Israel, Africa and the Gaelic Isles. . . . I do not like fake folklore, nor bittersweet harmony, nor six-part choruses, nor fidgety accompaniments, nor gefilte fish orchestration." Neither review came from Nazi Germany.

Sixty years later, a twenty-five-year-old guest critic reviewed a number of Korngold releases in the *New York Times.* He wrote of the "well-fed mediocrity" of Korngold's American music. "The serenade is charming on first hearing, less so when one realizes that the main theme is lifted from Ponchielli's *Dance of the Hours.*"

The critic, perhaps repeating the received wisdom of his professors, wants his readers to believe that an overweight Korngold stole the one thing he finds charming. (Would he have said that Brahms was "well fed," or did the writer mean Korngold was "well paid" for his music?) It should also be said that the two melodies in question, one by Korngold and one by Ponchielli, share only one commonality—an ascending minor third followed by a major second. After that, these two tunes go in entirely different directions and have entirely different rhythms and affects. There seems to be a larger point: Korngold, like all Hollywood composers, stole his music. But worse was in store for Korngold.

> A good way to put Korngold in perspective is to imagine what might have happened if he had died not in 1957 but in 1920, after completing "Die Tote Stadt." The twenty-three-year-old composer would have left behind him two sensational operas and several compelling instrumental works. He might now be extolled as a genius who died with far greater things ahead of him. A magical aura would attach to his name, comparable to that of Keats or Rimbaud.
>
> Korngold lived longer, and his reputation plunged. His few masterpieces, early and late, are flickering visions of what might have been. There is a vague, incoherent greatness here: a composer who lived after his time had passed, or died before his time had returned, or lived and died in the wrong time altogether. A love for Korngold will always be a guilty pleasure. But who can fault music for giving pleasure?[12]

A very good question. Thus, we find ourselves with major music critics feeling safe in suggesting that Korngold's music gives them the vapors, that Hitler was correct in condemning it, that his music is "pus," and that perhaps it would have been better had he died at age twenty-three, rather than sixty. Even Hitler did not come to that radical solution for another thirteen years.

With one critic passed out on his cot and another vomiting in the washroom, one of them at least finds "pleasure" somewhere in the morass of his responses to Korngold's music. Why it is a guilty pleasure, however, should be a source of sober reflection. When one major New York critic recently referred to Hindemith's first major American work, his heroic Symphony in E-flat (1940), as containing "industrial strength counterpoint"[13] and another in London stated, with astonishing insensitivity, that "in general, it was a bad thing for Schoenberg to go to America,"[14] we have to consider the prospect that these younger voices profoundly disdain this music—or feel they ought to.

Another possibility is that they have not freed themselves from the imprinting of their education and do not have the tools—or feel they have permission—to assess the greatness of the music they are reviewing. Composers do not go from being geniuses one year to incompetence the next when they move to another country to find work, or indeed to survive.

It may seem obvious to say this, but composers, like audiences, are people. Before the World War II exodus of the great Austro-German composers, other composers led traumatic and passionate lives. Composers fell in and out of love. They got sad and they worried. They were jealous and insecure. They lived in times of war and political upheaval. And when they needed money, they got it from donors: a king who fell in love with you (Wagner), a director whose politics you did not agree with (Bernstein), a repressive and threatening government (Strauss, Prokofiev, Shostakovich). The ones who needed money were naturally preoccupied with this condition, but they wrote music (Debussy, Mozart, Bach). The ones who got rich and famous could get ensnarled in scandal (Verdi, Puccini). Some went deaf (Beethoven, Smetana), some were homosexuals (Blitzstein, Tchaikovsky) and others might have been (Chopin, Ravel). Some were Jews who converted to Christianity (Mahler, Schoenberg, Rózsa) and some converted back (Schoenberg). What all of these composers did was write music, and no one excuses or dismisses the music of any of them because of these human conditions. Yet we continually hear a litany of these "explanations" as a way of dismissing or patronizing the music of the World War II refugee composers—whether or not they wrote for the movies.

There is no single appropriate response to trauma. Great composers tend to be survivors and transcend the conditions in which they find themselves—personal and artistic—and always have.

—⋅◦⋘⧎⧍⧎⧍⧎⋙◦⋅—

CHAPTER 11

Of War and Loss

Before the bullet was fired that led to World War I, the racial and religious policies of Europe and Russia had already started something that changed music forever. From its inception, the United States was the destination of choice for millions of oppressed peoples. Among them, a group of brilliant composers—frequently the sons of immigrants—would, along with former slaves from Africa, create what we call American music. The loss to Europe and Russia was palpable and arguably accounts for a draining of the "Old World's" cultural leadership in the twentieth century.

In the last years of the nineteenth century, the flight of émigré Jews out of the ghettos and fleeing the pogroms brought us the naturalized American parents of George Gershwin, Aaron Copland, and Leonard Bernstein. What would Russian music be today if these children had been born in Europe or Russia? After the Great War, it was the music of these children that made American classical music both American and classic.

It also goes without saying that the American Songbook would be quite different without its many immigrant composers—and those who were sons of European and Russian parents—such as John Philip Sousa, Irving Berlin, Victor Herbert, Jerome Kern, and Harry Warren (born Salvatore Guaragna).

Geniuses are, by definition, rare, and any country that ejects its creative class will be permanently diminished. After World War II, however, the classical music community accepted the artistic leadership of the countries that had ejected these men from their communities and then acted as if their moral and aesthetic positions were somehow intact and objective. As people disappeared from their positions in the Fascist, Nazi, and Soviet conservatories—as well as their orchestras, opera houses, radio stations, and music journals—others willingly filled those positions. When America got Kurt Weill, however, what did Berlin get in return? When America got Hindemith and Schoenberg, who replaced them to teach and mentor Germany's young composers? As a New Yorker growing up in the 1950s, the first conductor most of us regularly saw was Arturo Toscanini. What living Italian can claim that?

Germany, for example, has no living Kurt Weill tradition because he, his wife, and his entourage all settled in New York. The lineage of his theatrical tradition can be heard in the musical theater of John Kander and Fred Ebb (*Cabaret, Chicago,* and *The Visit*) and in the orchestral film scores of Nino Rota, who studied composition at Philadelphia's Curtis Institute, and Danny Elfman—but not in Germany.

Vienna has no living Mahler-Strauss tradition. It is now an American symphonic tradition because native-born composers such as John Williams, Jerry Goldsmith, Elmer Bernstein, and Bernard Herrmann—not to mention film directors such as Steven Spielberg—were inspired by Korngold, Waxman, and Steiner, just as Vienna was simultaneously "discovering" Mahler—conducted by an American, Leonard Bernstein. Bernstein knew the Mahler symphonies because, in America, he studied with refugee conductors such as Fritz Reiner and Mahler's assistant, Bruno Walter. And, lest we forget, it was anti-Semitism that drove Mahler out of Vienna in the first place. Where did he go? New York. Bernstein was busy building a bridge from New York to Vienna while new music by men who were trained in a direct line from Mahler and Strauss were mentoring young American composers in Los Angeles—the so-called Hollywood composers.

It is also important to stress that fascist policies were not simply a German issue. The Third Reich and Italian fascism found many eager supporters throughout Europe and America. Some musicians were willing and enthusiastic participants; others tried to "make accommodations" in the evolving political climate in order to save themselves and their families. And, of course, there were the quiet ones who kept their gaze downward and tried to get through it all. When "liberation" came, Americans were meant to believe that all the war-weary people of Europe had suddenly become pro-American, democracy-loving citizens of a new Europe. They were not.

More than a half-century ago—eleven years after the official end of World War II, when I was a first-time visitor to Europe—emotions were still raw. In London's Tube, I was asked a question by an inebriated man. My answer elicited a torrent of invective about "you fuckin' Yanks!" In Munich, when I could not remember the German word for mustard, I offered a bit of French and said "*moutard*," to which the man behind the counter yelled with fury in his eyes, "*Senf!!!*" Later, at the Wagner festival in Bayreuth, I wrote the following in my diary:

> Mark [Rubenstein, a fellow student] and I were in a milk bar when 3 German soldiers, each about 18 years old came in. We were all at a counter. One of them came over to us, with a gentle smile and said in perfect English, "We just got back and had no time to change out of our uniforms. We normally would have. Many people however think the Germans are fond of uniforms . . ." (August 7, 1966)

Three days later, in a letter to my parents, I wrote of a dinner I attended with Wagner's granddaughter, Friedelind, which her mother, Winifred, also attended.

> Friedlind [*sic*] left Germany at age 19 because of her hatred for the Nazis. She lived in England for a while and gave speeches on the radio and lived in America with Toscanini's wife. In fact she is an American citizen. Well, we asked, "You *can* get back your German citizenship now, can't you?" "Of course I could, but I'd rather be a Hottentot." She came back to Germany in 1953 but retains an apartment in New York. The U.S. returned the Festspielhaus to Friedelind and her 2 brothers, but she got 34%. As you know, Winifred was one of Hitler's favorites. Winifred is actually English (!) but raised in Germany. At one point, the old Winifred crossed the room to another table. "There goes Mother on to one of her Nazi friends," said Friedelind.

And it must also be said that the United States had many who secretly—and not so secretly—felt that there was something really good going on with Hitler (and Mussolini and Stalin, too). Whether this was ideology, business, practicality, careerism, or a level of "distaste" for the power of non-Aryan and non-Christian peoples (ranging from discomfort to outright hatred), there is a much broader accountability in this story. Europe had, after all, 1,500 years with anti-Semitism as an officially—or implicitly—sanctioned way of life. Hitler did not invent it. Neither did Richard Wagner.

Waves of intolerance and violence—whether racial, tribal, religious, or philosophical—are a significant component of the history of Europe, with its inquisitions, pogroms, and marauding armies fighting wars in the name of specific interpretations of the writings of Moses, Jesus, or Mohammed. This was normal, and it was not until after World War II that Europe had the longest period of peace in recorded history—even as an unseen war, the cold one, was being waged. And while America has been the recipient of centuries of creativity from immigrants and slaves, it is not and never has been immune to the very same intolerance carefully taught to us by our European parents.

John Waxman, the American-born son of composer Franz Waxman, remembers as a boy hearing his parents and fellow refugees, who had successfully escaped the Nazis' official anti-Semitism and were making a successful living in Los Angeles, discussing the sad fact that they were unwelcome to dine at certain restaurants in Los Angeles. These restaurants were, to use the euphemism of the day, "restricted." Jews certainly could not be members of most country clubs or serve on the board of the Los Angeles Philharmonic, which also disdained performing the music of their resident émigrés—whether or not they were Jews.

When the Los Angeles Philharmonic presented the West Coast premiere of Gershwin's *Rhapsody in Blue* at the Hollywood Bowl on August 13, 1927, the program notes by Bruno David Ussher surprisingly referred to him as "Russian-American composer George Gershwin" and said, "Gershwin's 'Rhapsody in Blue' has been 'legitimized' by arrangement for symphony orchestra. It is perhaps the first pretentious application in the concert hall of the combined principles known as syncopation and jazz purporting to establish the higher musical possibilities of these effects." It is up to the reader to decide what hidden meanings are buried in those words.

Anti-Semitism "was disguised and very evil," recalled John Waxman. "And this was America! They didn't expect this. It was the Wild West, where a bridle path still existed between Beverly Hills and Hollywood. There wasn't grass there. There was dirt where people would ride their horses. My parents were pretty upset. They would talk about it at dinner."[1]

Additionally, the fear of Communist infiltration subsequently led to a witch-hunt mentality that played into (and masked) the anti-Semitic traditions of the United States. Composer Alex North, for example, had his passport taken away and would not be hired because he was suspected of being a Communist. North's family had emigrated from Russia, changing their name from Seufer to North after they had moved "north" within the United States. Growing up poor in rural Pennsylvania, North needed scholarships to pay for his musical education at the Curtis Institute (in piano) and the Juilliard School (in composition). In order to pay his expenses in New York, he learned to be a telegraph operator, working from six in the evening until two in the morning, and then going to Juilliard during the day. Because he idolized Prokofiev and hoped to study with him someday, he accepted an offer from the Soviet Union, all expenses paid, to work as a telegraph operator there. Soon he was able to audition for the Moscow Conservatory, where he studied composition for two years—though, according to his widow Anna, he never got to meet Prokofiev.

As if this were not suspicious enough for the FBI, years before North's trip to Russia, his older brother had been the recipient of a citizenship award, and when it was discovered that he was Jewish, the award was rescinded. According to Mrs. North, his brother became an activist as a result and ultimately became an editor of the *Daily Worker,* America's Communist newspaper.

Alex North, the man who scored *A Streetcar Named Desire, Spartacus, Cleopatra,* and *Who's Afraid of Virginia Woolf?,* an alumnus of the Curtis Institute, the Juilliard School, and the Moscow Conservatory, had the center of his creative life cut out in America—the land of freedom that was a refuge for his parents, who had fled the anti-Semitism of Russia. Was North a Soviet fellow traveler, intent on bringing down the U.S. government? Apparently some people thought it was a distinct possibility.

While it is easy to express outrage at those who misjudged our own citizens and even misjudged the capacity of the Soviet Union, some might also whisper that perhaps this was the correct decision, for certainly we are not living in a world of Communist domination. And anyway, we are now far more enlightened than those who fought the culture wars of the last century.

Or are we?

AESTHETICS

We have all participated one way or another in creating today and perpetuating yesterday. We try to "make sense" of times past, drawing straight lines by connecting the dots of events, memories, and published accounts, but in actuality we can find arguments to explain and justify just about any theory. All eras are murky.

For example, we continue to criticize the aging Richard Strauss for having been a Nazi. As stated earlier, because his son Franz had married a Jew, his grandchildren were Jewish in the eyes of the German government. The borders were closed. He was being watched. What would you have done?

Igor Stravinsky made many accommodations to the Nazis in their early years, ensuring the flow of his royalties. He also wrote and said truly embarrassing things about Mussolini and fascism, as he did in an interview with the Roman music critic Alberto Gasco in *La Tribuna* in 1930:

> I don't believe that anyone venerates Mussolini more than I do. To me, he is the man who counts nowadays in the whole world. . . . He is the savior of Italy and—let us hope—of Europe.

There have been allegations that Sibelius was a Nazi sympathizer, too. After all, his music represented an attractive and muscular Aryan dream of Nordic heroism. It is now known, thanks to the work of American musicologist Timothy L. Jackson, that the Finnish master was kept on a generous pension by the Nazis throughout the war.

It is helpful to contextualize Finland's historically inimical relationship with Russia. The threatening and acquisitive Russian bear was the monster lurking in the subconscious of all Finns, and if Sibelius had to choose between supporting the Bolsheviks or the Nazis, he would have to side with Germany, much as Pope Pius XII did, but for different reasons. Sibelius was living through an immense writer's block and had ceased composing in the 1920s. His royalties were being withheld because of the war. Veijo Murtomäki, a professor of music history at the Sibelius Academy, has responded to the allegations by saying, "So, Sibelius was selfish and flattered by his fame in Germany and wanted the money. I am sorry for that." What would you have done?

Even as the day-to-day decisions of life and death during a century of war recede from living memory, we learn more of the complex situations that arose from them, as documents are released and historians do their best to clarify what happened. Are there fixed conclusions in anything other than fiction? Most stories begin and end with some version of "Once upon a time . . . They all lived happily ever after." In between those two oft-repeated lines is the truth: the process, the transitions, and the transformations. By its definition in physics, the inevitable conclusion of a revolution is to end up exactly where you started. Evolution is something quite different.

Throughout the past century music has been a weapon, a symbol, and a target. That said, it should not be viewed as collateral damage. Music is our collective story; it is how we can understand who we are; and it demands our attention and respect—all of it—because, quite simply, music contains the world's memories.

❦

CHAPTER 12

A Century Ends

December 31, 1999. Born as I was in the middle of the twentieth century, and having spent much of the intervening time interacting with living composers and their new music, it was particularly telling to see how arts institutions decided to wrap things up as we exited the old century.[1]

New York City prides itself on being a cultural capital of the world. On that New Year's Eve, the New York Philharmonic celebrated the end of the twentieth century by playing Beethoven's Ninth Symphony, completed in 1824. The program included nothing American, nothing from a century of Philharmonic commissions and history, and, indeed, nothing from the twentieth century itself. Only a pre-recorded twelve-tone bell motif—selected from the music of Schoenberg, Berg, Webern, Bernstein, and Stravinsky, and used by the Philharmonic to summon its audience into the hall—recalled the waning of the old modernist century, and not with a bang but a tinkle.

New York's Metropolitan Opera put on a "Millennium Gala" based on Act II of *Die Fledermaus* (1874). The music from the twentieth century performed at the gala was not from operas, but from the Broadway musicals *South Pacific, Carousel, On the Town,* and *Man of La Mancha.* To be fair, there were two arias from Puccini operas: "Vissi d'arte" (1900) and "Nessun dorma" (1924). And there were operetta arias by Victor Herbert and Franz Lehár, and a Hollywood song, "Because You're Mine," from the 1952 Mario Lanza film of the same name, which includes the lyric by Sammy Cahn "That isn't thunder, dear. It's just my heart you hear." No Berg, Henze, Stockhausen, or Berio. Not a note of the century's great opera composers: Richard Strauss, Erich Wolfgang Korngold, Kurt Weill, Benjamin Britten, John Adams, Philip Glass, Samuel Barber, or Gian Carlo Menotti. And no recognition of the thirty operas that the Metropolitan Opera itself had commissioned during the twentieth century.

Of course, institutional discussions went into choosing these programs, and one does not want to draw too much from these data. However, if we compare the two programs with, say, the opening of Philharmonic Hall in 1961 (Beethoven, Mahler, Vaughan Williams, a world premiere by Aaron Copland) and the 1966 opening of the new Metropolitan Opera House (the world premiere of Barber's *Antony and Cleopatra*), the contrast is quite startling. What does it say about the very greatest American institutions and their attitudes toward the art they commissioned—not to mention the hundreds, no, thousands of works composed during a 100-year span? Were there no works those institutions felt should be heard again, proudly displaying their commitment to new music and opera during an entire century?

That New Year's Eve in Berlin, Claudio Abbado conducted the Berlin Philharmonic in final movements of a number of symphonic works that just barely took its audience into the twentieth century—excerpts from the nineteenth century's Beethoven and Dvořák mixed with short excerpts from Stravinsky's *Firebird* (1910), the finale to Mahler's Fifth Symphony (1902), Schoenberg's super-Romantic sunrise from *Gurrelieder* (1900–1911), and some German operetta excerpts and dances. Every single piece of music ended with a simple major chord (A-major, G-major, B-flat-major), with the first half of the concert—the classical half—culminating in a thunderous, minute-long, triumphant C-major triad, the simplest chord every child learns to play on the white notes of a keyboard. No Webern, Boulez, Carter, or Morton Feldman. No living composer—German or otherwise—or a single note of classical music composed after 1911 was represented.

No world premiere commissions from any major institution were performed on that historic night. A search in various archives provides more sobering data on how classical institutions chose to end the century. Those facts directly confront what has been written about the twentieth century and what was deemed "important" from a philosophical and aesthetic point of view. It is as if we are living in two parallel universes: one that is what we actually experience, and one that seems more of a wish that keeps demanding to be true.

Thousands of books have been published on the two world wars, the run-up to each of them and their aftermaths, raising the uncomfortable possibility that wars never actually end. World War II's "hostilities" may have ceased in 1945, but the world did not go back to a sense of peace by September 12, 1945, the day I was born. Indeed, "hostilities" may be a euphemism to represent armies standing down and peace treaties being signed, but hostilities in the actual meaning of the word clearly continued—and will continue as long as there is memory. It was, after all, a world war, and in some respects it is a war that never seems to have ended.

Nearly every day brings some news about World War II. And yet there is no substantive discussion about how that war, still called "the war," impacts what we hear in concert halls and what fuels the aesthetic discussions available to us by those who write and get published on the subject of classical music and lyric theater. We should never forget it was both a war that *used* music and a war that was waged *against* certain music. It was a war that punished some musicians while it officially made heroes of others, extolling their music as representing, or at least supporting, political ideas.

Mostly, when it comes to classical music, the twentieth century was a century of loss, and that loss matters. One thing is clear to me: We have eliminated vast numbers of composers whose music was once played and appreciated. Some might say that this is a normal process. After all, many nineteenth-century symphonies, chamber works, and operas have fallen by the wayside, and we accept that as a normal weeding out of the crop. The difference, however, is that the mid-century weeding was done in spite of the continued successes of the works and the composers. Seventy-five years after the end of World War II, it is time for a reset. The so-called lack of repertory is a myth.

History is written by the victors. Then the revisionists, the rational balance-makers, and the logicians weigh in to help give a more nuanced view of the losers and the winners. Sometimes a writer will correctly point out that the vanquished have an immense influence on their conquerors. However, this process was accelerated after World War II and proved to be a unique example of the vanquished exacting justification and revenge when it came to culture and especially to classical music. America has always seen Germany and Italy as principal sources of classical music (true) and affords them the respect of knowing more than we do (sometimes), and because, although they lost the war, we needed them as allies in our fight with the Soviet Union (definitely). It proved to be a major aesthetic victory rising from the ashes of their otherwise humiliating defeat. And anyway, America could not force Europe to listen to its own music, composed on American shores, if it was not wanted. It was not, and when it was played, the music was excoriated in the dailies. Just ask the Korngold family what it was like for Erich in the 1950s when he brought his new music to Vienna.

A humiliated society's intellectual community living in the wreckage of its own failed dreams wrote books and reviews—and taught music to the young. One can replace the mayor and the chief of police, but you cannot replace everyone, and it has been well documented that many Nazi and Fascist professors returned to their jobs, as did the conductors, the writers and the performers. A few of the children of the disaster, brilliant and talented, joined their voices in rejecting the refugee composers of America, whose music confronted a European populace that was now without food and water, and where accountability was everywhere to be sought. Many displaced Jews in Europe, having barely survived, returned to what was left of their towns and villages only to be blamed for causing the war in the first place.

That is what I believe happened to the thousands of hours of musical works—some of which might be masterpieces—that disappeared. As the generations have passed, a source of these aesthetic judgments—the racial policies of the Nazis and the Fascists and the war against Soviet communism—has been forgotten, and post-war aesthetic conclusions have been accepted as objective. And after having removed so much music and so many composers from our lives, what have we gotten in return? Surely, we have erased the link to—and continuity with—the great masters of the past, which has forced our institutions to leap across the void toward newly composed works that continue an aesthetic position the public has not embraced for over a century.

Aesthetics and politics are connected, and in the twentieth century the former easily masked the intent of the latter. If our classical music institutions exist to perform a core repertory that stops in the interwar era and then skips to living composers who write in a certain style, then that is the business of these non-profit organizations. That the institutions also feel they must support the provocative and the fringe elements—making this natural part of the art world the very center of it—should be worth serious discussion. That isn't to say that the fringe and the provocative are not of value—but they are not the whole story, and never have been. We should always remember that building a never-ending embrace of the provocative, the ironic, the disruptive, and the incoherent will keep new classical music separate from all the other arts, which, unlike classical music, continue to thrive.

The very concept of "progress" is a relatively new one and should not be taken as a given. The Romans, for example, "regarded novelty with distrust and aversion," as Ronald Syme points out in *The Roman Revolution,* and the "myth of progress" has been part of intellectual discourse since the nineteenth century. The futurist fantasies of the 1900s are so old-fashioned—retro, if you will—as to be curiously touching. Even though a number of middle-aged multibillionaires are investing in brief tourist trips into space, we need to reconcile our science fiction dreams with the fact that the last man to walk on the moon, Eugene Cernan, died in 2017 at the age of eighty-two, and the 2019 restoration of Eero Saarinen's futuristic TWA Flight Center from 1962 is now a nostalgic trip into a future that never arrived. In the last decade of the twentieth century, a headline in the *Financial Times* seemed to reinforce my boyhood belief in UFOs and alien invasions with "Mars Wins Right to Sell Ice Cream in Germany." Imagine my relief to find out that Mars is the name of an American company that manufactures candy and pet food.

Progress may be a myth, but transition is not. A constantly repetitive artistic revolution is numbingly boring and ultimately irrelevant to most people. It is time to recognize the unstoppable process known as evolution. This is not an issue of liberal versus conservative. It is not about popular versus serious. And it is not about progressive versus retrogressive. It is about compassionate inclusivity rather than rigid exclusivity.

Even though our current music critics get breathless with excitement, one has to wonder if the world is really impressed by the prospect of a concerto for ping pong players and symphony orchestra[2] or a recording of "Philly cheesesteaks" on the grill as a compositional element in an orchestral tone poem played in Carnegie Hall by the Philadelphia Orchestra.³ Perhaps it's just fun. If it is fun, it is the same kind of fun as hearing the mechanical orchestras of the 1800s, the noise orchestra from 1913, and Nora the cat playing the piano on YouTube.

If you care to reread the incendiary words that made Pierre Boulez so famous in the early 1950s, you may begin to understand the universal acceptance of his pronouncements by the musical establishment of the 1960s, a time of great political upheaval in the United States and Europe. That Boulez subsequently spent so many years conducting the great Romantic works of Wagner, Brahms, Mahler, and Ravel, making them sound rational, cool, and controlled, was, perhaps, his way of returning to the center of the wheel of the art form he loved—great, descriptive, tonal music—without having to compose a note of it, unlike Schoenberg, Korngold, Shostakovich, Hindemith, and Britten, who were brave enough to do just that. Boulez just tried to make those Romantic works sound as if he had written them. This, too, is perfectly understandable. Boulez's performances also gave cover to those like-minded people who wanted to love the music that dared not speak its name in the modern twentieth century—the passionate music that could only be admitted into a modern world when cloaked in rational dispassion. This, too, might be seen as an expression of the era's counterculture that attracted many young people.

When Karlheinz Stockhausen expressed admiration for the 9/11 terrorist attacks as a brilliant work of art, I knew what he was saying, because it encapsulated the original, pre–World War I philosophical position of the avant-garde regarding the necessity of art to make a radical statement—one that ideally changes everything. He soon said that wasn't what he meant, knowing that no one would ever play his music again if he held to the truth of his response. This is what he originally said:

> Minds achieving something in an act that we couldn't even dream of in music, people rehearsing like mad for ten years, preparing fanatically for a concert, and then dying; just imagine what happened there. You have people who are that focused on a performance and then 5,000 people are dispatched to the afterlife, in a single moment. I couldn't do that. By comparison, we composers are nothing.⁴

We should not kid ourselves. Stockhausen was admiring the destruction of something that exists in order to create something new. That two airplanes taken over by a small group of religious fundamentalists could create an image of collapsing towers on a sunny morning when no one expected anything was indeed (for him) great performance art—"The greatest work of art imaginable for the whole cosmos."

In order to understand (if that is even possible) a mind like that of Stockhausen, here are a few facts. He was born in 1928 near Cologne. His mother had a mental breakdown when he was three years old. His father married the housekeeper and had two children by her. His biological mother was gassed by the Nazis along with other "useless eaters" while she was institutionalized. When he was a teenager, all of Cologne was carpet-bombed by the Allies. Look carefully at a photo of Cologne in 1945 and imagine a motherless seventeen-year-old.

This is where Stockhausen received his musical education. Ten years later, while much of Cologne was still ruins, Stockhausen took a position at WDR (West German Radio), which had opened an electronic music studio.

Perhaps we can understand a great deal with that brief outline—an outline that leaves out a thousand Thursdays and numbingly grey Februaries. What Stockhausen achieved is a miracle of human resilience and transformation, whether or not you like his music. Perhaps now that you know this story, you will open your ears to what he left us.

In 2001, Stockhausen was expressing an aesthetic philosophy that directly echoed ideas that had been promoted almost a century earlier, and that resonated within his mind and soul. It was in 1909 that the movement known as futurism was born. Its intentions were to "exalt movement and aggression, feverish insomnia, the racer's stride, the mortal leap, the slap and the punch. . . . We intend to glorify war—the only hygiene of the world—militarism, patriotism, the destructive gesture of the anarchists, beautiful ideas worth dying for, and contempt for woman. We intend to destroy museums, libraries, academies of every sort. . . . We shall sing the multicolored and polyphonic tidal waves of revolution in the modern metropolis."

These ideas, born in the pre–World War I cauldron and recycled in the post–World War II era, fueled Stockhausen's response to the attacks on New York's World Trade Center in 2001. He was not a bad man by any stretch of the imagination. Although he recanted, his words nonetheless express the continuing aesthetic of an avant-garde that is protected, curated, commissioned—bought and sold—by the very establishment that was its original intended target. In addition, as Joseph Epstein points out in his *History Meets Philosophy*, "At the birth of societies, the leaders of republics create the institutions; thereafter it is the institutions that create the leaders of the republic."

It is both dangerous and simplistic to look back at the 1960s and 1970s, smile, and say something like, "Well, that was a naïve time and we don't do that anymore." If you went to a concert of contemporary music that you did not like and, on cue, stood up and stopped the concert by blowing whistles and banging a hammer, as Boulez did with his fellow students in 1946, would you be a hero? I think not. Boulez was at war for the rest of his life. The philosopher Sir Roger Scruton called him "a byproduct of a disastrous war."

Surely, it is time for peace.[5]

CHILDREN OF PEACE

Restaurants, sports, knitting, politics, pet handling, sanitation, laundry detergents, movies, alternate-side-of-the-street parking, the weather—all are fair game, and everyone feels empowered to have a valid opinion about them. Ask most people about art, especially classical music, and you will get something like, "I really don't know anything about it." Here's the secret—you know *everything* you need to know about it. Art is not something you need to learn at school in order to understand, and of all the arts, music is the most personal and the most universal. You have been taught it every day of your life. You live in it and it lives in you.

If there is incipient optimism in all this, it is the beginning of a shift in the acceptance of a portion of the "missing repertory" on the part of the younger musicians who make up more and more of the personnel in symphony orchestras. With players born in the post–*Star Wars* age filling the ranks of orchestras, there is an emerging sense of profound joy in playing the music of their childhood—the music that, for many, inspired them to become musicians in the first place. If the Vienna Philharmonic can play the music of John Williams and honor its eighty-eight-year-old composer in 2020, that should count for something. This is music many musicians heard before they heard Beethoven.

Whereas there was tremendous resistance to Hollywood "movie music" in the 1990s by orchestra players who had been told in their various conservatories that this music was not good, we may have reached a tipping point. Adults born after 1975 have already bonded with this music and made it part of their adolescent playlist before anyone could shake that relationship, even if the music is, as one highly regarded critic wrote, a "guilty pleasure."

What might have started as an expression of barely concealed contempt for nouveau riche immigrant Jews who composed the founding music of Hollywood films, soon morphed into a generalized disdain for music composed decades later by American-born (but still primarily Jewish) composers. One "reason" to dismiss the younger generation of film composers was that they had not been properly trained in real conservatories (as opposed to film schools). Of course, if they attempted academic training—rather than apprenticeship with working composers—they would have experienced an ongoing battle with their professors and the pressures to reject the vast and ever-expanding lexicon of music necessary for success in the field.

Film music composers were emerging in the twenty-first century from their experiences playing rock and roll, like Howard Shore (*The Fly, The Lord of the Rings, Doubt*), Hans Zimmer (*The Lion King, Gladiator, The Dark Knight*), and Danny Elfman (*Batman, Edward Scissorhands, The Nightmare Before Christmas*). Snobbery against them for their lack of bona fide credentials led to a conversation with André Previn in 2017 about my preparing for the world premiere of Elfman's Violin Concerto. "Who's that?" Previn asked. As I was explaining who Elfman was, he interrupted with, "Oh, the whistler." "The whistler?" I asked. "Yeah. You know. He comes up with a tune and whistles it and his arrangers write the music." Although I defended Elfman as a man who composes every note and has the most astonishingly perceptive ears of any musician with whom I have worked, Previn remained unconvinced. (When Gershwin's *American in Paris* had its world premiere in 1928, there was a persistent rumor that his assistant knew more about the work than the composer did.) The public, it should be said, does not care about these "insider baseball" stories. They love the music.

Italy has recently begun to produce some of its pre–World War II operas—by Italo Montemezzi, Riccardo Zandonai, Alfredo Casella, Pietro Mascagni, and Franco Alfano—and at least one composer, Marco Tutino, is writing operas that admit to the traditions of Puccini. A 2018 production of Korngold's *Das Wunder der Heliane* in Berlin was so successful that it was immediately scheduled for a return in future seasons, and other productions have been scheduled throughout Germany. The German reviews were the very opposite of the drubbing it received from London's press in 2007. Suddenly, Korngold's opera is a masterpiece and, to quote one critic, "absolutely worth being rediscovered." This might indicate that Europe is taking the lead in restoring the music it removed from performance after the war. Meanwhile, in America the 2018 Pulitzer Prize in music was awarded to rap artist Kendrick Lamar, rather than to another composer of serial or minimalist music. These are first steps in reclamation and redefinition. This is just the beginning, however.

Consider the following as examples of the effect of fifty years of obliterating the music of so many great composers. On August 31, 2014, Zubin Mehta, who served as music director of the Los Angeles Philharmonic from 1962 until 1968, was quoted in the *New York Times* as saying he had recently attended a concert that "introduced, or reintroduced, a lot of the old movie scores in bits and pieces. Scores by Miklos Rozsa, Bronislaw Kaper, Erich Korngold, Max Steiner, etc. They were all fine musicians. Many were émigrés from Europe escaping Hitler who made their livelihoods in Hollywood. It was the most enjoyable and educational evening for me."[6] Mehta found it "educational" that these composers were fine musicians and had escaped Hitler.

In 2019, musicologist/conductor and college president Leon Botstein was quoted in the *New York Times* regarding the American premiere of Korngold's *Das Wunder der Heliane*—which I recorded in Berlin for Decca in 1992[7]—as saying it was "a complete discovery for all of us." This was followed by his astonished "Where does [his] film music come from, and how did he put it together?" Put it together? Surely, he meant "compose it." Later in the article, Botstein said that Korngold's 1944 music to *Between Two Worlds* "[is] a very unusual score. . . . There's something postmodern in it." Post-modern? Does that rather bizarre assertion make Korngold's music suddenly acceptable?

You, however, have already created a personal lifetime playlist and started it sometime before the age of fifteen. There is always more to learn from music and its extraordinary history. Luckily, you went to the movies and watched television. Maybe you had an aunt who took you to concerts and operas, too. Your music is bound into the fabric of your life and is connected to the lives of a thousand generations who have lived and listened before you.

It is too late to refer to my generation—of which I am proud to call myself a member of its vanguard—as anything but the Baby Boomers. That phrase means that there are a lot of us and that we are merely a bulge in the population statistics, moving inexorably toward our *finale ultimo*. One might consider, though, the reality of why this gigantic generation exists. We are the Children of Peace.[8] We were conceived during a time when it was clear to our parents that the war would be over and would be won by those who rejected totalitarianism of any kind. Many of us born in America were blessed with happy childhoods. When we were hungry, we cried, and we were fed.

That does not mean we have not been wounded. That does not mean that we, who never saw that war, are shallow and unfeeling. Many of us profoundly care about the music of our lifetime (perhaps too much) and aspire to find an objectivity that can bring clarity of judgment along with a demand for fairness. And before we all die, we are, as a society, obliged to make amends.

There is music being composed right now that will be seen as representing this time and this place—wherever and whenever this book finds you. There are fifteen-year-olds who are discovering music that they will make their own and that will travel with them to the ends of their lives, giving them a thread from which to weave a lifetime of experiences. They will hear music through an aural prism greater than mine and far greater than any music heard by Debussy or Duke Ellington. Whatever that music is will be their music and that makes it great, because it will be part of a great *relationship*. This will be their inner resonator. It will bypass the future the deceased futurists were trying to anticipate. You or I could tell them that this isn't good music and give them a thousand reasons for your opinion, but you might as well be talking in outer space.

The only question that remains is whether we can connect the world of those fifteen-year-olds to the source—connected, as it is, through the last century and leading directly into their life stories. The journey from Brahms and Wagner to John Williams, Danny Elfman, and the video game music of Austin Wintory is actually quite easy to demonstrate. All you have to do is listen.

SOMETHING REALLY NEW THIS WAY COMES

Unlike the rituals of the eternal adolescence of the avant-garde, something truly new *was* emerging in the first decades of the twenty-first century, though it is not to be found where you think. It is not robots—artificial intelligence—composing the next wave. It is not another concert in which guitars sound like trash compactors or the chemical processes of plants are transformed into notes. Nor is it the music generated by translating into tones the genetic code of the novel coronavirus by MIT professors.[9] It is the interactive music composed for video games.

In its infancy and due to its limited technology, game music was a series of bleeps and blurps, as simple as the sounds we were composing at the Yale Computer Center in 1970. But, like the grand orchestral scores employed in successful science fiction epic films, big orchestral music gives contemporary video games a gravitas and "reality" that has become the new normal.

But here is where things change. A composer of a video game must write music that can morph to accompany the individual journey of the player of that game. In other words, the compositional challenge is to write dramatically appropriate thematic materials that can transform seamlessly with the progress of the game. The music can change at any time and in a split second. No two games will play out the same way, and no two renderings of the music will either. As with all dramatic music, there is a musical goal, but it may never be reached, or if it is reached, it will never be reached the same way twice. The score is therefore co-performed by the player and the author of the music. It carries within it the indeterminacy of chance music while expanding Wagner's leitmotif theories into the twenty-first century, with implications for interactive classical music that is absolutely new.

This, perhaps, is the biggest and most exciting challenge for a composer since the invention of sound films in the 1930s, and it has a huge future (and present) for some very talented musicians. If there is such a thing as an avant-garde in this century, it will be found in composing music for an interactive delivery system, something that never happened before in the history of music. Forget the music made by a woman tethered to the inside of a piano—or like it, if you want. New music has a new and magnificent challenge. As composer

Austin Wintory recently said, "At its best, game music turns the player into a co-storyteller."

In addition, the passion shown by millions of gamers for live orchestral concerts of game music, like those presenting music from the fifteen scores to *Final Fantasy* (mostly composed by Nobuo Uematsu), is rooted in an unprecedented application of the musical materials: the themes themselves become personal in role-playing games. Once you have chosen who you are in a game—which can last between twenty and forty hours *each time you play it*—your character's theme is you. It belongs to you in your quest. For opera-goers, it would be as if you chose whether to be Siegfried or Hagen, Gutrune or Wotan, *before* attending a four-day *Ring* cycle. The music and the story would be told from your point of view, and the importance of your motifs would shift accordingly.

Something new and something old is always happening. In every era there seems to have been a great thinker writing about how this is the end of life as we know it. At the same time, there inevitably is another great thinker who is writing about all the new and great things that are happening or are about to happen. Both are correct.

The story of the music from the last century is complicated by the plethora of music that was accessible to a worldwide public—and every composer writing for it—all in an environment of turmoil. Human nature—why we make and listen to music, and how we perceive sound—does not change. Wars and propaganda machines played music throughout the last century as if it were a shuttlecock in a badminton game. If, as one theory goes, music is not about anything but the notes, it certainly was used as a representation of a lot of things and ideas—and power. Perhaps the simple answer to this complicated story is: play the music.

The officers of the Monuments, Fine Arts and Archives program of the United States Army—the so-called "Monuments Men"—did not search for the lost music, just the art works looted by the Nazis. How do you find something that is invisible? We must all be the Monuments Men and Women of Music. Restitution will return the music to its public—or rather, the heirs of the public from whom it was stolen. Us.

We can read the names of many composers and their works and have absolutely no idea who they were and what their music sounds like. What symphonic works were composed in Europe, Russia, South America, and the United States—*indeed, the entire world*—that is excluded from the books we read and the music that is played in our concert halls?

In America, our opera houses and orchestras were commissioning works throughout the century, and practically none of those works has survived. Were all those dedicated commissioners, those who sat on juries, and those who ran the most important cultural institutions of our country 100 percent wrong? If that is not true, is there anyone willing to do the work and let us hear the most likely candidates for rescue?

Will there ever be major grants to restore our own collective cultural legacy? If the artistic institutions in each city of the world looked at their own history; if musicologists, open-minded critics, and music directors—with their orchestras and opera companies—committed to uncover and explore at least one forgotten composer each year, we could actually begin to refill the emptiness in our repertory, a repertory that lost its continuity due to a series of alliances and coalitions created in a century of European warfare, beginning with the run-up to World War I and ending (perhaps) on December 31, 1991, when the flag of the Soviet Union was lowered over the Kremlin for the last time.

I long to hear the music of Heitor Villa-Lobos, Egon Wellesz, and Mario Castelnuovo-Tedesco in concert. I hope to experience a fully staged production of Hindemith's *Die Harmonie der Welt* (The Harmony of the Universe), which, as of this writing, has never even received a concert performance in the United States.

Howard Hanson's symphonies, a restored *Antony and Cleopatra* by Samuel Barber, the works of Ernst Toch and Franz Schmidt, the operas of Nino Rota, the works of unknown masters from Brazil (Walter Burle Marx), Ukraine, and Argentina—all fill the imaginary aural landscape I have created from the readings I have undertaken in the past half-century. And what about all the women composers? During World War II, for example, both Hindemith's and Schoenberg's classes were full of young women, and yet we know so little about them and how they passed on their knowledge and talent to future generations.

After so many decades of repertorial choices that have erased certain composers and brought others forward, audiences have been taught to shy away from composers whose names they do not recognize. Others, such as Hindemith and Schoenberg, have such a bad reputation that programming them will mean major challenges at the box office. The American period of both men includes some of the greatest music of the last century.

This means our institutions and cultural leaders must re-establish a trust with the public. Surely we need to encourage the new generation to play and champion this music, especially in our most prestigious venues and with our greatest ensembles. It will take time, leadership, and a real commitment, but classical music should not be a niche industry.

Maybe we can get away from our yes/no world of classical music, stop thinking in terms of pops versus serious, and refuse to ghettoize movie music. We can create organic concert programs that demonstrate continuity based on ideas and styles, instead of sandwiching a new complex piece between two well-known warhorses, which only confounds the brain and its ability to absorb musical information. Music has always been and will always be an ever-developing connector, not a disrupter. Perhaps we can open our arms to a greater definition of what the music of our lost time actually is. Maybe, as we encourage our living composers to sing to us in their personal voices, we can also bring back the music that was taken from us a half-century ago and give it a chance.

We might all benefit from accepting without guilt the music we already love and let our natural curiosity lead us to music we do not yet know. If we cannot find it, demand that it be played and support the small recording companies that explore the forgotten and the unknown. If you are very fortunate, that music will take you to all those places and states of being that the physicists are trying to explain and prove—parallel universes, non-linear time, and the vast majority of things that exist but we cannot see or hear and that connect us from today into the very reason we love music, the heart of the matter.

Charles Ives made a distinction between the Unknown and the In-known, the latter being what we profoundly sense but cannot prove or even explain. Just widen your embrace and listen without prejudice. What is the *sound* of it? No metaphors. No similes. No false criteria. No imposed walls: a gateway to the thing that is infinite, curved, expanding, and imploding—that always existed and will always exist as long as humans walk the earth. It is right there invisible to the eye, yet palpable to your ear, your mind, and your heart.

It is called music. It is yours, and because it is yours, it is great.

Appendix

A PERSONAL DIARY

Here are four great twentieth-century composers whose music has cast both a shadow and a light on my life, encouraging the process of discovery and pursuit that became the book you have just read.

PAUL HINDEMITH

Paul Hindemith, who emerged in the 1920s as one of Germany's most lauded and influential composers and teachers, once used the phrase that music could be made for specific use (*Gebrauchsmusik*). This was a perfectly reasonable and accurate thing to say, since so many works by the greatest composers were written for specific occasions. After World War II this term was used as a sword against him. Music was not useful! The post-war critics and avant-garde polemicists determined that Hindemith had composed too many useless pieces of "useful music." He had become an academic whose American works were of no value or interest. In 1950 he said, "It has been impossible to kill the silly term and the unscrupulous classification that goes with it." The eminent music critic Peter G. Davis summarized Hindemith in a *New York Times* review from 1979:

> At one time considered to be a key figure of early twentieth-century composition, along with Stravinsky, Schoenberg and Bartok, Paul Hindemith has pretty much vanished from the concert scene since his death [in 1963]. Save for a handful of instrumental sonatas, little of his music is played nowadays. Even once-popular works such as the *Symphonic Metamorphoses on Themes of*

Weber and the *"Mathis der Maler"* Symphony turn up less often than they used to.

Born in 1895, Hindemith rose to the heights of fame as an avant-garde composer and one of the most important teachers (along with Arnold Schoenberg) of the last century. His early works were complex and provocative, but he soon renounced them and began developing a personal theory of composition that explained Western music in a new way, maintaining the function of tonality and harmonious conclusions. As a Lutheran, he was not an immediate target of the Third Reich, and like many, he attempted to work within the new regime, although he was always under suspicion because of his early works. Ultimately his music was banned. His wife was a Catholic with Jewish ancestry, which made it essential that Hindemith emigrate, first to Switzerland and then to America, where he was welcomed as one of the most famous émigrés to arrive from Germany. Physicist Albert Einstein went to Princeton; architect and founder of the Bauhaus Walter Gropius went to Harvard; Hindemith went to Yale.

Unlike other German classical composers of his time, Hindemith studied and restored the music that preceded Bach and Handel, requiring his Yale students to play "ancient" instruments or sing in his Collegium Musicum. He therefore was a pioneer in early-music studies. He also composed new music that expressed a sense of continuity with the very first music we can "decode" from European manuscripts—the music of the Middle Ages and the Renaissance.

During my Yale years (1963–83), two events encouraged me to look into the music of Hindemith, who taught at the Yale School of Music from 1941 until 1953. His death in Switzerland during my first year at the college resulted in my singing in a chorus for the first performance in America of the composer's very last composition, a Mass for unaccompanied choir that he had completed a few months before. In the summer of 1966, while I was at the Wagner festival in Bayreuth, Germany, Friedelind Wagner told me that her brother Wieland was thinking about producing operas at the Festspielhaus that were not composed by their grandfather, Richard Wagner. (This is now illegal, but not in those years.) The first opera Wieland was planning was Hindemith's *Mathis der Maler.* That was astounding to me, given the hundreds of choices he could have made. It was time to find out more about Hindemith.

The result was simply overwhelming. There were symphonies, operas, concertos, sonatas, and choral works—composed in America. One result was to program a concert for the Music School's orchestra consisting of Hindemith's *Sinfonia Serena,* composed just after World War II; the orchestral settings of his song cycle devoted to the Virgin Mary called the *Marienleben* songs—astoundingly, an American premiere; and his magnificent 1951 symphony based on music from his last opera, *Die Harmonie der Welt,* completed in 1957, which tells the story of Johannes Kepler and his discovery of planetary motion.

We brought this program to Carnegie Hall in the spring of 1979, where it received unanimously favorable reviews. Neither symphony had been played in New York City since the years of their composition, and, as of this writing, they have not been performed there since. They contain music of profound heroism, spirituality, rigorous construction, and delightful humor. Andrew Porter in the *New Yorker* wrote, "I hear Hindemith's music, and especially of his American years, as inspired, warm, joyful, even passionate." The *New York Times*'s Peter G. Davis said, "His scores are not only superbly crafted but also filled with wonderful and often extremely beautiful music."

Hindemith's music triumphed that night. Nothing, however, followed, with the exception of a performance in 2010 by Riccardo Muti and the New York Philharmonic of the Symphony in E-flat, a heroic and magnificent work, composed just after the composer's arrival in the United States. On March 6, 2010, a *New York Times* headline said, "Seldom-Heard Symphony Resurfaces as a Novelty." Unlike Muti, who has championed the work, the reviewer described Hindemith's music as "academic," "pedantic," and "ponderous." Hindemith is considered box-office poison, and few conductors and artistic directors seem willing to explore/interested in exploring this once-heralded composer's works.

KURT WEILL

Kurt Weill was born in 1900 in Dessau, Germany. The son of a cantor, Weill studied music with a number of famous composers, including Wagner's former assistant, Engelbert Humperdinck (mostly famous today for his opera *Hänsel und Gretel*), and the Italian futurist composer Ferruccio Busoni. Weill had just turned twenty-six when his opera *Der Protagonist* brought him widespread acclaim within Germany (one critic called him "a creative power of the first order," and another said his music was "technically of quite astonishing perfection"). Once he altered his musical style from densely modern expressionism into a uniquely lyrical language that was easily understood yet complex enough to express many emotions, Weill's *Die Dreigroschen-oper* (The Threepenny Opera; 1928) and its early sound film (1931) brought him international notoriety and a modicum of commercial success. With the rise of Nazism in 1933, he left Germany and ultimately arrived in New York, where he composed for Broadway, dying in 1950 at the age of fifty. Unlike his sardonic and brilliant German works, the American works brought out a big-hearted optimism and were viewed by European critics as simplistic commercial compromises that pandered to common Broadway audiences—works that had no true cultural background. Sometimes, America was blamed for this fall from grace. Weill, it should be said, collaborated with many of its greatest poets and lyricists, among them Ira Gershwin, Maxwell Anderson, Ben Hecht, Langston Hughes, and Alan Jay Lerner.

As a boy, "Speak Low" was the first Weill song I heard. (The film version of his

1943 Broadway hit, *One Touch of Venus,* was occasionally shown on television.) Then, in high school, I attended a performance of his 1947 Broadway opera, *Street Scene,* which the New York City Opera occasionally revived. Once again, the music—mysteriously foreign and yet appealing—cast a spell. It is therefore no surprise that I jumped at the chance to conduct another revival of *Street Scene* at the City Opera in 1978. Directed by Jack O'Brien, the production opened during a newspaper strike. There were only four performances, but the word got out after opening night and all subsequent performances were sold out. The production was hastily scheduled for the next season and telecast on the public television series *Live from Lincoln Center.* I was able to spend time with the composer's widow and muse, Lotte Lenya, and among the many thousands who saw the production was Leonard Bernstein. "I am not convinced," he said, to my surprise and disappointment. He expressed the opinion held by a number of American composers (and European critics) that Weill's "American" voice was somehow fake.

More than a decade later, I led the first professional staging of *Street Scene* in Great Britain, its first complete recording, and its country premieres in Portugal and Italy. I also wrote articles and gave speeches about Weill's American works being a continuation of the Weill who created *Die Dreigroschenoper* in Berlin—a work that, after all, was also composed for the commercial theater and not a government-sponsored opera house. This was in direct contradiction to the received wisdom that Weill had compromised and dissipated his style for Broadway. In his case, the phrase "sold out" referred not to ticket sales but to a fatal artistic compromise. The most current assessment of his work at that time, published in the *New Grove Dictionary of Music and Musicians,* said, "It was Weill's misfortune that a radical transformation became unavoidable as soon as he was left without an alternative to Broadway." *Street Scene* was nonetheless conquering audiences throughout America and Europe some fifty years after it closed at the Alvin Theater in 1947.

Meanwhile, in West Germany, Decca was recording Weill's music, and usually it was a first for the local musicians. I recall seeing a kiosk in West Berlin announcing a production of *The Threepenny Opera.* It said (in bold print):

Bertolt Brecht
DIE DREIGROSCHENOPER

Underneath were the names of the stage director and designers, and below that the various roles and performers. At the very bottom, almost as an afterthought, were the unforgettable words:

Musik: Kurt Weill

I still remember the recording sessions of *Die Sieben Todsünden* (The Seven Deadly Sins) in the months just before the Berlin Wall fell in 1989. Not a single musician in the RIAS Berlin Sinfonietta (members of what is now called the Deutsches Symphonie-Orchester Berlin—the German Symphony Orchestra of Berlin) had ever played this major work by Weill, composed in 1933.[1]

For the centenary of Weill's birth in 2000, I was invited to participate in a panel discussion, broadcast on German Radio (MDR) from Dessau. A goodly sized audience attended what was essentially a press conference regarding the German premiere of Weill's 1935 Bible play *Der Weg der Verheissung,* known in America as *The Eternal Road.*

Sitting behind a table in the Bauhaus—the great design school built by Walter Gropius, who escaped from Germany in 1934—with other Weill experts, we spoke mostly in English to this group of Germans. The panel included David Drew (English), Teresa Stratas (Canadian), Kim Kowalke (American), and myself (American). One representative from the Chemnitz Opera spoke in German. And here is a point that cannot be dismissed: There was no true Weill tradition in Germany. The so-called German Weill tradition was a post-war invention of Bertolt Brecht, who had returned to East Germany and created a talk-sing style, in which the musical lines were erased to focus on the playwright's texts. Weill's most trusted interpreter, the conductor Maurice Abravanel, was adamant on the subject. He told me, "Weill insisted that every note be sung! This so-called talking style is disgusting."[2]

The painful truth was sitting behind the table: a group of English-speakers telling Germans about their own culture. We were being broadcast live on the radio, so I took the opportunity to implore young German composers to follow in Weill's footsteps and compose accessible and politically active music theater works.

Der Weg der Verheissung received its long-awaited European premiere, its Israeli premiere, and its return to New York, after sixty-five years, in a fairly good production that was greeted enthusiastically in Chemnitz, but with muted approbation in New York City. One member of the audience in Chemnitz said that he was surprised by the story, which tells, in flashback, the history of the Jewish people beginning with Abraham. Having been brought up in atheist East Germany, he said, "Very interesting, but I thought Jesus was in the Bible." Critics seemed unable to "place" it, and there was more discussion about its ending—in which the Jewish community leaves its little town rather than fight—than about the magnificent two-and-a-half-hour score and the work's position not only in Weill's life but in cultural and political history. The Israeli orchestra was particularly difficult to rehearse and openly disdained the music. One player (a Russian Jew) asked me, "Was this Weill a Jew? We never heard of him in Russia." I said, "Let's have lunch and talk about World War II."

ERICH WOLFGANG KORNGOLD

Born in 1897, Erich Wolfgang Korngold astonished all of Europe by composing mature works beginning at the age of eleven. Mahler called the child "a musical genius,"

Richard Strauss championed his early orchestral works, Sibelius referred to him as "a young Eagle," and Puccini called him "the greatest hope of German music." At the age of twenty-five, his opera *Die Tote Stadt* (The Dead City) became an international hit, with productions throughout Europe as well as at New York's Metropolitan Opera.

Korngold worked closely with Europe's greatest stage director, Max Reinhardt, and their adaptations of Viennese operettas were performed with enormous success. When Reinhardt was asked to adapt Shakespeare's *A Midsummer Night's Dream* for Warner Bros., Korngold traveled to Hollywood and became fascinated with the new medium of sound films and the synchronization of music to image and drama. Because of the annexation of Austria into the Third Reich, Korngold and his family moved to Los Angeles, where he continued to compose during the war, convinced that the films for which he wrote music would not be screened in the Third Reich. Once the war was over, he returned to composing for the concert hall. His attempt to return to Vienna, where formerly he had been hailed as a hero, was disastrous, with his music—both old and new—judged to be passé. His musical style developed naturally but always maintained a complex Romanticism that was similar to the tone poems and early operas of his mentor Richard Strauss but made a unique use of "shadow" notes within his tonal language and had a roiling emotional underpinning more like the symphonies of Gustav Mahler.

It was generally said in classical music circles that Korngold—a founding father of Hollywood's Golden Age—"was always writing for Hollywood even before he went there." The word Hollywood had been given a new post-war meaning of derision. In 1956, months before his death at age sixty, he wrote of the Vienna State Opera, "It is as if I have been totally obliterated, yes; in three or four books about the Vienna Opera, I am totally ignored." He died convinced that his life could be summed up as a transition "from genius to talent."

Like most classical music snobs, I thought that movie music wasn't worth my serious attention. I have no idea how I "knew" this, but I did. Like many people, I believed that Hollywood film music was mostly stolen from real classical composers. Sometime in the 1980s I had been blindsided by happening upon a recording of a dramatic and extraordinarily beautiful cello concerto broadcast on the radio. I had no idea who had written it, but it was terrific, carrying within its DNA the music of Wagner and Strauss, and yet different—more complex and contemporary. It was, I suppose, evolutionary rather than revolutionary. The announcer said it was the Cello Concerto of Erich Wolfgang Korngold from the 1945 Bette Davis movie *Deception*. I realized at that moment that I needed to go back to the drawing board about film music. Quite simply, this was great music.

As stated at the beginning of this book, in 1990 I was investigating music composed in Los Angeles for a brand-new symphony orchestra to play at the Hollywood Bowl, just as the Decca Record Company asked me to be a principal conductor for a proposed series devoted to *entartete Musik*—the music banned by Hitler that would be restored and recorded in Berlin. Here is where the two worlds collided: *The Adventures of Robin Hood* in Los Angeles and *Das Wunder der Heliane* in Berlin: the music of Erich Wolfgang Korngold.

These two masterpieces, composed under entirely different circumstances and in two countries, became a common denominator of confusion. They were both enormously complicated. They were both magnificent and, apart from an occasional excerpt, neither had been heard "live" in over a half century. *Wunder* would be a world premiere recording, though it had been composed in 1927, and *Robin Hood,* I would soon learn, actually saved Korngold and his family's life, since they were in Los Angeles in 1938 and expecting to return to Vienna when it became clear that Austria was about to become part of the Third Reich.

I got to know Korngold's son Ernst and his daughter-in-law Helen, and met the grandchildren and the great-grandchildren when I programmed Korngold at the Bowl. His music had not been heard at the Bowl (or in Los Angeles, for that matter) since Korngold had conducted a single concert in the 1930s. One of his great-grandchildren shared an essay he had written for his sixth-grade class in which he said, "If it weren't for my great grandfather coming to Hollywood, I would not exist."

I began to learn his music for the Berlin recordings and the Hollywood Bowl concerts. There was no biography to study. There were few recordings. Grandson Leslie had Korngold's private recordings in the garage, and I was able to hear the composer play his Symphonic Serenade on the piano, intended as a way of helping Wilhelm Furtwängler know his intentions for the work's world premiere in 1949 with the Vienna Philharmonic. I would use the same "instruction" to inform the recording we made in Berlin.

When I stood before the NDR (North German Radio) Orchestra in Hannover, there was not a single member of the orchestra *who had ever heard of Korngold.* When I made my debut with the Boston Symphony, I played a program of Hindemith, Weill, and the great Symphony in F-sharp by Korngold. Nothing on that program had ever been played by the Boston Symphony. I brought the *Symphonic Serenade* to the New York Philharmonic for its first New York performances in 1995 in a program that also included the Theme, Variations and Finale of Korngold's colleague, the Hungarian émigré Miklós Rózsa—famous for having composed the scores to such films as *Spellbound, Ben-Hur,* and *Madame Bovary.* Theme, Variations and Finale had last been played by the Philharmonic on a Sunday afternoon in 1943 at the debut concert of Leonard Bernstein.

There were two concerts of this program at Lincoln Center, both sold out. This was the first time in the history of the New York Philharmonic that live orchestral accompaniment was used in showing sound films, even though live-to-picture only amounted to half the concert. The instantaneous cheers and the standing ovations felt like we had achieved something historic. The *New York Times,* however, published no review of the event, and by doing so buried its moment for future researchers looking into the emergence of bringing these composers into mainstream concert life. Anyone looking for information on the beginnings of reclaiming the forgotten music of the twentieth century would find no record of this event in America's "paper of record."

Similarly, during the period from 1991 to 2006, when the Hollywood Bowl Orchestra and I performed hundreds of first concert performances of film music and my colleagues and I developed the techniques that are used today for live-to-picture concerts, the Los Angeles Philharmonic refused to call these restorations "premieres" or "first concert performances" because the music could be heard on films. Needless to say, the *Los Angeles Times* mostly ignored sixteen seasons of concerts heard by four million people. After a concert of music to Alfred Hitchcock films by five different composers that included mostly first performances, the *Times* answered the question of why it had not been reviewed with "We have already reviewed Mauceri conducting Hitchcock"—as if Hitchcock were a composer.

When I learned that during 1997—the centennial year of the birth of Erich Wolfgang Korngold—there would be no concert in the United States celebrating his life and music, I felt some echo of the frustration he and his family must have felt during his lifetime. Imagine my delight, then, in being asked to conduct the official centenary concert in Vienna.

I soon learned that Marcel Prawy, the greatly beloved and elderly impresario, would be the "host" of the concert, which would be televised. As a friend of Korngold during his Vienna years, Prawy knew what he wanted, and this amounted to music written before the war and before Korngold's escape to America. But how could a concert—a single concert—that was to consist of excerpts erase the years in America, which included more than a dozen film scores, a symphony, and two concertos? Prawy would not give in, because he felt Korngold's American music was not "on a high enough artistic standard."

My conversation with Christof Lieben, who ran the Vienna Konzerthaus, was a painful one. I told him to find "a nice young Austrian conductor who was willing to do what Prawy wants, because I, as an American and a musician, could not pretend that Korngold did not live and compose in America." A few days later, I got a phone call: "I hope you still want to do this concert because Prawy is out."

Thus, in April 1997, I conducted Vienna's tribute to Korngold, which ultimately did include the devastating Adagio from his Symphony, as well as extended excerpts from *The Adventures of Robin Hood,* shown with the film. The concert was sold out and enthusiastically received, even if there were audience members who thought we had added the Technicolor to the print, since they had only seen it on black-and-white television, in German, and without Korngold's music.

However, it was a Pyrrhic victory. There was no press coverage. The principal critics did not attend. Television withdrew, and the delayed radio broadcast with Prawy's narration deleted the American music. He had replaced it with pre-war recordings from Korngold's Vienna days.

ARNOLD SCHOENBERG

If you are a classical music lover, there is no more frightening name than that of Arnold Schoenberg, the "father of atonality" (a phrase he hated). Born in 1874, he was the oldest of the generation of young radical musicians. At first his music sounded as beautiful and unique as that of anyone growing up in the shadow of Wagner and Mahler until, as stated earlier, in 1908 he jumped into a new and unregulated world that would soon make him internationally famous.

Fleeing the Nazis, Schoenberg came to live in Los Angeles and, as he had done in Berlin, made his living as a professor. Like Hindemith at Yale, he taught hundreds of American students, many of whom were women, and like Hindemith, he taught music—whatever the level his students required—but not how to imitate his style. His impact on music of the twentieth century is enormous, even if performances of his twelve-tone and non-tonal music are relatively rare.

Schoenberg remains far more complex to assess. On the one hand, he was the father of the musical avant-garde, internationally regarded as the leader of the most progressive musical movement of the era that straddled World War I. Although he had, in the early 1920s, begun orchestrating the music of Bach, once he came to America he composed new music that occasionally made use of his early avant-garde methods and also occasionally explored older music, such as Baroque dances, albeit refracted through a complex and imaginative prism.

As with Igor Stravinsky, who also lived in Los Angeles, Schoenberg's music was being newly recorded in the 1960s and thereby becoming available to young American musicians of my generation. The popular image of him was of a stern and unforgiving martinet whose music was both fascinating and occasionally profoundly unpleasant to hear. That image held true for me until I discovered his Second Chamber Symphony in 1987.

Rarely played, it is in two movements. The first movement, dark and *Tristan*-haunted, was completed in 1908, just before Schoenberg moved into non-tonal explorations. While in Los Angeles, he picked up the old score, left incomplete thirty years before, and composed a second and final movement. This movement starts as a surprisingly happy scherzo, one that no one would guess is the music of Schoenberg, which gradually becomes crazier and crazier until it just stops, and the sad flute melody of the first movement returns, now on an elegiac trumpet, as we feel the inexorable march of time and the awful reality of being at the start of another war. The last bar of the symphony is dated October 21, 1939. England and France had already declared war on Germany the month before; Austria was part of the German Reich; Warsaw had fallen; and the first concentration camps were in operation.

I first conducted the Second Chamber Symphony in 1988 with the Scottish Opera Orchestra, in a concert that started with Richard Strauss's tragic waltz *München* (Munich), composed in 1940 after the bombing of the city. The Schoenberg followed it, with the rest of the program devoted to a concert performance of Kurt Weill's 1940 musical play *Lady in the Dark*. The Schoenberg and the Strauss had not been announced, and the sold-out hall in Edinburgh responded to the Symphony with enough enthusiasm to bring me back to the stage for a second bow. One critic, in reviewing the concert, wrote, "One way to get people to like the music of Arnold Schoenberg is to spring it on them as John Mauceri did last night at Usher Hall."

What makes this work so important is that embedded within the silence that falls between the first and second movements is what most people think of as "Arnold Schoenberg" and his legacy. Those twenty seconds in which we turn a page and we performers collect ourselves contain thirty years in his journey into non-tonality and the twelve-tone methodology. When the second movement begins, the composer has come to another place, one in which consonance is once again a viable part of his expression. Humor and beauty, if only for a few minutes, return to his musical universe, and all his tumultuous life experiences become tools for continuing his musical story—not into some future that never would exist, but into his own reality, one that he finally embraces, staring into its face: October 1939, when he lived on Rockingham Drive in Brentwood, California, with his wife and children, and his native Austria was at war with him.

The Chamber Symphony No. 2 is not considered a major work, though it most certainly is. When it was recently reviewed after a rare New York performance, one major critic seemed insensitive to what it contains, referring to it as "amiable." When Decca and I talked about a Schoenberg record for the *Entartete Musik* series, I suggested "Schoenberg in Hollywood" as a provocative enough title to confront what had previously been hidden: that Schoenberg composed astoundingly beautiful and complex music during the last thirteen years of his life.

Learning music comes with the job, of course, but learning an entire segment of a truly famous composer's output otherwise unknown to me, and seemingly to almost everyone, was a journey filled with exclamation points and question marks. On the one hand, given the composer's reputation, the Berlin orchestras were concerned that Schoenberg's music would be just too difficult to play and record. On the other hand, no one seemed prepared to accept what they were playing as actually being the music of Schoenberg.

In 1996, the Arnold Schoenberg Institute was housed at UCLA, in Los Angeles. It was there that I listened to private recordings of the works I would record, and was able to look at manuscripts, study performance materials with markings from the composer, and read various documents. Here is when more curious information presented itself to me: the fact that the music written in Los Angeles was not played there, much to the frustration of the composer. The Hollywood Bowl Orchestra's first recording of Hollywood music, *Hollywood Dreams* (1991), had begun provocatively enough with a fanfare by Schoenberg. Composed in 1945 for Leopold Stokowski, it is called *Fanfare for a Bowl Concert.* It had never been played. Anywhere.

Now, five years later, I was preparing a Schoenberg record for Berlin that included the Second Chamber Symphony, the Suite in G Major, and the Theme and Variations, Op. 43b. The Suite had been commissioned by the Los Angeles Philharmonic and performed under the direction of Otto Klemperer in 1935, and shortly afterward under the composer's direction—which was the last time it was performed by the orchestra that commissioned it.

In a conversation with Schoenberg's two sons, Lawrence and Ronald, in 2014, they recounted the performance history of their father's music at the Los Angeles Philharmonic. The Violin Concerto had been performed once, "forty years ago"; the *Prelude to the Genesis Suite,* once; Theme and Variations, Op. 43b, never. Lawrence wrote to me (January 30, 2014), "I think that Schoenberg pretty much currently 0 for 3 as far as the Los Angeles Philharmonic is concerned." The numbers, given in terms of baseball statistics, refer to the interest of the current and past music directors of the orchestra.

In 2018, the Los Angeles Philharmonic announced its centenary season, including fifty new works that would be given world premieres, along with a traversal of its extraordinary history. Stoically, but with more than a touch of unbearable sadness in his voice, Lawrence Schoenberg said (October 11, 2018) that the situation with his father's music in his adopted city was now "less than zero." Lawrence Schoenberg is a retired mathematics teacher and understands what numbers mean. In this case, for the one hundredth anniversary of the Los Angeles Philharmonic not a single note of Schoenberg's music was to be played and no reference to him exists in any of their print materials.

In a 2021 conversation, Lawrence confirmed that Arnold Schoenberg, the composer credited for creating the overriding sound of classical music in the twentieth century, still had not been programmed in his adopted city, and hoped that something would be played by the Philharmonic in 2024, the 150th anniversary of his birth.

Hearing the children and grandchildren of the refugee composers speak English with an American accent tells a profound tale. While I was recording "Dawn" from Schoenberg's *Gurrelieder* with the Hollywood Bowl Orchestra in 1994, a man came up to me during a break on the MGM (Sony) Soundstage—where, once upon a time, Judy Garland recorded "Somewhere, Over the Rainbow," and Miklós Rózsa recorded the score to *Ben-Hur*—and said, "Hi, John. I'm Larry."

Notes

INTRODUCTION

1. New York Times Editorial Board, "What's So Great About Fake Roman Temples?," *New York Times,* February 9, 2020.
2. "The [Los Angeles] Philharmonic has played a significant role in the music that has been a part of films for the past 80 years," says Smith. "So, there's been this intertwined nature. When you think about back in the '30s when the exiled composers like Max Steiner and Franz Waxman were coming here, those were composers that the Philharmonic was playing their concert works from when they were living and working in Europe. Out of that filmic symphonic sound was also born the sound of our orchestra. . . . The idea that the L.A. Philharmonic can exist in this space without having a deep relationship with the community of art makers that have made Los Angeles the center of creativity would be silly." Maxwell Williams, "L.A. Phil Plans Centennial Season Featuring Oscar Performance," *Hollywood Reporter,* February 7, 2018.
3. Rich Cohen, "Liberty Island's Hidden History," *Wall Street Journal,* July 13, 2019.

CHAPTER 1. A VIEW FROM 30,000 FEET

1. Anne Midgette, "People Are Upset When an Orchestra Closes. If Only They Went to the Concerts," *Washington Post,* July 19, 2019.
2. Coming out of the pandemic that shuttered musical performances worldwide for more than a year, the *New York Times* reported on June 9, 2021, that Carnegie Hall's 2021–22 season would be a "mix of familiar works and experimental music," as if those were the only two options in classical music programming in the twenty-first century.

3. Jonathan Haidt, "2017 Wriston Lecture: The Age of Outrage: What It's Doing to Our Universities, and Our Country," Manhattan Institute, November 15, 2017.

4. Pierre Boulez's influence cannot be overstated. He served as musical advisor and principal conductor of the BBC Symphony (1971–75), music director of the New York Philharmonic (1971–77), a principal conductor at the Bayreuth Festival during the 1960s and 1970s, and guest conductor with some of the world's major orchestras (Chicago, Vienna, Berlin, and Los Angeles). The French government supported his experimental institute for "research and acoustic/music coordination" in Paris (IRCAM), which opened in 1977, awarding it 40 percent of the nation's budget for contemporary music. The *New York Times* published two obituaries on January 7, 2016 and a photo on its front page.

5. David Brooks, "The Retreat to Tribalism," *New York Times,* January 1, 2018.

CHAPTER 2. BRAHMS AND WAGNER

1. This should not be confused with futurism, which was unveiled in 1909 and articulated elements of the avant-garde. Wagner was writing about the future of music, which he saw as a return to the very beginnings of music drama by the ancient Greeks and the fusion of poetry and music in a state of endless transition.

2. Max Kalbeck, *Johannes Brahms,* Vol. 2, Part 1 (2nd ed., 1908); trans. Piero Weiss in Piero Weiss and Richard Taruskin, eds., *Music in the Western World: A History in Documents* (New York: Schirmer Books, 1984), 122–26.

CHAPTER 3. STRAVINSKY AND SCHOENBERG

1. The Bloomsbury Group consisted of English writers, artists, and intellectuals in the first half of the twentieth century—including Woolf, E. M. Forster, and John Maynard Keynes—many of whom lived in the West End of London in an area known as Bloomsbury. Many of them advocated for feminism, pacifism, and a liberal attitude toward sexual profligacy and gender fluidity.

2. Anne Midgette, "'Written on Skin' Brings Theater to Opera Stage," *Washington Post,* August 12, 2015.

CHAPTER 4. THE LURE OF CHAOS

1. Margaret MacMillan, *The War That Ended Peace: The Road to 1914* (New York: Random House, 2013), xxiv–xxv.

2. Western music is based on an extremely simple matrix of rhythms and note lengths (whole notes, half notes, quarter notes, etc.) that are presented in consistently repeated groups (measures) of pulses. Entire works exist as a series of two beats per measure, while others might be exclusively in in three or four. By 1900, this simplistic pulse/rhythmic system was made exciting and complex by a performance practice that changed the pulse matrix by subtly slowing and speeding up—accelerations, distended "up beats," the addition of a sudden breath (a *luftpause*). The new music from America

confronted this tradition with a motoric, one-tempo music that found its energy in breaking up those twos, threes, and fours so as to create surprising inner rhythms. Imagine the European model as graph paper, with the size of the boxes being made wider or narrower, and then imagine a strictly even graph in which the boxes are colored in different-sized groups. The latter would be ragtime.

3. Next Level, an initiative of the U.S. Department of State, "Uzbekistan Final Concert," Residency Recap," posted August 5, 2018, https://www.nextlevel-usa.org/sca/uzbekistan.

4. Philipp Blom, *Fracture: Life and Culture in the West, 1918–1938* (New York: Basic Books, 2015), 370–71.

5. Notes can be imagined as the white notes on a piano—C, D, E, F, G, A, B. The black notes add the other five notes within the octave and are given names in relation to the white note nearest them. Each black note has two names—one based on the white note to the left, the other based on the note to the right. Thus, the same black note can be called F-sharp, because it is a little higher than (i.e., to the right of) the F key, or it can be called G-flat, because it is a little lower than (i.e., to the left of) the white note called G.

6. At the same time, a new political force, inspired by the Bolshevik Revolution, was developing in China,—which would set the standard of international Communism in the twenty-first century. To celebrate the hundredth anniversary of the founding of the Chinese Communist Party in 2021, President Xi Jinping announced plans for 300 officially approved operas, ballets, plays, and musical compositions—all of which would hew closely to the aesthetic demands of the Party, with music once again used as a symbol of a political system, a country, and its people.

CHAPTER 5. HITLER, WAGNER, AND THE POISON FROM WITHIN

1. Elisabeth Noelle-Neumann (1916–2010) survived the war, joined the Christian Democratic Union, and successfully entered the post-war West German business of political and market research. She was hired to serve on the faculty of the University of Chicago in 1978 and stated that she had fought the Nazis by "working from within." She remained a highly respected figure in public opinion polling right up to her death at the age of ninety-three.

2. Sigmund Romberg (1887–1951) was trained in Vienna, came to America in 1909, and became an American citizen in 1919. The 1924 *Student Prince* was the longest-running show on Broadway during the 1920s and 1930s—running longer than *Show Boat* and every show by George Gershwin. In 2012, I performed the score with the WDR (West German Radio) Orchestra in Cologne. Although the work received a standing ovation, the head of the WDR told me that he had never heard a note of Romberg. The city's chief music critic bested him by confessing that he had never even heard of Romberg's name.

3. In other words, Abraham Lincoln was president of the United States when Strauss was born, and Harry Truman was in the White House at the time of his death.

CHAPTER 6. STALIN AND MUSSOLINI MAKE MUSIC

1. See John Mauceri, *For the Love of Music: A Conductor's Guide to the Art of Listening* (New York: Alfred A. Knopf, 2019), 21–22.
2. Respighi's *Pines of Rome* may have "passed" through the Fascist filter thanks to the fact that the anti-Fascist Arturo Toscanini had conducted its American premiere in 1926.
3. John Mauceri, "Un incontro con l'uomo, un incontro con la sua musica," *Teatro Regio: Stagione d'Opera 1998–9* (1999), 97–100.
4. Harvey Sachs, *Music in Fascist Italy* (New York: W. W. Norton, 1987), 129.

CHAPTER 7. THE MIRACLE OF A SECOND EXODUS

1. For the 1927 world premiere of the silent film adaptation of *Der Rosenkavalier* in Dresden, the projectionist (who was operating a hand-cranked mechanism) changed speeds to synchronize with Strauss's conducting of the orchestral score! This system proved impossibly awkward and unacceptable because of the disruption of the image speed for the public. Strauss was, however, able to bring the silent film to London, and even recorded some excerpts from the film score for the Electrola label. He and his librettist Hugo von Hofmannsthal—who had significantly changed the story by giving it a *Marriage of Figaro* ending with disguised lovers in a formal garden—had hoped to bring their operatic masterpiece into small cities, where the opera could not otherwise have been mounted. For this purpose, two orchestrations were made: one for the big cities that replicates the orchestra complement of the opera, and a much smaller "salon orchestra" version. While negotiating an enormous fee to bring the movie to New York's Metropolitan Opera, the entire project became moot because of sound film technologies (and the film company, PAN Film, went out of business). The American premiere had to wait until March 29, 1974, when the Yale Symphony Orchestra and I presented it to an audience of undergraduates (black tie requested) and two important guests: the famous Viennese opera expert Marcel Prawy and the favorite soprano of Richard Strauss, Giacomo Puccini, and Erich Wolfgang Korngold, Maria Jeritza (who was living in New Jersey at that time).
2. Steven C. Smith, *Music by Max Steiner: The Epic Life of Hollywood's Most Influential Composer* (New York: Oxford University Press, 2020).
3. The entire sequence of Ratoff's death on the operating table lasts approximately ten minutes and consists of two musical sequences. The first, lasting six minutes, accompanies the main character's preparation to operate on his father. The operation itself is performed without music—a breathtaking two minutes and fifteen seconds of silence and sound effects, followed by one minute and forty-five seconds of music accompanying the isolation and horror of Ricardo Cortez's character, who is left alone in the operating theater.
4. As an example of the enormity of the public that hears music composed for film, consider the national television broadcast of *Ben-Hur* on CBS (Columbia Broadcasting System). Although the film had already been seen by millions of people since its pre-

miere in 1959, the telecast was viewed—and Miklós Rózsa's two-and-a-half-hour or-chestral score was heard—by 84.82 million people on one night, February 14, 1971.

5. Anno Mungen, *"BilderMusik": Panorama, Tableaux vivants und Lichtbilder als multi-mediale Darstellungsformen in Theater- und Musikaufführungen vom 19. bis zum frühen 20. Jahrhundert,* 2 vols. (Remscheid: Gardez!, 2006).

6. A *tableau vivant* is a silent and stationary re-enactment of a scene or painting with living actors in costume in a painted setting.

7. In 1984, I managed to convince the legendary Stella Chitty, long-serving stage man-ager at the Royal Opera House, Covent Garden, to follow this important indication in the score. She thought it might "break the mood" and that once the curtain began to move, there would either be applause or the audience would think she had made a mistake. I prevailed on her to give it a try, which she did. No one broke the mood. The audience immediately understood what was happening and the effect was indeed magical.

8. The question of how Hitler experienced *King Kong* was addressed by author/musicol-ogist Brendan G. Carroll in a private email to the author on August 24, 2017: "King Kong was made in 1933. This is an important year as far as sound films are concerned because it was the year when the technical capability of post-synchronization of a sep-arate music track finally became possible. . . . I cannot think of a reason why RKO would make a different version for Germany with stock music. So I think we can be sure Herr Hitler heard Maxie's music."

CHAPTER 8. A NEW WAR, AN OLD AVANT-GARDE

1. In 2016, contemporary artist Jeff Koons donated a sculpture, *Bouquet of Tulips,* to the city of Paris. However, it was actually a donation of an *idea* of the work—which re-quired 3.5 million euros to make and install in October 2019.

2. Seventy years later, the *New York Times* published an article about the "entrepreneurial revolution" in the "new" music by Vick Chow for a soloist "armed with kitchen utensil noisemakers." Steve Smith, "Make Your Selection of Sounds (Kitchen Utensils Are on the Menu)," *New York Times,* September 7, 2013.

CHAPTER 9. A COLD WAR DEFINES CONTEMPORARY MUSIC

1. Once the "Copland" sound was replaced in the concert hall with the international non-tonal style, it was preserved in film music. In 2016, composer Ennio Morricone accompanied the on-screen reading of a forged letter from Abraham Lincoln in his Academy Award–winning score to *The Hateful Eight,* making use of this American language in a musical cue called *"La Lettera di Lincoln."* Composers such as Elmer Bern-stein, Alfred Newman, Bruce Broughton, and John Williams have kept it alive in scores that accompany stories of the American South and West, and as W. G. Snuffy Walden did for the long-running television series *The West Wing.*

2. A few years later, on May 14, 1959, President Eisenhower would break ground on Lin-coln Center for the Performing Arts, a multi-million-dollar arts campus in mid-town

Manhattan that projected America's commitment to the arts during the Cold War, announcing that its "beneficial influence . . . will not be limited to our borders."

3. Frances Stonor Saunders, *Who Paid the Piper?: The CIA and the Cultural Cold War* (London: Granta Books, 1999), 408.

4. Vincent Giroud, in his biography of Nabokov, cites Nabokov's 1953 article, after the death of Stalin, for *Encounter* magazine: "Why, [Nabokov] asked, had the expected musical homage to the dead dictator failed to materialize seven months after his death? . . . Taking the example of Prokofiev's posthumous canonization, Nabokov suggested that 'the only indispensable qualifications for entrance into the Pantheon of Russian classics were that (1) the composer must be dead and (2) he must on no account have composed any music that could be described as dissonant.'" "No Cantatas for Stalin?," in Vincent Giroud, *Nicolas Nabokov: A Life in Freedom and Music* (New York: Oxford University Press, 2015), 276.

5. We are not talking about marches and hymns with political words to them, since that "style" was precisely the same in every country, no matter what side of the political discourse one was on. Karlheinz Stockhausen demonstrated this with his 1967 score *Hymnen* (Anthems), which is a kind of electronic tour of the world. Stockhausen's conceit is to imagine he had a shortwave radio and could pick up broadcast signals from every region of the planet to hear its various national anthems. With few exceptions, they all sound exactly the same.

6. In 1950, the *New Yorker* published an interview with Ernest Hemingway in which he said, "I use the oldest words in the English language. People think I am an ignorant bastard who doesn't know the ten-dollar words. I know the ten-dollar words." Lillian Ross, "How Do You Like It Now, Gentlemen?," *New Yorker,* May 6, 1950.

7. Ben Brantley, "Review: 'Moulin Rouge! The Musical' Offers a Party and a Playlist, for the Ages," *New York Times,* July 26, 2019.

8. Arnold Schoenberg, *Verklärte Nacht,* Op. 4 (1899), *Friede auf Erden,* Op. 13 (1907), and *Erwartung,* Op. 17 (1909).

9. See Chapter 1, note 4.

10. Corinna da Fonseca-Wollheim, "MATA Festival's Sounds of Play," *New York Times,* April 16, 2015.

11. Frank Wilczek, "The Hidden Meaning of Noise," *Wall Street Journal,* May 28, 2020.

12. Jon Pareles, "Where Guitars Sound Like Orchestras or Brawling Geese," *New York Times,* January 19, 2014.

13. Ernst Toch, "Glaubensbekenntnis eines Komponisten" (A Composer's Credo), *Deutsche Blätter,* March/April 1945, 13–15. Ernst Toch Collection, Performing Arts Archive, UCLA, Box 106, item 22. Translated by Michael Haas in *Forbidden Music: The Jewish Composers Banned by the Nazis* (New Haven: Yale University Press, 2013).

CHAPTER 10. CREATING HISTORY AND ERASING HISTORY

1. Hollywood is a district in central Los Angeles. After World War II, the word started to mean (in music) overblown, unacceptably melodic, melodramatic, superficial, manipulative, stolen, venal, the home of charlatans, and, by extension, anything a music

writer does not like. Note: The European word *cinema* is for good things, *movie* is bad, and *film* is neutral. A *cinematic* performance would mean something is thrilling and epic, whereas a *Hollywood-sounding* piece of music, or a piece of music that sounds like *movie* music, is a bad thing. In 2014, the *New York Times* published the following: "As the piece [*Triple Resurrection* by Tan Dun] evolves, repeated-note rhythms signal a coming mood shift. Soon, percussive blasts and wailing orchestra chords lend the concerto a little 'Crouching Tiger, Hidden Dragon' action. The instrumental writing includes the captivating amplified sounds of water being poured into basins. The piece is alluring until it turns Hollywoodish, when a soaring theme for strings breaks out." Anthony Tommasini, "Ringing In the Chinese Zodiac's Year of the Horse," *New York Times,* February 2, 2014.

2. In March 2014, Pierre Boulez managed to take both sides in an interview posted by the international financial group BBVA's Foundation, which had given him a €400,000 award in 2013. When asked if contemporary music is for an elite, he answered oxymoronically, "Of course. But the elite should be as large as possible." Norman Lebrecht, "Pierre Boulez Video Interview," March 12, 2014, https://slippedisc.com/2014/03/pierre-boulez-video-interview-i-am-a-composer-i-still-am-a-composer/.

3. Stravinsky, Schoenberg, and Korngold—not to mention Toch, Rózsa, and many others—lived in Los Angeles as American citizens. Weill and Hindemith were living in the same time zone on the East Coast. These composers were not friends in Europe and they were not friends in Los Angeles and New York—and why should they have been? However, quoting one to discredit the other is an effective technique to destroy both composers and justify not playing their music. Tchaikovsky didn't think Bach was a genius, and Mahler thought Tchaikovsky was "shallow [and] superficial." It is doubtful that changes your mind about Bach, Tchaikovsky, or Mahler—because you know their music.

4. Paul Goldberger, "Cuddling Up to Quasimodo and Friends," *New York Times,* July 23, 1996.

5. Inspiration from other music has always been a fundamental part of the process of composing music. What made the twentieth century unique was the proliferation of source materials. It was possible for a Stravinsky to be inspired by the music of Carlo Gesualdo (1560–1613), Giuseppe Verdi (1813–1901), Johann Sebastian Bach (1685–1750), and Anton Webern (1883–1945); to subscribe to publications of ragtime and jazz; to incorporate tangos and marches into his aesthetic world; and to collaborate with the Ringling Brothers and Barnum and Bailey Circus, Walt Disney, and Breck Shampoo, all the while maintaining an air of bemused and elegant detachment from popular culture. He lived in Hollywood but is buried in Venice, Italy—not Venice, California.

6. The Cooperative Remittance for Europe (CARE) was created in 1945 for private citizens in America to send food relief to Europe.

7. According to the OREL Foundation, which encourages interest in composers suppressed as a result of Nazi policies, Krenek became a professor and head of the Department of Music at Hamline University in St. Paul, Minnesota, in 1941, where his music was performed by the Minnesota Orchestra. He departed for the West Coast in 1947,

where he continued to conduct, teach, write, and compose some 100 works before his death in 1991.

8. James Coomarasamy, "Conductor Held over Terrorism' Comment," *BBC News,* December 4, 2001.

9. Boulez's abusive letters have been quoted in many sources, including Hugh Wilford's *The Mighty Wurlitzer* and Vincent Giroud's *Nicolas Nabokov*. See Hugh Wilford, *The Mighty Wurlitzer: How the CIA Played America* (Cambridge, MA: Harvard University Press, 2008), 110; and Vincent Giroud, *Nicolas Nabokov: A Life in Freedom and Music* (New York: Oxford University Press, 2015), 286.

10. Hans Werner Henze (1926–2012) was a German composer of international renown and strong political opinions. A Marxist and Communist, he left West Germany in 1953 to live in Italy as a protest over his country's attitudes toward his politics and homosexuality.

11. Quoted in Stephen Hinton, *Weill's Musical Theater: Stages of Reform* (Berkeley: University of California Press, 2012).

12. Alex Ross, "A 'Serious' Composer Lives Down Hollywood Fame," *New York Times,* November 26, 1995.

13. Anthony Tommasini, "Seldom-Heard Symphony Resurfaces as a Novelty," *New York Times,* March 6, 2010.

14. The author begs the indulgence of the reader. This sentence appeared in the *Guardian* (1996) in a review of his Decca recording *Schoenberg in Hollywood*. The author generally does not keep his bad reviews, preferring to memorize them.

CHAPTER 11. OF WAR AND LOSS

1. Recorded interview with author, 2015.

CHAPTER 12. A CENTURY ENDS

1. The twenty-first century actually began on January 1, 2001, not January 1, 2000, but few paid much attention to that fact, with the exception of Arthur C. Clarke.

2. *Ricochet* by Andy Akiho, performed by the New York Philharmonic; see Joshua Barone, "Watch Ping-Pong Make Its New York Philharmonic Debut," *New York Times,* February 19, 2018.

3. *Philadelphia Voices* by Tod Machover, performed by the Philadelphia Orchestra; see Michael Cooper, "How a Philly Cheesesteak Goes from the Grill to Carnegie Hall," *New York Times,* April 1, 2018.

4. Stockhausen's comments at a press conference in Hamburg on September 17, 2001, were recorded by North German Radio (NDR) and published the next day by various news organizations such as the BBC and AP. See Julia Spinola, "Monstrous Art," *Frankfurter Allgemeine Zeitung,* September 25, 2001.

5. The behavior of the young and angry European youth who grew up in the rubble of World War II still reverberates in the obituary columns in the first quarter of the twenty-first century. On July 2, 2021, the *New York Times* ran a half-page article (with

a photo) of the Dutch composer Louis Andriessen (1939–2021), referring to him as an iconoclast who then became "one of Europe's most important postwar composers." In 1969 he and a group of like-minded composers sabotaged and disrupted a concert of the Concertgebouw Orchestra with noise makers because they objected to the orchestra not programming the kind of music they were writing—post-war serialism. He went on to hold faculty positions at Princeton, Yale, and the University of Leiden.

6. Kate Murphy, "Zubin Mehta," *New York Times,* August 30, 2014.

7. Seth Colter Walls, "Korngold's Rarely Heard Opera Hints at His Future in Hollywood," *New York Times,* July 29, 2019.

8. Not all of us Baby Boomers are children of peace. Some of us are the children of sexual violence. It has been well documented that the Soviet army was responsible for raping approximately two million German women in their offensive that ended in Berlin in April 1945 and continued for a number of years afterward. German doctors subsequently performed an alarming number of abortions and reported the rise in venereal diseases among their female patients. It is estimated that somewhere between 100,000 and 300,000 living Germans are *Russenkinder* (Russian children), but because of the shame attached to this period, the real number will probably never be known.

9. Robert Lee Hotz, "Tuned to Music, the Coronavirus Sounds Like Zappa," *Wall Street Journal,* June 27, 2020.

APPENDIX

1. RIAS stands for "Radio in the American Sector" of Berlin.

2. John Mauceri, "A Conversation with Abravanel," liner notes to *Die Sieben Todsünden,* Decca, 1990.

Acknowledgments

This book is the culmination of more than thirty years in pursuit of something that made no sense to me, both as a music lover and as a musician. How could it be that the same repertory that was beloved when I was born in 1945 is the same music that is universally beloved now, and most of what was composed in between remains contentious?

Ever since Michael Haas uttered the question that appears in the dedication of this book, I have tried to understand. Why, for example, when I was invited to conduct a New Year's gala in Munich in the late 1990s, which would inevitably be considered a "pops" concert, was a message from the presenter relayed to me which read, "Please tell Mr. Mauceri no film music"? Only when I contacted the presenter and played some of the music of Waxman and Steiner to her on the phone did she relent. Why, after seventy-five years of tenured composition professorships, are we not the beneficiaries of hundreds of beloved masterpieces composed without the pressures that beset Mozart, Beethoven, Wagner, and Debussy, that is, the need to earn a living from their music?

Many people participated in the creation of this book. They include composers, musicians, critics, teachers, and fellow music lovers. When the elderly uncle of my German manager spoke to me about the "American" music of Hindemith and Schoenberg, he got suspiciously agitated when he shouted, "We HAD that music after the war! It was no good!" He—a retired conductor—and his generation are hereby acknowledged.

As a New Yorker, my local newspaper will always be the *New York Times*. For the past thirty years, I found myself having less and less connection with what I was reading in their music section, even though I continued to read with great interest everything else the paper covered and evaluated. Why was that? I therefore acknowledge—without irony—the *Times* and every other journalist throughout the world who has written about music and, in doing so, inspired me to think.

Many peers have read this manuscript, some of whom were enraged. Their comments, along with those who thought "it was about time" for this book to be written, are gratefully acknowledged. What was hated—and why—taught me a great deal. Thank you.

The families of the forgotten and erased composers—Helen Korngold, John Waxman, Larry Schoenberg, Juliet Rózsa, and so many others—are hereby acknowledged and thanked for their shared stories. I am a privileged man to have heard John Waxman refer to Franz as "Father," Helen Korngold refer to Erich as "Papa," and Larry Schoenberg refer to Arnold as "Daddy." Thank you.

And thank you to the orchestras, many of whom dreaded the repertory I brought to them—and yet played fully committed performances, perhaps changing a few minds. I well remember hearing a member of Leipzig's Gewandhaus Orchestra mutter, "*Schönes Stück!*" (Beautiful piece!) to his stand partner after a first reading of a work by Miklós Rózsa, who had, after all, studied music in their city. And whether the players openly resisted, as the New Israeli Opera's orchestra did with Weill's *Der Weg der Verheissung,* or merely played the notes put in front of them—their job—I knew that they were at the forefront of deciding if this music would stand or fall. They know what music is, how it is constructed, and whether it is worthy. They are the ones at the heart of the change for those composers who have re-entered the consciousness of the world. We need more, of course.

My young musician colleagues, Thiago Tiberio, David Gursky, Francesco Cilluffo, and Michael Gildin, willingly read segments of the manuscript and sent corrections and comments. Michael Mungiello at InkWell Management is a hero to me. Above all, my literary agent, Michael Carlisle, loved this book from the very beginning, when we simply called it "our book." Yes it is, Michael. Thank you.

Index